D0368810

BORGLUM'S

unfinished dream

MOUNT RUSHMORE

BY JUNE CULP ZEITNER AND LINCOLN BORGLUM

Library of Congress No. 76-5651
ISBN Number 0-87970-135-8

North Plains Press
Box 910
Aberdeen, S.D. 57401

Printed in U.S.A.

Acknowledgments

The primary source of information for this book has been the Gutzon Borglum papers, telegrams, notes, speeches, brochures and manuscripts, which together with hours of Lincoln Borglum tapes, and the memorabilia in the Borglum Museum and Studio, record the entire story of Mount Rushmore as the Borglums knew it.

Special thanks go to the South Dakota State Library for their files on the animal life and vegetation of the Rushmore area, and to the South Dakota College of Mines library for geological references. The *Rapid City Journal* and the South Dakota Tourism Division provided much information about the continuing story of Mount Rushmore, the Borglum family, and the Borglum Ranch and Studio.

Others who have been of special help are Mary Anne Borglum, Albert Zeitner, Paul and Pat Ellsworth, William Tallman, Kay Riordan, and Irene Herren. Rushmore superintendents, McCaw and Wickware were also most helpful.

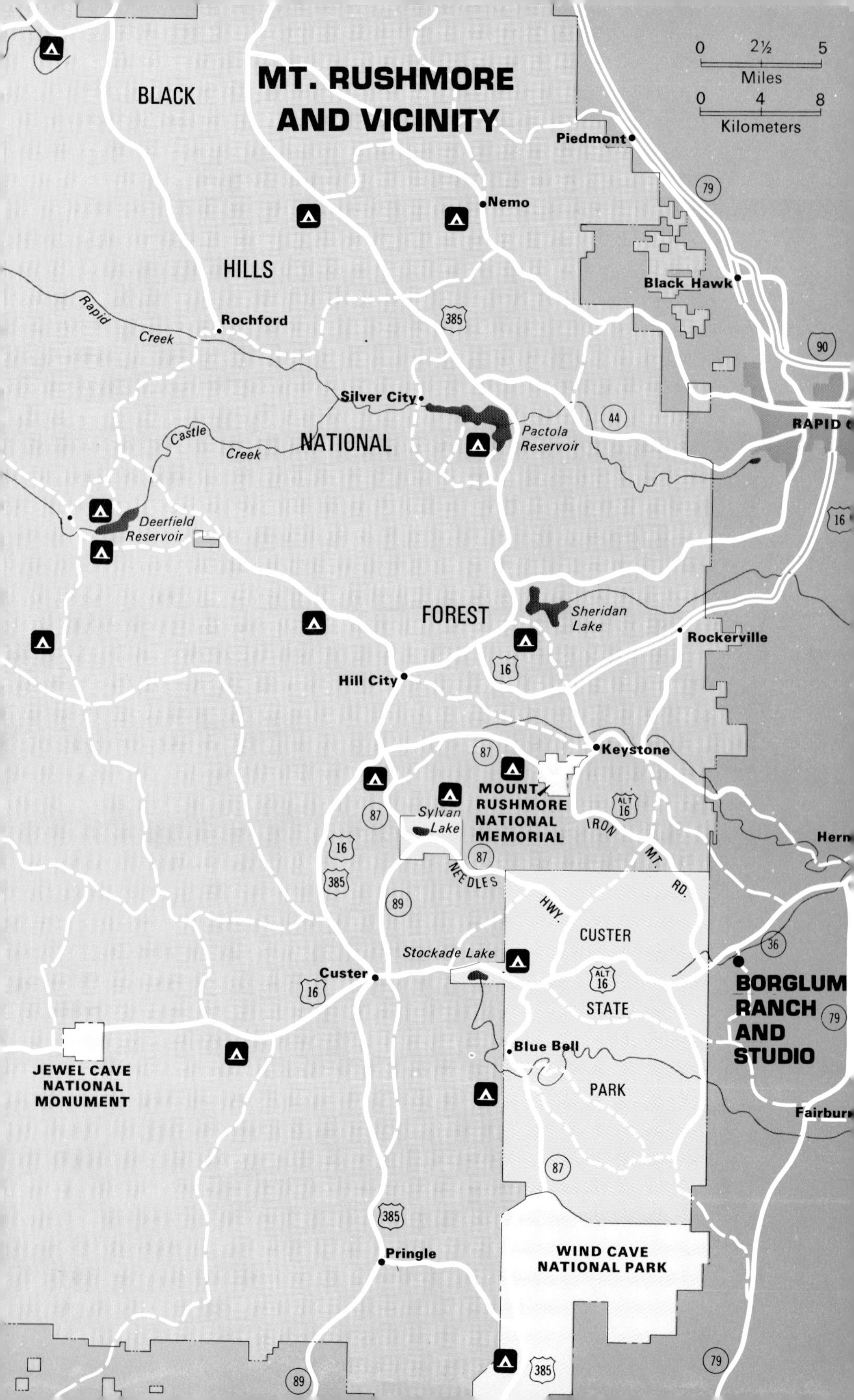

MT. RUSHMORE
AND VICINITY
0 2½ 5
Miles
0 4 8
Kilometers
BLACK
HILLS
NATIONAL
FOREST
Piedmont
Nemo
Black Hawk
Rochford
Rapid
Creek
Silver City
Castle
Creek
Pactola
Reservoir
Deerfield
Reservoir
RAPID C
Sheridan
Lake
Rockerville
Hill City
Keystone
MOUNT
RUSHMORE
NATIONAL
MEMORIAL
Sylvan
Lake
IRON
MT.
RD.
NEEDLES
HWY.
CUSTER
STATE
PARK
Stockade Lake
Custer
Blue Bell
BORGLUM
RANCH
AND
STUDIO
Fairburn
Hermosa
JEWEL CAVE
NATIONAL
MONUMENT
Pringle
WIND CAVE
NATIONAL PARK

Dedication

This book is dedicated to Mary Anne Borglum and Albert Zeitner for their patience, understanding, inspiration, and love.

Foreword

Gutzon Borglum loved America and the West. An artist and a genius, he was also concerned with ecology, sports, transportation, and politics. How Gutzon and his son Lincoln changed a lonely spot in South Dakota to a National Shrine, thus reawakening patriotism in this country and changing forever the life of the State, is the subject of this book.

Table of Contents

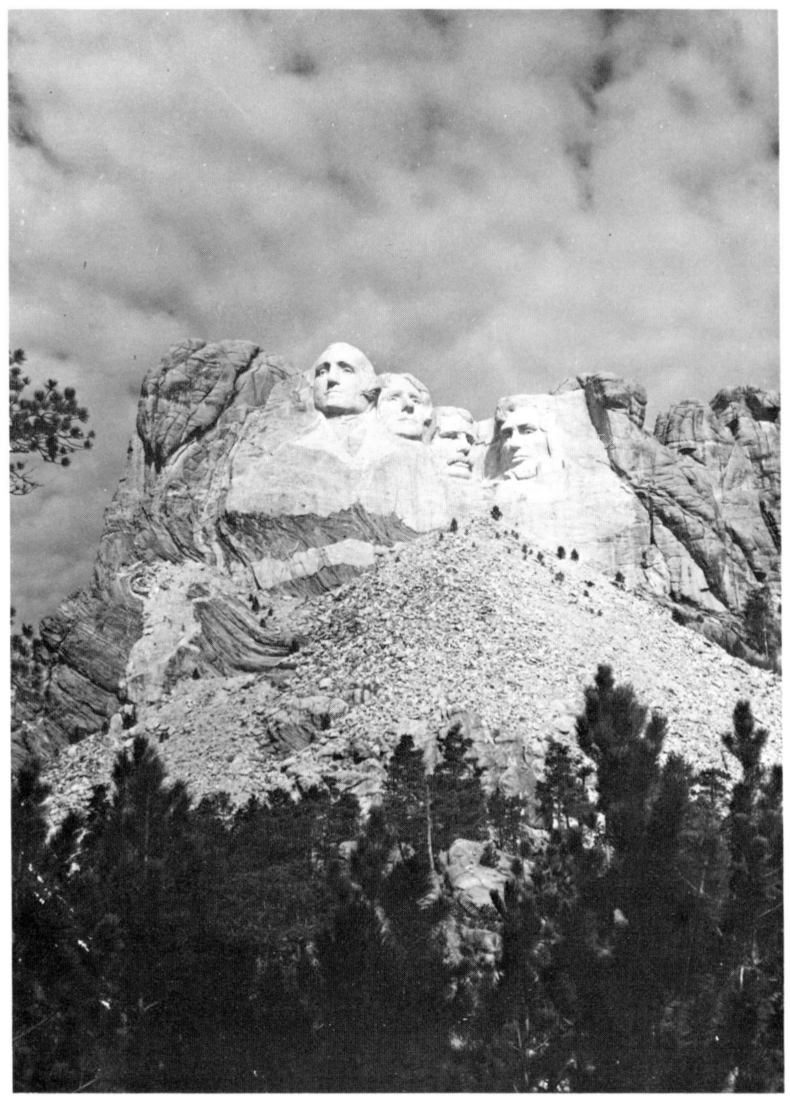

At its best in the morning sun, the Shrine of Democracy is carved from durable granite which will wear away at the rate of only a fraction of an inch in years. The mountain is 500 feet higher than the surrounding peaks, and one of the highest in ancient Harney Range.

Preface

Much has been written about the nation's Shrine of Democracy, Mount Rushmore, and this is as it should be, as there is nothing else in the world to equal it. As a National Memorial, designed to endure and tell its story of a remarkable civilization, it has no peer. Still this shining jewel of the nation's culture, set in the ponderosa forest of the ancient Black Hills, has not been fully described. Although the past has been described in painstaking detail there are many tales which have not been told, a vast amount of information which could be lost to posterity. And what of the present? And the future? The sculptor, Gutzon Borglum, and many of the men who helped build the mountain, are dead. But to the survivors, the blasts of dynamite, the sun against the granite, and the cutting winds of winter, are as real as yesterday.

The era which produced Borglum, his crew, and the great carvings has changed. Although Borglum was a man of vision, as were most of the leaders of the project, he could not possibly foresee a time when automobile traffic to the Memorial might have to be barred. When Borglum first glimpsed the mountain which was to become his immortal masterpiece, there were no litter problems, no parking problems . . . indeed, there were no roads. The aluminum beer can and other disposable marks of our times had not been invented. How different, our ecology today.

There was only the mountain, massive and gray, surrounded by other ancient peaks, rising above the sea of pine. The area was isolated and unspoiled. Only a few independent, mountain-loving descendents of miners and pioneer ranchers lived nearby. The real inhabitants were the deer, the elk, the chipmunks, the eagles and the bluebirds. Instead of modern highways, the trails of wild animals wound through a shag tweed carpet of moss, lichen and pine needles, penetrated by craggy boulders of granite.

The entire story of how the mountain got to be the way it was at that point in time, and how the artistry and toil of man succeeded in creating a monument particularly meaningful in these surroundings, has not been told. This primitive mountain was destined to enhance this environment, and to become a focal point for the 200th Anniversary of the United States.

It is not really possible to grasp the full significance of Mount Rushmore without a knowledge of American history and a respect for this land. We must be able to realize that Mount Rushmore does not portray the likenesses of 4 presidents in eternal granite. We must understand the times which produced the planners, the artists, the builders, and now the keepers. Likewise, the whole picture is not complete without some knowledge of this mountainous part of southwestern South Dakota, in the central part of our nation, which is the appropriate and unique setting for the Shrine of Democracy.

The mini-world of Mount Rushmore is roughly a quadrangle with Rapid City, Pactola Lake, Custer, and Hermosa, located at the four corners. The area lies within Pennington and Custer Counties. Within this region there are facilities now for all types of recreation. There are plush motels and gourmet restaurants. There are wildnerness campgrounds by clear streams. There are museums, playhouses, mine tours, art galleries. And then there are the shops which sell Japanese made Indian jewelry. Frankly, in many ways, it is a cross section of almost any area which has become a famous vacation center.

Tourists, if they will learn something about the area, can avoid the unpleasant commercialism. In addition to the well beaten paths they must travel to Rushmore, there are hundreds of miles of peaceful, scenic drives. There is a surprising abundance of wildlife. There are meadows blazing with native flowers. There is pure air, blue sky, bright sun.

The success and fame of Mount Rushmore has helped create the new world around it, and is responsible for the tremendous influx of tourists which has made tourism the second ranking industry in the agricultural state of South Dakota. Mount Rushmore itself is one of the most visited of all National Parks or Monuments, and it will probably draw more and more people, and thus continue changing its environment. The mountain, as you see it today, is the center of a panorama in time and space.

To fully appreciate the meaning of Mount Rushmore, the visitor is anxious to see the total picture. The typical visitor is full of wonder, awe, and questions. He wants to be able to visualize the hardy men in their slings attacking the resistant rock. He wonders about the icy winters, about the dizzying heights. He thinks about where the funds could come from and what part the government might have played. But it is difficult for him to conceive of the constant frustrations which eventually made the triumph so great. To sense the inspiration of the past, and to stand in awe of the present, invokes in the on-looker, curiosity about the future of Rushmore and its environs, and for our democracy as a whole.

It is the purpose of this book to bring to light facts never told about this greatest wonder of the free world, and to be a new kind of book about Rushmore-land. The book is designed to be both a guide book and a reference. It is written with the armchair traveler in mind, who wishes to enjoy a vicarious trip to South Dakota in his chair by the fire. The tourist who wants instant information about the rocks, the flora and fauna, the men, the statistics and the legends, will find the subtitles a helpful guide. The hobbyist or researcher may reread certain chapters without having to study the whole book.

For the vacationer, the book hopes to add to your pleasure and to your understanding. For the student or historian it will present the problems which still beset the mountain and project possible future solutions.

The book deals with the primitive and the contemporary, with nature and with people, because it is the story of the world of Rushmore, which natives proudly call "the mountain". This is an infinite story, squeezed into the media of paper and ink. We hope the story will answer old questions and awaken new interest.

1

Geology, Rocks, Minerals, and Gems

First there was the dream. Then there was the mountain to match the dream. Deep in the towering Harney Range in South Dakota's incredibly ancient Black Hills, there stood until the Twentieth Century, a nameless peak of rugged gray granite. No road led to the majestic peak. Few people had seen it, and fewer still knew that it was informally called Mount Rushmore. To the naked eye there was little to distinguish this peak from many surrounding peaks of weathered rock, all dominated by the stark and imposing Mount Harney, which at 7,242 feet is the highest peak east of the Rocky Mountains.

Perhaps the name *Black Hills* is an unfortunate misnomer. It is taken from the Sioux name for the area, *Paha Sapa*, hills of black. But these are not hills in the usual sense. Parts of the Appalachians look like rolling hills. The Ozarks look like hills. But the great granite peaks of the Black Hills are true mountains . . . and appear just the way every new adventurer hopes that mountains will look.

The entire range of deeply fissured, rough, weathered granite of tarnished silvery tones, accented with rich mineral pegmatites and sparkling metamorphic schists, rises abruptly from the prairies and can be seen for many miles. Rough rock forms the backbone of the spectacular scenery. There are great boulders thrust out of surrounding earth at dramatic angles. There are balanced rocks, blocky rocks, pointed rocks. There are needles and spires, reminiscent of ancient castles or the pipes of a colossal pipe organ. But in spite of being angular and jagged in appearance, the edges of the strange, rock shapes have been worn smooth, attesting to the endless battles with the elements.

The Needle's Eye is one of the gray granite shapes Doane Robinson originally envisioned for a series of western sculptures.

Many tourists are surprised at the beauty of the rocks around Rushmore. They often stop at their first sight of flat books of silver mica shimmering in the sun. Or they compare the soft, silken gray of the carved faces with the weathered, surrounding rock. They wonder at the jointed rock forms, at the rocks standing on end, at the massive peaks. So the questions about the rocks are natural and many. "How did these mountains get here?" "How old are they?" "Why was granite chosen for the Memorial?" "Why was this particular granite peak chosen?"

And of course the inevitable question of men first looking at shining rocks . . ."Any gold?"

The Black Hills, at a venerable 40 million years, are the nation's oldest mountains. Geologists tell us that at one time these mountains may have been twice as high as they are now. The fantastic spines of bare granite we now see are the enduring inner cores of the ghost peaks, long since eroded away. Mount Rushmore, with an elevation of 6,200 feet, stands 500 feet higher than the peaks nearest it.

Elliptical in form, and rather like a gigantic distorted layer cake, the Black Hills region is roughly 125 by 60 miles. Coming from the east, the visitor will pass through sedimentary formations, ancient limestone deposited by long extinct seas and lakes, and by floods whose only record is in the rock. Then you will climb through the red sandstone, which is a redeposition of eroded harder rocks. After the sandstone comes the schist, and topping the whole cake are peaks and candles of granite.

To the east of the Black Hills in eroded areas, some of the finest vertebrate fossils are found, giving clues as to what this land was like eons ago. The Oreodont skull is from a ruminant which roamed this area during the Oligocene.

Although the Black Hills are beautiful green mountains, the nearby Badlands are desolate, arid, and forbidding. Badlands and Black Hills vegetation overlap near the Borglum Ranch. Photo by S.D. Travel Division

Granite is igneous rock, which means that it was born of fire. Molten rock, known as magma, smolders deep within earth's furnace. The lava erupting from new volcanos is an example of the power of this core of superheated liquid rock. The magma which created the Black Hills was forced upwards with unimaginable pressure. As it rose, it broke up and lifted existing formations. Like a huge blister on the earth's surface, it kept rising and struggling, ever higher above the earth's crust. Since the process of mountain building is not instantaneous, man is seldom aware that mountains are constantly being built up or destroyed in various parts of the globe.

After the magma pushes up it crystallizes and hardens. Then it may lay dormant for millions of years, when again the uplift may resume. But even as soon as it crystallizes, forces are at work to tear the peaks away. One of the greatest is ice. The contraction and expansion of water with the change of seasons, flood waters dissolving rock and carving canyons, heat causing rocks to flake, the acidity of rain, vicious winds laden with sharp sand . . . all these are the enemies of the mountains.

The events, which brought this old and deeply buried magma to tower above western South Dakota, began some one and a half billion years ago. The limestones and shales, which were disturbed by the igneous rock, were softer rocks and more subject to the erosion of the elements. But the granite itself has been succumbing, which accounts for the surrounding schists, and the rounded edges of the jointed spires. So nature was the first sculptor of Rushmore and its surroundings, and the entire Harney range is an incomparable gallery of art.

When winding through the scenic routes leading to Mount Rushmore, visitors see that many of the roadcuts are hewn from solid granite. This gives them a closer look at the rock from which the faces are carved. Granite, as rocks go, is hard, tough, and resistant. It is composed of grains of crystallized minerals such as quartz, feldspar, and mica. Mount Rushmore, Harney Peak, Mount Coolidge, the Needles . . . and the other great rocky peaks and shapes, are granite. So slowly does granite wear away that it is estimated the area will still look much the same two million years from now. That is, barring cataclysmic events.

Often tourists see a slanting, light colored "dike" of coarser rock in the granite, with big veins of white or pink quartz, blocky peach or ivory feldspar, or shining mirrors of mica. This coarse granite is called *pegmatite*, and it is from the pegmatites, which crystallized more slowly, that the commercial minerals and gems of the area are found.

Many mines surround the Mount Rushmore Memorial, and in fact, there are mineable ores in the Memorial itself. Some of the mines are ghosts of the bonanza west, and others still play a part in the economy of the region. Granite is even classed as a commercial mineral. The mining industry of the United States has been in doldrums for many years, because it has been cheaper to buy ores from foreign countries than to mine our own resources.

Some of the largest crystals of valuable minerals in the world have been found near Mount Rushmore. These were the giant spodumene crystals from Keystone, one of the nation's greatest sources of space-age lithium and beryl. Tin, another expensive mineral, is also found near Keystone.

Some of the mines in the area produced copper, silver, lead, and in latter days, uranium. A famous gem mine, the Scott Rose Quartz Mine is nearby.

But the mineral which brought men to the Black Hills and lured them to stay was *gold*. Custer's expedition of 1874 opened the territory to one of the wildest gold rushes of them all, culminating in the discovery of the Homestake Mine, which for many years has been the nation's leading gold producer. The Holy Terror gold mine is only a few miles from Mount Rushmore. Still seen on the roadside in old Keystone, this mine yielded almost 1 1/2 million dollars in gold, which for those days was quite a lot of gold. There were both placer (gravel) mines and underground mines. There was low grade ore, and there were pure bright nuggets.

While it is certainly true that all that glitters is not gold, there is plenty of gold left in the Black Hills. Each summer finds determined tourists and hobbyists panning for gold in the clear streams of the area, and being rewarded for their patience with grains, and flakes, and sometimes nuggets, of the precious yellow metal. Sometimes old mines are open on a fee basis for tours, and some entrepreneurs will rent gold pans to the tourists, and give lessons and demonstrations of panning, sometimes resulting in the novice finding a little pyrite or a flake of gold. Some of the gravels may be salted, some are not.

It was an unexpected problem in the carving of the presidents, when removal of the deep surface fissures revealed well mineralized veins. A deposit of high grade lead-silver ore was encountered near the end of Abraham Lincoln's dignified nose. George Washington's aristocratic collar was difficult to carve because of huge geometric crystals of feldspar. If there is an almost ruddy glow to one of Roosevelt's cheeks, it is due to the presence of the red mineral, allanite.

Native stone has widely and wisely been used in the exterior and interior of buildings of the Rushmore complex. The excellent roads have also made use of native rock. Often shoppers see souvenirs of so-called "Rushmore-granite" in area gift shops. This does not mean that the granite was taken from the mountain itself, since this is prohibited by law. However, the same type of fine-grained, hard, gray granite outcrops in places outside of the Memorial proper.

Next to granite, the most common rock seen along Rushmore trails is mica schist. This is a metamorphic rock, which is to say a *changed* rock. The darkly shimmering schist is composed of thin plates or layers of quartz and mica in minute flakes or folia. Feldspar, hornblende, and carbonaceous materials are also present. Schist has been altered from igneous or sedimentary rock to its present form, by movement, pressure, heat, and water. In the Rushmore area the schist is frequently studded with dark red crystals of tiny gem garnets. Schist eventually decomposes to shimmering clay, and thus thousands of brilliant little garnets are released in streambeds where children eagerly gather them in vials.

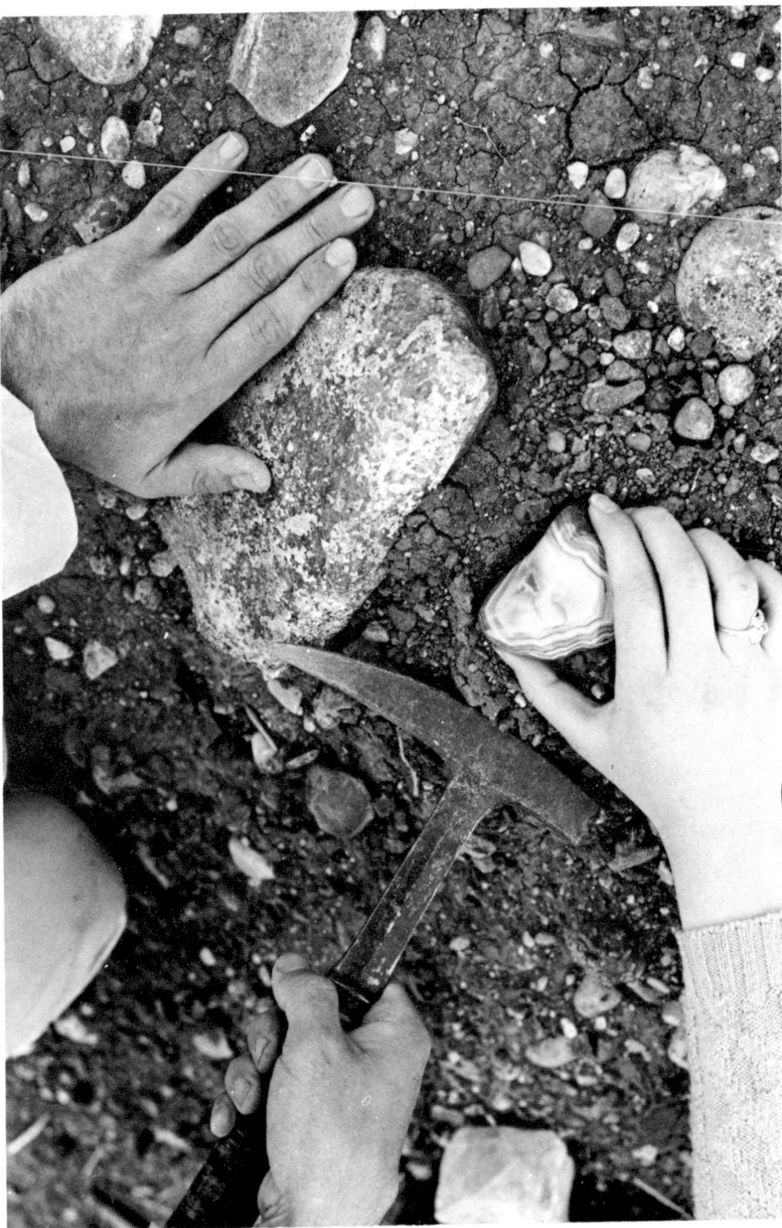

A rockhound brings out his pocket rock, a genuine Fairburn agate to compare to the rough rock his companion is wondering about. Fairburns are the State gem, and are scattered in the alluvial gravels of Custer and Pennington Counties.

Photo by S.D. Travel Division

Magnificent views of Mount Rushmore, framed by arched tunnels of granite, are a feature of Iron Mountain Road. Iron Mountain is an immense iron deposit just southeast of the Memorial on the scenic road to the Borglum Ranch and Museum. Great quantities of iron ore, another mineral heritage of South Dakota, are of possible commercial value, but the present use of this mountain as a scenic outlook and approach, far outweighs the monetary value of the iron. Alternate U.S. 16 goes straight to the top of this mountain of iron. Some of the mineral specimens from the mountain are as iridescent as the wings of a tropical butterfly. Rose quartz and other minerals are present on the route.

Gems have been found in the Rushmore vicinity, but not, so far, diamonds, emeralds or rubies. If someone shows off a "Black Hills diamond" it is quartz. If anyone offers a "native ruby", it is garnet. But at the mines in surrounding mountains, gem crystals have been found of faceting quality golden beryl, and ice blue aquamarine. Both are the same as emeralds, except for color. Precious tourmaline has also been found in local mines in a rainbow of colors, rose, blue, and deep green. Needles and pencils of black tourmaline are common in the white quartz of the area. Smoky quartz is another facet-quality gemstone found here.

South Dakota's State Mineral is rose quartz, a lovely pink decorative stone and gemstone found in abundance in the Black Hills, perhaps in greater quantities than in any other state. Many of the old mines of the southern Black Hills near Mount Rushmore, ran into bright massive veins of this popular stone. Locally favored for everything from rock gardens to jewelry, the mineral has been exported in quantity for carvings for foreign artisans.

Custer State Park is noted for a brightly banded agate, which is called, appropriately enough, Park agate. It is a vivid finely banded gemstone found in connection with widely scattered chunks of limestone of deep buff color. Numerous colorful gems have been found on rocky hillsides during trail rides, camp outs, or the filming of western movies.

South Dakota also has a State Gem, and was one of the first states to honor the mineral kingdom in this manner. The official gem is the Fairburn agate, a brilliant stone of gypsy colored intricate stripes and bands. Named for the tiny hamlet of Fairburn, not far south of the Borglum ranch, the prized agates have been found along French Creek, and Lame Johnny Creek for many years, and can still be collected in remote spots.

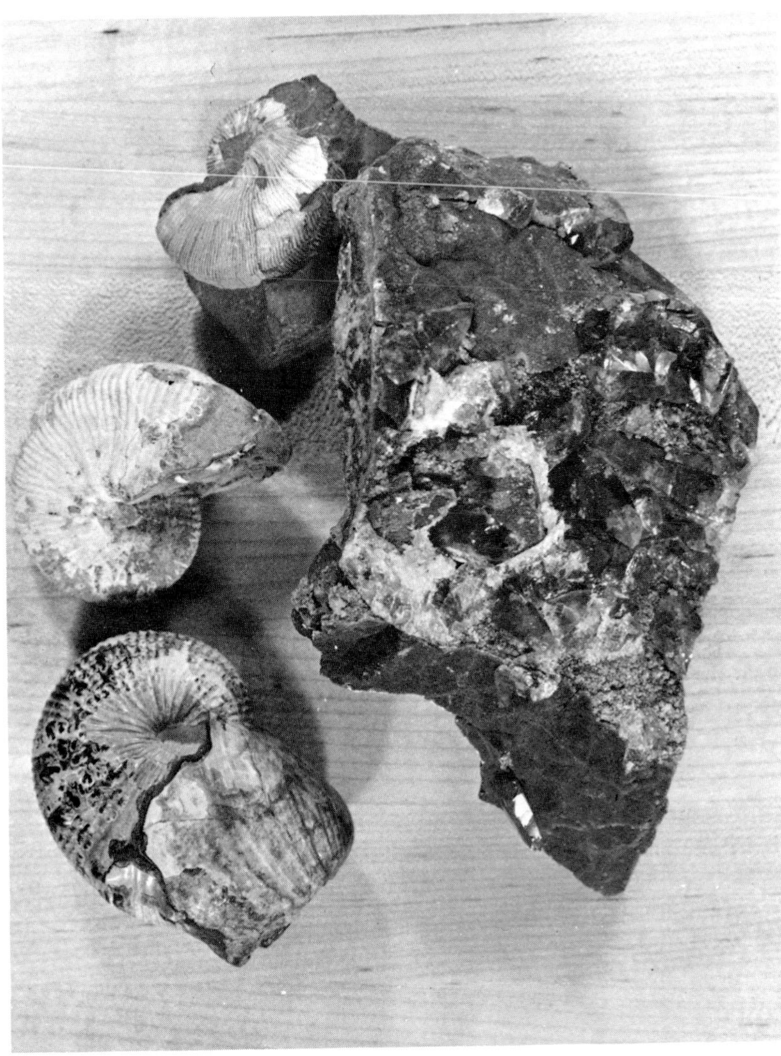

Lacy patterned fossil shells and golden and velvety crystals are found in the Pierre Shale concretions in the western part of South Dakota, to the delight of scientists and students of geology and earth science. Photo by S.D. Travel Division

Near the Borglum Museum on the edge of the State Park, a rare and unusual type of petrified wood has been found. Known as cycad, this intriguing petrified wood with its bold, diamond-shaped patterns, is one of the most valuable of such fossils. As the ancestor of both palm and pine, it is earth's first known flowering plant. More fossil cycads have been found in South Dakota, and in a better state of preservation, than any other state. Other species of petrified wood are common in the Black Hills. Careful collectors have even found fossil pine cones and hackberry seeds from the ancient forests of the area.

Other gems of the region are jasper, carnelian, chalcedony, sardonyx, prairie agate and Tepee Canyon agate. These are all members of the quartz family, so when the color and quality are good, they are hard enough and durable enough to be fashioned into gems and jewelry.

The visitor to the Black Hills will probably find more rock and mineral shops, rock and mineral museums, mineral and gem departments in stores, and front yard rock piles, than anywhere else in the nation. Some stores display carvings, jewelry, and elegant original gifts made from genuine Black Hills gems. There are several lines of native pottery made from Black Hills clay, (which is decomposed rock). And often tourists can buy rough pieces of good local gem material from which they can make their own mementos. On the other hand some shops are little more than tourist traps. Among the gems sometimes claimed for the area are goldstone, jade, turquoise, dendritic agate, and "black diamond" hematite. Not one of these is native. In fact goldstone is not even a real stone. The best of South Dakota's gemstones are not cheap, but this is true all over the world. Decorative stones and ornamental rocks, however, are inexpensive.

A part of the habitat of the Rushmore world are the many caves which underlie large areas of the Hills. These fascinating domains of "inner space" were sculpted and built from limestone by underground water. Some of the caves are administered by the Government, some are private commercial ventures, and many are unknown and unexplored save for bats or mountain lions.

Best known is Wind Cave, which is open the year around, and has tours showing the stony boxwork unique to this cavern. A new dramatically planned and well lighted tour takes visitors through beautiful Jewel Cave, also administered by the Park Service. Jewel Cave also has rare and exotic cave formations, such as calcite bubbles, delicate helictites, and vivid crystals. New explorations indicate that Jewel Cave is much larger than previously estimated, and that it might even connect with Wind Cave, which would make it one of the largest underground mazes anywhere. Although many Black Hills caves are dormant, parts of Jewel Cave are live, which adds to the sparkling beauty of this trip.

Many caves have had their names changed from time to time, for commercial purposes. Among these are Rushmore Cave, Crystal Cave (now Bethlehem), Wildcat Cave (now Diamond), and Stagebarn. Sitting Bull Cave is well known, but does not advertise as heavily as Rushmore Cave, which is 7 or 8 miles from Keystone on a scenic trail.

There are many undeveloped caves, some far from the main road, or otherwise inaccessible, and some too treacherous to encourage exploration. Some caverns of the canyon country preserve the picture writing of ancient man. An intriguing cave near Moon is the cool "Ice Cave" with walls which are said to be icy cold all summer. "Caving" is a scientific pursuit, and should not be attempted without trained speliologists as guides.

The Park Service is charged with the responsibility of keeping the environment of Mount Rushmore as near as possible to the way it was when it was first seen by the Borglums in 1925. It is for this reason that the removal of any rock from the Memorial is strictly prohibited. The presence of each ancient rock, whether laced with lichen, or adorned with rosettes of tourmaline, or jagged and bare, is an important part of the total ecology of the National Memorial.

Of course, in the carving of the faces, and in the making of parking lots, and other facilities, a considerable amount of rock had to be removed. Not to mention the thousands of tons of rock which had to be removed during the work on the Memorial. Which brings us to quite another kind of controversy, the non-removal of rock. Visitors will see a great pile of sections of rough granite at the base of the carvings. This is the rock rubble pile blasted from the surface of the mountain. Borglum's plans were for this rock to be removed at the completion of the sculpture. As he saw it, the faces on the mountain would seem higher and larger, and more dramatic, the mountain would be more majestic, if the loose rock were removed. There were many ways this could be used, such as fill, paving, buildings, or even to sell to raise funds for unfinished tasks like the Hall of Records. For some reason the bureaucracy never could agree to such plans. Now hundreds of baby ponderosa pines grow among the rocks, and in fact, one was plucked not long ago from George Washington's lapel.

The gems and minerals of the Rushmore environment are important to a full appreciation of the Memorial. Not only is the sculptor's work the prime example of art in stone, but there are few other places in our land which afford a better understanding of the nature of the rocky globe we inhabit. A tower of fine granite, standing in isolated grandeur in the Harney Range, this mountain is the best choice Borglum could possibly have made. Here Americans come face to face with their ideals and culture as they study the carvings, and become aware of the virtually ageless granite, and of the ancient geological events which made all this possible.

2

The Rushmore Years

In the early 1920s Gutzon Borglum was working on a Confederate Memorial at Stone Mountain, Georgia, when he received a letter from South Dakota which interested him. It was from South Dakota State Historian, Doane Robinson, suggesting that Borglum might like to come to the Black Hills to talk about the possibility of carving some Western figures on the sharp granite needles which crown the Hills like organ pipes. Borglum had taken his bride, Mary, to South Dakota on their honeymoon. He remembered the odd rock forms of the Black Hills. He recalled the spectacular scenery. An admirer of all things Western, he liked Western movies and stories and legends and heroes. With Mary's encouragement he decided to go to talk with Robinson. Accompanying Borglum was his son, and constant companion, Lincoln, then a lively boy of twelve.

Robinson had proposed his idea of a Western carving to a woman's club in South Dakota. On the spur of the moment the women had passed a resolution fervently endorsing the idea. When, a short time later, they had another meeting, they decided the idea was foolish, so they voted to rescind their former action. This had irritated Robinson so much that he became all fired up, and absolutely determined that it could and should be done.

The Borglums, father and son, went to the ancient Black Hills uplift by train, stopping in the Capital, Pierre, to pick up Robinson, for the last leg of the journey. This first visit was to have been kept secret, but one of the Stone Mountain workmen had a brother in Rapid City, so the news got out, and Borglum was met by the business leaders of Rapid City, as well as the press. For the scouting trip, the Borglums and Robinson were joined by Cleophas O'Hara, then president of the South Dakota College of Mines, and Dr. Joseph Connally, an author,

The men who worked on Mount Rushmore have had several reunions to recall the smiles and tears of the years they worked on changing a mountain into a memorial.
Photo by National Park Service

professor, and geologist.

Borglum had been plagued by difficulties in Georgia, but was still intrigued at the idea of carving an immense mountain, a rugged mountain in the West. He had written, some time before this, "Somewhere in America, in or near the Rockies, backbone of the continent, removed from succeeding selfish, coveting civilizations, and out of the path of greed, an acre or two of stone should bear witness, carrying likenesses, a few precious words pressed together, an appraisal of our civilization, telling of the things we tried to do, cut so high, near the stars, it wouldn't pay to pull them down for lesser purposes."

Robinson had speculated that a few figures could be easily carved on the granite spires called "needles" near Harney Peak, highest peak in the United States east of the Rockies. With a little imagination most of the needles already resembled exotic objects.

When Gutzon saw the stone needles after spending a night under the stars at lovely Sylvan Lake, he told Robinson, "Figures on those granite spikes would only look like misplaced totem poles. We will have to look farther."

Gutzon was dreaming of a specific mountain, although he did not know exactly where it would be. Of a mountain and a subject big enough to exert all his skills, to burn his energies, to test his genius to the limit. He did not find the mountain of his dreams on this trip, but he did react to his destiny. He praised what he saw, the quiet, darkly forested, granite mountains, barely emerged from the pioneer days of Indian Wars and Gold Rushes. He felt anew a devout love of America, and a fierce desire to serve it in a daring and creative way. He carefully surveyed the surrounding from the highest vantage point, and in his heart he knew he must come again.

The next year, 1925, Borglum returned, still accompanied by his shadow, Lincoln. "This time," Gutzon told Robinson, "we will spend at least two weeks exploring the highest peaks of the Harney Range and the mountains to the north." Then he gave his prerequisites for his ideal mountain to his companions on the pack trip. "The peak should be higher than the surrounding peaks, and well separated from them. It has to be a mountain of solid rock. For maximum sunlight, the major mass of rock should face the southeast."

A westerner who had once worked for Theodore Roosevelt, Theodore Shoemaker, was the guide, and again Dr. O'Hara joined the group. Good naturedly, Borglum explained that he was not impressed by bigness for its own sake. "The Washington Monument," he said, "is just another Egyptian obelisk, only bigger."

After two weeks on horseback, the party came to an opening in a rugged wilderness east, and slightly north of Harney Peak. There, ahead of them, was a sheer, gray cliff, venerable and warm in the sunlight, jutting upwards a good 500 feet above the surrounding mountains, with a vast rocky exposure opening to the southeast. This was Borglum's mountain, and he knew it. He insisted on a tortuous climb to the top, where he rested, looking out over the prairies and the pine clad peaks. Time stood still for him. In this lonely silence he knew the reality would be a difficult test for the dream. These still moments revealed to him the immensity of the mountain and its setting, and the terrible responsibility he was setting for himself, to match the awesome scale of the mountain. To equal this grandeur with the hand and the mind and spirit of man, he knew he was committing himself to toil and burdens almost beyond endurance, but he also was sure he had no other choice. Before he left, the party's horse wrangler, Ray Sanders, had planted the American flag on top of the rock.

When Borglum returned to the others he said, "It came over me in almost a terrifying manner, that I had never sensed before the dimensions of what I was planning. This new burden suddenly isolated me, as this mountain is isolated from the valleys below."

Borglum was not surprised that his choice did not meet with the enthusiasm he felt. The press, who joined the party, complained loudly that the site was "too remote." There were no good roads anyplace near, and officials from Rapid City and South Dakota, direly predicted that no one would be interested in this lonesome mountain, deep in the wilderness. Furthermore the mountain was unknown. Indeed, none of the guides could even recall its name—if it had one. Later research showed that it had been named, almost in fun, for a young New York attorney named Rushmore, who was doing some legal work for a mining company. When asked the name of the peak, his companions had answered lightly, "Hanged if we know! Let's call the damned thing Rushmore."

Officials tried to dissuade Borglum and get him to look farther. Some suggested trying the Deadwood area. Some suggested going closer to Custer. Some argued about roads, some about the rough appearance of the stone, some about the distance from the city. Not a few stated that the whole thing was impossible.

The geologists were impressed, however. They assured the sculptor that the ancient granite was extremely hard, and incredibly durable, and that the fissures were probably only skin deep.

Norbeck was momentarily disappointed, but Robinson was quite agreeable. After all, the main thing was to get an artist of unquestioned competence to start some kind of gigantic sculpture in the Black Hills. If the artist could find a way to sculpt the mountain, Robinson was determined to find a way to bring people to it.

So the mountain was selected, and Robinson, Norbeck and countless others started telling Gutzon what they thought should be carved on the granite pinnacle.

Likenesses of important western heroes such as Lewis and Clark, Frémont, or Chief Red Cloud were first suggested. But Borglum had other ideas. He felt his task was not to portray human beings in stone. What he was going to do was to tell a story in stone. He wanted to show the spirit of democracy, the ideals of the nation, its trial by fire, its bold expansion. To express his belief that man has a right to be free and to be happy. He was going to build a memorial. A message on the scale of the mountain. A shrine.

Gutzon Borglum came to South Dakota, not as a man in need of work (although by then the long smoldering fuse under Stone Mountain had blown up that job), but as a busy and enormously successful artist at the height of his career. He came to try a new challenge, to reach for an even greater goal than any sculptor had ever attempted. He already had 12 statues in the National Capital and many in civic centers and parks. He was represented in major museums around the world. He was sought by his friends, the famous and the wealthy, for his advice, his opinion, and for important commissions.

He didn't want to carve just any mountain, nor a subject which was not near and dear to him. New York Jewish leaders had asked him to carve a Jewish history on the Palisades, and he had refused. He had not been paid for the 10 years he had worked at Stone Mountain, Georgia, so he knew that carving a mountain would not make him a fortune.

Actually Borglum had not expected to spend the most of his hours for the rest of his life turning his mountain into a memorial. He had the inspiration, the skills, the experience, and the executive ability needed for a big job, and he didn't dream that he would never be free of the anxiety of every detail of the project, from the family problems of the workers to the financing of the carving, from battling a bureaucracy to protecting the carving from the ravages of weather. He never really expected he was sealing his own doom.

Lincoln Borglum had been with his dad most of the time. Gutzon wanted his son to understand all he felt as the work was about to start. He told the wide-eyed lad, "Nothing but the hand of the Almighty can stop me from completing this task." But even *he* thought of such statements as mostly oratory. He was strong, vigorous, and in his prime.

When he signed the first contract in 1927, after being paid a total of $250 for three years consultation, he fully expected that the actual supervision of the workmen and the translation of his plans from clay to granite, would be done by his trusted and trained assistant from Stone Mountain days, Major Jesse Tucker. In fact he so wanted Tucker to take over the burdensome day-to-day toil of stone removal, that he voluntarily deducted 10% of his commission to assure Tucker of an annual salary of $10,000. As further incentive to Tucker he later gave him a piece of land in the Black Hills.

The first contract, negotiated after much discussion, was with the Mount Harney Association, an organization of South Dakota boosters, businessmen and politicians. Borglum and Tucker were already at work on the preliminary survey when the contract was final. Fifty thousand dollars had been raised, largely through Borglum's lively powers of persuasion. The Association agreed that Borglum should start on a memorial of national scope. The sculptor eagerly made arrangements to use an abandoned slaughter house for a studio.

He found a sparse one-room home in a small hotel in the primitive hamlet of Keystone, which less than 40 years before, had been a rough and booming gold mining camp. This sparsely furnished room was a far cry from the spacious and exquisite Connecticut estate, Borgland, but he was lonesome for Mary and little Mary Ellis, and this was the only home he could find to bring them to. Mary left her gracious home for a room in the wilderness with no reservations. She had given up her career to dedicate her whole life to her husband and she was ready to make a home for him and ease his load, wherever fate should take him. Mary was used to making long, hard trips alone, to manage the mortgaged property in Connecticut, and to keep creditors, salesmen and schemers away from her husband. Gutzon and Mary were never happy apart, and they tried to bridge the chasm with stacks and stacks of Western Union telegrams.

Borglum, although he had spent many years abroad, was the staunchest of patriots. In choosing the subject for his mountain masterpiece he was motivated by love of country. He was also influenced by the artist's precept of unity, harmony, and the fitness of things. To him this great towering peak, near the center of the nation, could not be a memorial to individuals with all their human frailties, but only a memorial to the ideals and accomplishments of a great people.

The first model, completed in his winter studio in San Antonio's Brackenridge Park, was of three figures: Washington, a natural choice, since he represented the birth of the nation, the noble spirit which started a courageous people on an untried course; Jefferson, through whom he would show the youthful inspiration of the Declaration of Independence, and the foresight which expanded the country with the Louisiana purchase, of which this area had been part; Lincoln, his favorite subject, who represented the humanity, the suffering, the compassion and the eternal unity of the nation.

Lincoln Borglum and a Texas school buddy, Allan Day, loaded the model in the back of Lincoln's car, at his dad's request, and started eagerly on the trip north to South Dakota. Teen-aged Lincoln was proud to be asked to carry out a job of this importance, but both boys were full of confidence. The long trip, mostly over open prairie, became somewhat boring, so they wanted to get it over with as fast as possible, and drove for too long periods of time, and perhaps too fast. They came to a sudden stop. Lincoln had fallen asleep at the wheel, and the car had turned over. The dazed boys, now wide awake, determined that the three heads were all right, although the base was broken. Then they walked back and forth on the country road to get some air and wait for

The old studio houses this first concept of the National Memorial, which was modified and changed many times before the mountain, still unfinished, was brought to its present state.

help.

Some travellers stopped. "Are you boys all right?"

"Yes, thanks," replied Lincoln, "we're fine, and thank goodness, so are the three presidents we had with us on the back seat."

"You boys better rest," was the dubious reply.

After comparisons were made with the original model and the mountain it became apparent that there was plenty of rock for a fourth figure. When Theodore Roosevelt was chosen for the fourth figure, it brought forth a flood of controversy.

Roosevelt had only been dead 8 years. Since he had split the Republican party, he still had many political enemies left. Others didn't want Roosevelt for the simple reason they had other favorites to propose. Some felt that Roosevelt was not up to the caliber of the other three, and Borglum had to reiterate that it was not the man that counted but his part in the history of our democracy.

Borglum had been a close personal friend of the late Rough Rider, and could well have been prejudiced, but it was really Calvin Coolidge who suggested that Roosevelt would properly round out Borglum's saga in stone. Coolidge thought that Roosevelt's enthusiasm for the American West, and his measures to preserve the nation's beauty, his efforts in behalf of labor, and his building of the Panama Canal, which truly linked East with West, all proclaimed that Roosevelt was the logical choice. Borglum agreed, and the matter was closed.

Asked about the controversy later, Borglum reminisced that the choice of Lincoln had also been slandered when first brought up. He testified that a few had called Jefferson a despicable character, and at least one politician had mentioned that he had always thought of Washington as being a cold and unapproachable man.

But Borglum reaffirmed the rightness of his choice. "Regardless of what biased people may think of these four as human beings, they were the ones at hand when our destiny as a people was shaped. They were the ones who personified certain basic elements, crucial to our survival and growth as a nation."

The controversy over the subjects was not the only trouble the sculpture faced. Although this was long before the days of the radical ecologist groups, there were abundant harsh protests by self proclaimed nature lovers, insisting that the mountain was more beautiful and meaningful as it was, standing alone in the wilderness. "Man," they proclaimed, "has no right to desecrate a mountain."

Most of these writers had never seen this particular mountain, and since there were no roads to it, few would have ever had the chance or the desire to see it. Even some South Dakotans screamed that the state could get along without this "preposterous undertaking."

Curiously enough, it was some of the cities which stood to benefit the most, which voiced the loudest opposition. Even the Rapid City Journal, only newspaper of the city which was to boom because of the carvings, opined that "The Black Hills can sell themselves without any alteration of nature's handiwork."

Most hostile were the stories written by Cora B. Johnson of nearby Hot Springs. Her attacks in the Hot Springs Star were incessant and bitter. They were widely reprinted as representing the prevailing attitude of South Dakota. Nationally circulated papers printed cartoons deriding one man's attack on a mountain. "Borglum is about to destroy another mountain," one eastern paper announced. "Thank God it is in South Dakota where no one will ever see it."

Added to this was the vengeful aftermath of Stone Mountain. Literally tons of spiteful and untruthful literature about Borglum was mailed to South Dakota by Stone Mountain people. Borglum was maligned as a vandal and a thief. He was described as being flighty, temperamental, and violent. He was said to be impractical, undependable, and lacking in business sense and ethics. Much later he was exonerated, and Georgia leaders pleaded with him more than once to return and finish Stone Mountain under his own terms. A few South Dakotans may have been permanently influenced by this hate broadside from Georgia.

The major problem though, in the beginning and all the way through the 14 long years, was finance. Borglum's first estimate that the figures could cost around $200,000 each was amazingly close, but where was the money to come from?

Times were good when the project began and he trusted that sufficient private money would be forthcoming. This was not the case. He had to spend much of his time and talent and vigor soliciting funds, when all he wanted was to be working at his art. To add insult to injury he was not given much credit for his fund raising, and detractors attributed each new appropriation or donation to local politicians and businessmen. It is significant that after Borglum's death *not* one more cent was ever raised for the carvings. Much later, more than half the cost of the entire monument was easily appropriated for a National Park Service Administration Building and Visitor's Center at Rushmore, and a quarter of the cost of the memorial was spent enlarging the concession building.

Borglum was hired as a designer and artist. He had no intentions of being an accountant, a bookkeeper, a public relations manager, or a fund raiser. But the project was important to him, so when he saw that money was going to be a problem, he had to become the major fund raiser, in addition to his other jobs. Money was unpredictable, and the hardest part for him, was to be satisfied with a succession of small funds, interspersed with long drouths. Virtually every penny had to be prayed for and argued over. It was a nerve-wracking, frustrating, ever present problem. The very qualities which made South Dakota an ideal location for this undertaking, also made financing harder. South Dakota had, and has, a very small population, with very few millionaires or nationally influential people. The remoteness of the state from major population centers and prime transportation routes made the state of little concern to most Americans. Borglum was widely known and had many friends on both coasts, but to most of them South Dakota was a minus. Most of the work on the project was done after the crash of 1929 during the depression years in a farm state which was simultaneously suffering from the most devastating drouth in its history. South Dakota was known as a cautious, thrifty, and conservative state, but not without good reason.

John Boland of Rapid City, who was Secretary of the Commission, often came out better than the sculptor financially. Boland had a regular salary for his work and part of his business secretary's salary was paid from Rushmore funds. He was in the appliance and implement business, and was able to sell large orders of supplies to the Rushmore work.

A real boost was needed to get the mountain carving started, and to convince people that it should and could be done. South Dakota's far-seeing Senator Peter Norbeck invited President Calvin Coolidge to vacation in the Black Hills. Intrigued by the West, and the possibilities of reported fantastic fishing in the trout streams of the mountain forests, Coolidge accepted the invitation. He announced that his summer White House for 1927 would be the State Game Lodge in Custer Park in South Dakota's Black Hills. The preliminary work at the mountain, paid for by various private and civic donations, was already bogged down and Borglum was exuberant at the approaching Coolidge visit.

This was the time, he felt, for the big drive. Perhaps if Coolidge became a friend of the Rushmore project, he would back a bill to grant Federal aid to the mountain. Congressman William Williamson, Senator Norbeck, and Borglum worked feverishly to solicit more donations to pay for getting ready to start the actual carving while Coolidge was there. Charles Rushmore, for whom the peak was named, was quite flattered by the project, and wrote out a check for $5,000.

The very first major contribution for the Memorial was made by Herbert Myrick, publisher of The Dakota Farmer of Aberdeen, South Dakota. Borglum had known Myrick in Connecticut, and was delighted at his friend's support at this critical time.

The general manager of South Dakota's colossal Homestake Gold Mine, Bruce C. Yates, was a distinguished man who was sympathetic to Borglum's ideas. Under his direction, Homestake donated a check for $5,000, and in fact, this was only one of several gifts from the mine. Yates was helpful in many ways in the early Rushmore days. He had worked in the Black Hills since 1897 and knew the climate, the men, and the rocks, as few others in the region.

Relatives of Theodore Roosevelt were also generous, and a few businessmen and publishers, even some of the previously indifferent men from Rapid City, came up with timely donations. These contributions, together with the gift, by Samuel Insull of Chicago, of a 200 horsepower diesel engine, made it possible for Borglum and Tucker to get the rock ready for the pointers which would mark the layout of the Washington face. They then hired a few hard rock miners and began a

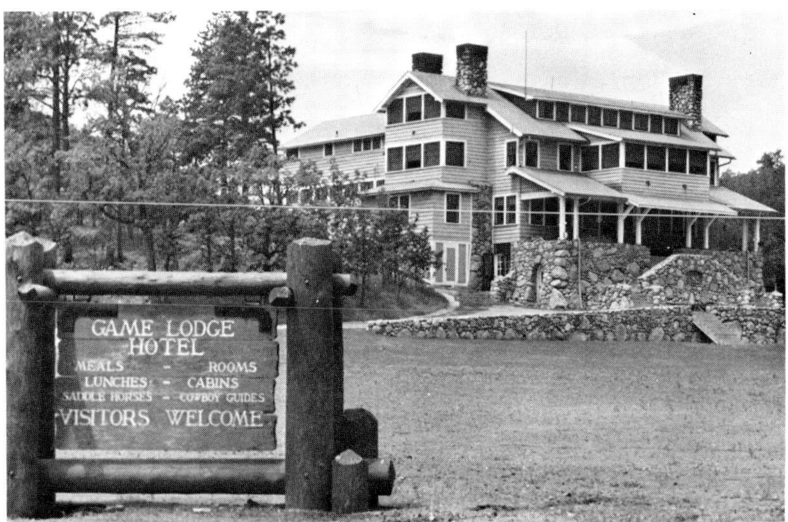

The State Game Lodge, near the Borglum Ranch, was the summer White House for Calvin Coolidge at a crucial time in the history of the Monument.
Photo by S.D. Travel Division

frantic preparation.

Coolidge arrived in South Dakota on June 15, but it was not until August 10 that the careful plans paid off. A big ceremony was held at Mount Rushmore with Coolidge as the heralded guest of honor. Many of those present, including the disgruntled press, had to walk 3 miles, but the President, wearing a cowboy hat and cowboy boots, rode through the pine wood on a gentle horse. The unique Presidential salute was a series of reverberating explosions from the blasting away of tree trunks which stood in the right of way of the new road to the mountain. Before the waiting crowd, the sculptor invited Coolidge to be the one to write the inscription to be chiseled on the mountain.

The President handed Borglum 4 steel drills, and the artist was suspended in a swing harness of leather and steel in front of the granite cliff, high over a deep ravine. It was a tense moment as metal started grinding rock. Each of the drills was used briefly on what was to be Washington's forehead. The first historic drill was presented to the President, the next two went to Senator Norbeck and Doane Robinson, and the last one Borglum kept for himself. (It may now be seen in the Borglum Museum.)

Coolidge was carried away by the dramatic moment. In a short talk, mostly impromptu, he termed the proposed memorial a "National

Shrine" and called on the government of the United States to support it. Borglum was given a personal invitation to come to Washington, D.C. to discuss with Treasury Secretary, Andrew Mellon, the prospects of federal funding. Even the tired and grumbling reporters were impressed.

Coolidge's stay in South Dakota was lengthy. Squaw Creek was stocked with 18 to 20-inch brown trout, cleverly confined to the Presidential fishing area. In honor of the gracious First Lady, it was renamed Grace Coolidge Creek. The hand-fed fish were ready to jump into his creel, and Coolidge bragged that South Dakota fishing was truly sensational.

His famous statement to the press in regard to a second term, "I do not choose to run," was made from his South Dakota White House, the State Game Lodge. His visit to South Dakota was a real turning point in the fortunes of Rushmore, with his visit bringing millions of dollars worth of publicity to the Black Hills.

A short lived elation followed at the mountain. Then Borglum began the first of an almost endless series of treks to Washington for funds. Borglum proposed the acceptable idea of private donations to be matched by Federal funds. People should feel that they had a real part in the memorial, he reasoned. Norbeck berated his friend for not seeking the full amount, but Norbeck was ill, and even the modest bills he and Williamson took before Congress were not immediately passed, so no work was done in the summer of 1928, and even former boosters quickly forgot the work on the mountain.

The Mount Rushmore bill finally passed in the winter of 1929 on George Washington's birthday, and one of Coolidge's last acts as President was to name the first Mount Rushmore National Commission. The bill, as passed, agreed to provide up to half the minimum $500,000 estimate, on a matching basis.

Joseph Cullinan, a Texas oil man, was elected president of the first commission. John Boland of Rapid City was chairman of the smaller executive committee, which was put in charge of the financial administration of the project. Mount Rushmore was designated a "National Memorial" with this bill, which also specified that there never be any charge made to visitors at the mountain. In addition, the bill named the four heroic figures and endorsed the entablature to be written by Coolidge. "Such Memorial to be constructed according to the designs and models of Gutzon Borglum."

Asking Coolidge to write the text eventually precipitated another crisis. The styles of "Silent Cal" and the flamboyant artist were entirely different. Although Gutzon told Coolidge that the words should be Biblical in their simplicity, he also mentioned what should be included, and then edited some of Coolidge's words. Borglum felt that the inscription should be a part of the art, so the artist should have the final say. The publicity resulting from these differences, which were really minor, was exaggerated and prolonged, so a rift developed between Borglum and Coolidge, and the entablature was postponed.

As he worked, Gutzon pointed out that no monument in the history of the world was so conceived. The great monuments of India, China, Egypt, and Greece had been planned for other purposes, for worship, to mark graves, or possessions, or scenes of conflict, but never to tell the story of a nation.

In 1929, when things were finally going well, Major Tucker resigned. In spite of constant worry about Rushmore, Borglum had accepted other commissions, and had relied on Tucker for routine progress. He was working on a statue of Woodrow Wilson for Poland. He had completed the wonderfully poignant North Carolina memorial for Gettysburg Battlefield, a group to be similarly made in real life many years later at the flag raising at Iwo Jima. Other commissions were General John Greenway, Sidney Lanier, and "Pawnee Bill", Major Gordon W. Lillie.

Although he quickly replaced Tucker with J. C. Densión, his new assistant lacked training and experience, so Borglum realized he would have to spend most of his time in South Dakota after all. He decided to buy a 1500-acre ranch near Hermosa on Squaw Creek near Custer State Park. Here he could have a comfortable home for his family. He could build a big studio for his other work, and he could have a few horses, which were always dear to him.

When Tucker left, all the responsibilities became Borglum's. The original agreement was not changed so Borglum was still getting only the designer's and consultant's fees, instead of the additional fees he should have as engineer and manager of the entire work. He had taken less money in the first place to insure adequate remuneration for Tucker, and he pointed out his fee should be increased when Tucker left. It was Borglum, not Denison, who was taking over Tucker's job. His maximum commission had originally been set at $87,000, but this had been signed under the erroneous assumption that the work would progress rapidly without interruption and that Borglum's presence would not be constantly required.

Boland continued to think the sculptor was overpaid, and wanted him put on a regular salary, as if he were only an engineer. The total amount paid Borglum was less than $10,000 a year. Much of this went for promotional trips, lobbying, helping workers, and trying to keep a roof over the head of his family.

Borglum had planned that the head of Washington be dedicated in July of 1930. In order to have matching funds ready he designed and published a *Mount Rushmore* book, complete with advertisements. Expertly done, the book became very popular. The commission also organized a Mount Rushmore Society limited to 500 memberships at $100 each. So again a financial hurdle was past, and the face of Washington began to emerge from the gray granite wall.

First, a scale model was made, with the ratio of one inch to one foot. Then measurements were made on the rock itself. A relative point was found for the top of each head by intersecting lines. At the center of these lines a level metal plate was installed with degrees accurately reading from 0 to 360. A protractor-like arrangement was the 32 foot steel boom from which hung mercury plumb bobs. By dropping the boom ten degrees at a time, it was possible to get a rough basic outline

A series of tunnels, blasted from the hard, ancient granite, frame the Shrine of Democracy exactly as Senator Norbeck planned. Photo by S.D. Travel Division

of the proportions to be transferred to the mountain. The model was similarly equipped with a measuring device and every measurement was multiplied by 12 before it was transferred to the rock. Red paint marked the measured points, telling the workers what amount of rock to remove in each spot.

The first part of this process of rock removal was the drilling of vertical holes on a sloping plane of rock. The rows of holes were not haphazard, but were done in a definite pattern, dictated by the amount of rock to be removed, and the throwing power of the designated explosive charge. One pound of dynamite will remove one cubic yard of rock, and a drilled hole one foot in depth and 1 1/8 inches in diameter will hold .69 of a pound of dynamite. So the explosive in this hole would remove .69 of a cubic yard of rock. With a large jackhammer weighing 60 pounds and a new drill, an experienced workman could drill a foot a minute under ideal conditions.

The *du Pont Magazine* of December 1930 featured a story about Mount Rushmore and gave details of the use of company products for this work of art. For the head of Washington alone 2000 yards of granite were removed by 6000 pounds of 40% du Pont gelatin dynamite set off by 40,000 mercury blasting caps activated by electricity. As little as 1/64 of a pound of explosive with a single cap alone was sometimes used.

To prevent costly errors in the early stages, horizontal holes were drilled with a jackhammer to the correct depth so that when workers, who removed the first masses of rock, came to the horizontal hole they would immediately stop. About 1 1/2 to 2 feet was the maximum depth they could drill before removing the drill for resharpening. The drill could last two feet only if the stone were softer than average, while if the granite was unusually hard maybe only one foot could be attained. The drilling was done with pneumatic drills operated by compressed air with electricity as the power. The air was transported by 3 inch pipes and rubber hoses.

Soon the technology was improved and the horizontal holes were abandoned. A selected crew of three men did nothing except make constant measurements, telling the workers exactly how much rock to remove in each spot. Four hundred drills or more were used in a single day. The first overburden of rough and scarred rock was taken off by drilling holes 8 inches apart and about 8 to 10 feet deep. Into each hole the proper amount of dynamite was placed. Echoing blasts removed 50 to 60 tons of the old, gray rock at once. As the work progressed closer to the egg shaped mass which was to become the face, the holes became shallower and the dynamite charges smaller. Some work was done with only jackhammers. Rock between closely spaced holes could easily be removed with caps. The process was so highly refined that the drilling and blasting could be correct to within a quarter of an inch on a 21 foot nose. On a massive mountain this was an infinitesimal amount. An electric detonator set off many blasts at once.

At the extreme projection of a face, the tip of the nose, a marker of paint was placed. This defined the center of the face horizontally, so for the eyes and cheek bones the boom could swing from left to right, accurately locating other vital points. The frontal cheek bones were the second points. The measuring device was referred to as the pointing machine. A constant menace in the use of this machine were the gusty Dakota winds. Extra stone was left in all areas to allow for mistakes, and for the subtle nuances of later exact modeling.

It was at Stone Mountain, Georgia, that a Belgian visitor first suggested to Gutzon, that rock could be sculpted by the precision use of dynamite. Borglum had been looking for the best way to remove large quantities of rock to prepare the surface for carving. He thought the dynamite idea was feasible. A conference with the du Pont Company in Wilmington, Delaware, was followed by du Pont experts coming to Stone Mountain to instruct the sculptor in techniques worked out for his needs.

Engineers, who were interested in the mechanics of the removal of rock for such a unique purpose, first suggested elevator-like machines with steel arms holding cages which could be electrically moved at will over the entire mountain face. Such machinery would have cost more than the entire estimated cost of the project. Techniques such as painting the face on the rock or projecting pictures by powerful lenses, had been tried at Stone Mountain, but were not adaptable for the Rushmore work.

The method devised for moving the men was a safety harness of steel and leather, similar to a boatswain's chair, suspended by a 3/8 inch 300 foot cable from a winch at the top of the head. Banks of 6 or 7 winches were located in winch houses on the tops of the Washington, Jefferson, and Lincoln heads. Firmly buckled in, the men could not possibly fall out. Prototypes of these chairs, invented by Gutzon, were used at Stone Mountain.

When the mass which was to become the face was reached, it was divided into thirds horizontally, with the eyebrows, the bottom of the nose, and the bottom of the chin representing the three divisions. Then each face had the measurements transferred by scale from the model, so that points every 6 inches horizontally and vertically were marked. Later points would be as close as 2 inches.

Gutzon was not just a studio artist. He was out on the mountain in any weather inspecting every task. Photo by S.D. Travel Division

As the work came closer to the actual surface for the face, holes were drilled close together like a honeycomb, each to a specific depth. In this way large pieces of rock could easily be removed without damage to the solid stone underneath.

Since the work on Washington was to be first and become the gauge for all of the work to follow, Borglum supervised each detail with care, so that each step would be carried out with exact accuracy. He did much of the work himself, becoming so involved in it that he would forget the wind, and the rain and the time of day.

The great egg shaped mass of stone had to be studied for some months before much work on the features could be attempted. Gutzon had to study the play of light on the mountain. Then, looking at the mass from different angles and distances, he had to note the perspective of the mass in relation to its environment. The quality of the resistant stone itself helped to determine the attitude of the head in relation to the rest of the peak. Here, a studio enlargement of the Washington head could be used, only as long as it was in keeping with the design dictated by the mountain itself.

Borglum noted that the Rushmore cliff was not perfect. Aging and weathering had produced in it a series of cracks running from top to bottom at angles of 30 degrees to 45 degrees every 70 feet. These cracks could not cross any projecting features. At the same time, to arrange the figures to avoid the cracks, like four fingers in a row, would hardly constitute good art.

Borglum felt that the essential nobility, honesty and strength of the Washington character could best be expressed by an erect face looking straight ahead. Washington was given the best location on the mountain. By the time the chin line of the Founding Father was reached, the artist was 30 feet into the stone cliff.

The 7 winches housed in the shack behind the center plate at the top, were under the watchful eye of the "call boy", strategically placed where he could view the workmen and the operators of the winches. The call boy, using a microphone, relayed messages for drills to the "steelman" who would swing the tools to the workmen as needed, but his main job was to interpret the signals of the men who wished to be raised or lowered and to instruct the winchmen, who had speakers in the winch houses. All tools and supplies were transported by cable 1500 feet, and the men climbed 760 steps before starting work.

Borglum was the one who found the best means for stone removal. He was the one who designed the machines and tools. Borglum had to find and train and supervise the men. Then, as he worked, he had to check the stone, and redesign the models to adjust to the stone. He was the indispensable man all the way.

After the granite was down to within 6 inches of the final surface, the actual process of carving began. This process, called *bumping,* was done with pneumatic tools called *bumpers.* The steel bits used in the tools were each about 1 1/4 inches square and had two sharp triangle shaped impressions. The bits were made at the Rushmore blacksmith shop, located just across the ravine from the stone work area. Not a

Machinery on top of the mountain controlled the men who were swung over the face of the cliff in their safety harnesses.

rotating bit, the function of this tool was to bounce up and down on the surface of the rock and flake off small shards. A few workers were so skilled with the jackhammers that they preferred to do finish work with them. Jackhammers weighed from 25 to 65 pounds, with the smaller ones used for final stages. The bumping machine was also a small easily controlled machine. Both methods cut the rock rapidly and accurately. The surface produced was not unlike a concrete highway which appears smooth as ivory from a distance, but up close has a finely pebbled grain. Bits wore away fast, but the blacksmith annealed, sharpened and retempered them as needed.

This final work was done from a moveable cage constructed of rough

2"x4"s. The sturdy cage, suspended from steel cables, was a remarkably steady platform for the workman, his tools, and a supply of water. After a given amount of work was done from the cage, the cage could be raised to assess the accuracy of the progress. If more work were needed, it could be returned to the same position. If the artist and superintendent were satisfied, it could be moved to a new location.

The work of translating exact measurements could be done mechanically from the scaffolding, but the cage was necessary to make the ultimate refinement of the project a matter of art rather than engineering. Both Gutzon and Lincoln Borglum did much of the finishing work. Such work was time consuming. The effects of light and shadow, of distance and angle, always had to be considered. Much time was spent analyzing each detail before those last bits of rock were removed.

Although it was later found that some work could be done at the mountain under most weather conditions, Borglums knew that the best time to accomplish demanding goals was between 10:00 A.M. and noon during the summer months. Records of the effects of light and shadow were followed by studying plaster models, and by the liberal use of cameras. Lincoln Borglum could often be seen in some precarious perch trying to get a difficult shot with his camera.

Actual completion of any part of the carving was painstakingly slow, mostly because the entire project was underfinanced and understaffed. In all the Rushmore years, less than a dozen men were employed who were skilled at any form of art. Among these, in addition to the Borglums, were Tallman, Villa, Bruner, and Bianco.

Luigi del Bianco, an Italian by birth, had worked with Gutzon since Connecticut days on the "Wars of America Memorial." The 42 foot statuary, largest ever cast in bronze up to that time, was too big for Borglum's studio. Bianco at that time was a rough stone worker and Borglum asked him to construct stone walls for a new studio to house the huge sculpture. Bianco finished the building up to the roof, and it was then topped with canvas. To keep the clay from freezing, a furnace was installed in the unique studio. Here Bianco helped get the masterpiece ready for casting and learned something of the sculptor's art from the master. He was to become one of the few previously trained workers at Rushmore.

Borglum instituted an on-the-job training program on the South Dakota project, and this produced about 6 more skilled stone carvers. By and large, most of the workers were unemployed miners, lumbermen who couldn't make any money selling posts at 25 cents each, or ranchers who had lost their herds to the drouth. They were courageous, hard working men, who became dedicated and able workers, all captured by the magnetism of Borglum and his dream.

The first figure on the mountain, appropriately Washington, was the key figure. Borglum did most of the rough sculpting of the Washington face in about ten weeks. Although dynamite could remove a lot of rock in a hurry, the definitive appearance of the features, the lifelike expression of the countenance, and the overall effect, were achieved only with the patience and care of the artist. Borglum would study the largest face ever carved from a distance. He would watch it in the pink Dakota dawn, and in the violet shadows of dusk. He would study it in the full blaze of morning sun, and when clouds of mist were hanging low. He knew exactly where he had to take off a bit more rock and exactly when the right amount had been removed. He kept refining this face for several years. Borglum was never truly satisfied with this face, or any of the others, but eventually he said that to him the "Bold features took on the elemental look of the timeless gray peak."

The head of Lee on Stone Mountain was 20 feet high, so Borglum knew from the beginning that to be consistent with the greater height of Mount Rushmore, these faces would have to be on a larger scale. He originally marked out 30 feet on the mountain and then went back to take a look. He reported "Thirty feet on that mountain looked like a small potato or a large peanut." So he doubled that to come up with the dimensions of the largest sculpted heads in the world.

Washington's nose was left one foot longer than the correct scale proportions. Geologists estimated that the extra foot might add 100,000 years to the life of the monument. Borglum was positive that with a face proportionate to a man 465 feet tall, one foot more on the nose would not even be noticeable. He was accutely aware of the immortality of his creation.

Soon it was time for another dedication. Borglum loved dedications. An eloquent speaker, he had a flair for planning and producing programs, which thrilled the crowds, imbuing them with his powerful optimism and great enthusiasm for this mountain. For the unveiling of the Washington face, set for July 4, 1930, he sent out engraved invitations to prominent people. He found ways to keep up the momentum of local publicity so that everyone in and near South Dakota feverishly anticipated this great event.

The native log studio Borglum used, was at the foot of Doane Mountain (named for Doane Robinson) directly across the valley from Rushmore. On the appointed day a crowd gathered here on the pine shaded terrace. Across the ravine and above them they saw a 72 foot long, 40 foot wide, 48 starred flag covering the first face. Commission

President Cullinan referred for the first time, to the work, as America's "Shrine of Democracy." Others on the program were Dr. O'Hara, and Robinson, who was then 74. But it was Borglum the crowd was waiting to hear. He did not disappoint them. He told how he was influenced by the Houdon mask of Washington, how he studied the famous portraits by Peale and Stuart, but how in the last analysis, he had to do something new, he had to breathe dimension and animation into an enormous mask of cold ancient rock. The problem of how to give the noblest of human qualities to such sheer bulk had never been solved before. Then he reiterated that this particular moment in time, marked the dedication of a face which would outlast all of the civilization it represented. All was silence as the stars and stripes were suspensefully withdrawn, and the summer sun shone dazzlingly on the largest carving of all time. Thunderous applause soon followed, but it could hardly be heard for the sharp salutes of rifles, and the roar of approaching planes.

The New York Times gave front page coverage to the ceremony, and part of it was filmed for the newsreels which every cinema featured. People who were formerly quite negative about Mount Rushmore were suddenly disposed to be cordial. In spite of overwhelming public approval, a carping minority continued to scoff and deride.

Mrs. Johnson of Hot Springs loudly denounced the carving through her news reporting, and she was joined by art critic, Florence Davis of Michigan, who proclaimed that though the figure was stupendous, it had nothing to do with art. Both declared that the mountain might better have been left as it was. Other editors and cartoonists forecast the mountain carving could become a fad and ruin all of the fine peaks of the Black Hills and Rocky Mountains. Jealous artists referred to the work as an engineering feat. But the *people* loved it. They were impressed by the lovely scenery, the graceful new road, and the magnificent likeness of the first President high on a granite cliff. Soon as many as 400 cars a day were winding their way to this spot. Visitors stood in awe as they glimpsed the soul of the land they loved. For them the monument had meaning.

But new work had to proceed. Denison was not a satisfactory replacement for Tucker. Borglum decided to promote William S. Tallman. This young man had considerable ability. He had studied under Borglum as a boy in Connecticut and was a friend of Lincoln Borglum and the whole family.

Another person hired by Borglum was Hugo Villa, an Italian sculptor who had previously assisted him, and who had a studio of his own in San Antonio. Villa was the son of a wealthy Italian family, who

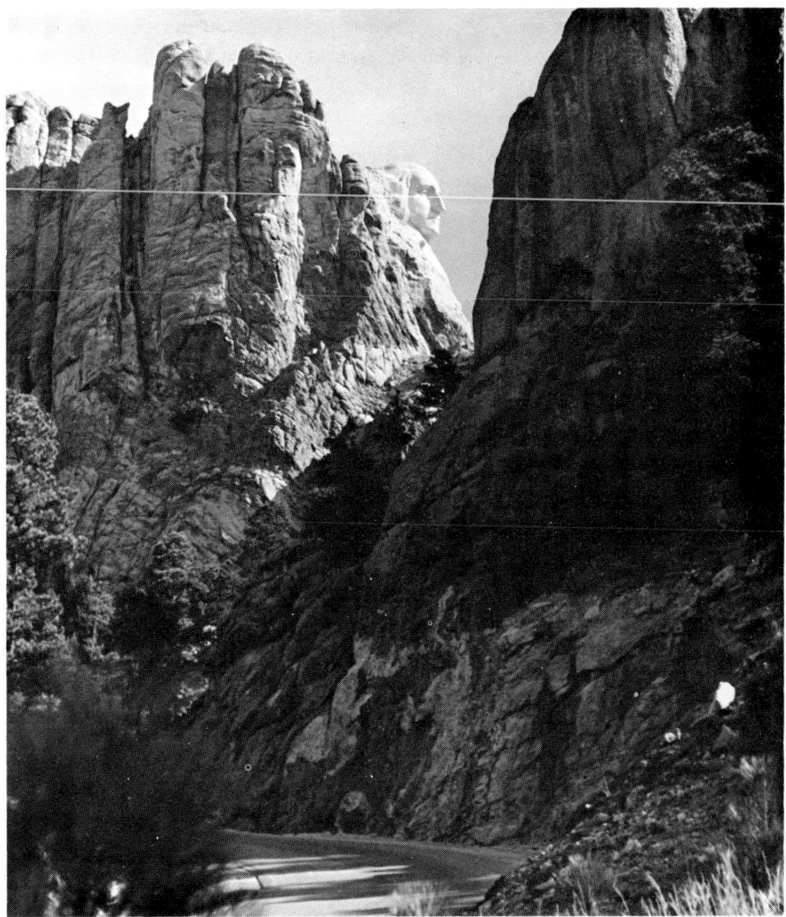

Viewed from the Borglum Memorial Highway, the profile of George Washington is a dramatic sight, particularly at night with the floodlights on. Mount Rushmore is a part of the Harney Range, the highest part of the Black Hills. Photo by S.D. Travel Division

had left his native land for the freedoms of America. He was well educated and talented. Besides working at sculpting he had a hobby of making "Stradivarius" violins. He got old and authentic wood from Italy, and patiently he concocted just the right glues and varnishes. His artistry was exacting and his "Strads" were great and valuable "discoveries" which made news in music circles for a number of years.

For awhile it looked as if progress might be rapid after the excitement of the Washington dedication, but the "out of funds" monster rose again.

John Boland warned that unless additional funds were immediately forthcoming it would be necessary to shut down the work, so only a few weeks after the triumph of the dedication, work came to a halt.

One money-making plan had been the selling of memberships in the Mount Rushmore National Memorial Society at a hundred dollars each, so Gutzon dug into his own pocket, as he frequently did and bought five memberships to the society and contributed $1,500 in addition. He wanted the work to continue, and he wanted the men to be able to stay on the job, and to get paid. He did not look for approbation in such acts of generosity, and didn't even think about them in that way. He only knew that if he happened to have money and the project happened to need it, that is where it should go.

Work was resumed in the middle of August in 1930 and continued until early in November, when ice and snow added to the general gloom, which prevailed before the commission meeting which was called for November 19.

It was then that a volunteer fund raiser came up with an idea which was emotionally packed. It was to have school children across South Dakota and later the nation, bring dimes and quarters to do their part to preserve the history of our era. Many children actually took part in this drive, which was carried on through the schools. It was easy for children to understand why a man would want to leave a message on a mountain. But this was the big depression, and the dimes and quarters turned out to be only pennies. By the time the certificates of appreciation, the advertising, and the mileage were paid, the net was under $2,000, so the success of the campaign was not financial. Few children ever forgot bringing pennies to school to help the memorial, and many great grandchildren have now heard of their family founder's participation.

At the annual Commission meeting, which was held in Chicago, Borglum suggested that a professional fund raising company be hired to solicit money to be used for matching funds for the Lincoln figure which was now being planned. He felt that Abraham Lincoln was a particularly beloved President, and that a drive ending on Lincoln's birthday, would be more successful than any financial plan to that time. The Commission turned this plan down. What they did was to authorize Borglum to publish another brochure. Then the Commissioners and the sculptor dug into their own pockets and eventually scraped together enough money to start work another season.

Borglum laid out precise and detailed plans for a large volume of work for the summer of 1931. Borglum and Lincoln were going to Posen, Poland for the unveiling of the artist's Woodrow Wilson statue which had been commissioned by Paderewski. The artist Hugo Villa was to do the more specialized work while Borglum was gone.

Villa was unusually adept at plaster work, an important part of sculpture. He taught Lincoln Borglum, as a boy, about the intricacies of this specialty. Once when Villa was casting a model which Gutzon had finished of Harvey W. Scott of the Portland, Oregonian, Villa decided to take a shortcut by leaving his plaster mold in Squaw Creek overnight for the clay residue to be washed out, instead of using the customary tedious sponging. The next morning, the entire mold had dissolved, and the vexed Borglum had to remake the back end of the statue which had been damaged in making the destroyed cast. The whole process had to be done again, and it was back to the sponges for Villa. Borglum disapproved of shortcuts, but the daring Villa was willing to try anything.

The major part of the work Borglum left to Villa was blocking out the Jefferson features, to the viewer's left of Washington. Villa's carving techniques varied from Borglum's, too, but he was an artist with training and experience, and the giant sized job had great attractions for him.

When the Borglums returned from Europe and reached the baseball diamond, about two miles from the monument, Gutzon looked up expectantly for his first glimpse of progress on his mountain. Gutzon exploded in a rage. He rushed to the studio, where he sent at once for Villa and Tallman.

"See," Villa muttered to Tallman as they entered, "didn't I tell you he'd notice it at once?"

"How did you ever manage to make such an irrevocable mistake?" Borglum demanded. But he hardly waited for the explanation for the damage had already been done. What happened was that Villa had cut too deeply into Jefferson's forehead. A sculptor can remedy a situation when a cut is too shallow, but there is nothing to do if it is too deep.

Borglum had worried casually before about the Villa method, but didn't think Villa would try it on work so meticulously laid out. Villa liked to find a low spot and work out and up from it. Borglum always found a high spot and worked carefully down. At this point the only "cure" was to blast the emerging Jefferson off the mountain and start anew in a different spot. (The rock in this spot was also found to be inferior.) Villa hastily left the scene and returned to his San Antonio Studio. On this day Lincoln was drafted by his father to work as chief pointer.

Up to this time Lincoln had been spending his winter months at the Valley Ranch School for boys near Cody, in neighboring Wyoming. He had spent his summers in the Black Hills with his family, and had been a keen observer of every phase of the work on the mountain and in the studio. Lincoln had expected to go to a University after finishing school at Cody, and he planned to study engineering. He had chosen the University of Virginia and had been accepted. His other interests were flying, athletics, and art. He thought, when he told his dad that he would help at the mountain, that he was only temporarily postponing his pursuit of an engineering degree. Gutzon was overjoyed to have his son on the job, as he was at his best with Lincoln around, and of course Lincoln had always enjoyed being with his father. The only drawback with the job was that it carried no salary. With funds so short, Gutzon did not dare put his own son on the payroll.

Lincoln was assisted by another pointer, Jim La Rue. He was more or less the mystery character on the mountain. A good worker, he did not mingle with the others and no one knew where he came from or anything about him. In fact, some were not even sure his name was La Rue.

When work resumed again on Jefferson, Villa's mistake was compounded, when it was found that the stone for the alternate location was unsound. Carving it was impossible. The rock had to be blasted away to a depth of 60 feet before solid rock was found. In the end, this proved to be a blessing in disguise, since the increased depth between the two faces now allowed light to come in from behind Washington to light up the Jefferson features.

The shifting of Jefferson made it necessary to modify the position of Washington's shoulders with relation to his head. This entire episode was intriguing and mystifying to the general public, who came in greater numbers than ever, half expecting to see the vast heads being shuffled about on the mountain. If nothing else, the procedure proved that mountain carvings are in reality more art than engineering, for no one but a trained artist would have the ability to redesign the entire composition at this stage of the game. To make it look as if it were planned that way. In effect to bend the cold, hard stone to his will.

Gutzon Borglum believed that labor needed to share in the creative efforts of civilization, and should be given pride in the results of its efforts. He never asked a worker to do something which he would not do himself. He climbed the mountain with his men. He visited with them, ate with them, instructed them, helped them and praised them. He knew their problems, at home and at work. He knew their potential on the job. He was rewarded with love and respect, and an atmosphere of true cooperation.

In the early years drillers on the work were being paid 50 cents to 60 cents per hour, while the few trained carvers earned $1.00 an hour. Even though the work period was only about 6 months, the workers were more fortunate than most Dakotans. Great numbers were on relief, and others, penniless and despondent, were losing their farms, and moving west.

The charge was made by Commissioner Boland and others, that Borglum wanted to hire more skilled carvers in order to bolster his own pay, which was on a percentage basis of the total amount spent. This was not borne out by the facts, since there never were enough trained artists for the higher pay scales.

The physical plant of Rushmore included several buildings on Doane Mountain. The workers even had to organize their own fire department to protect these miscellaneous temporary buildings. The chief of the Rushmore Volunteer Fire Department was Lincoln Borglum.

Nineteen thirty two was the year of the Washington bicentennial, but

While work at the Mountain was in progress this studio served as visitors head quarters. The working model is still in this building which is lower on Doane Mountain than the present Visitor's Center.

lack of funds shut down the work on the mountain after only two months. Borglum was particularly bitter, since this was the same year in which South Dakota spent $300,000 building roads to a monument on which it had never spent a penny. He was kept busy rebuilding the large model in the studio. The granite mountain seemed almost to be a dictator at times, as the rock was unpredictable. The model had to be completely redesigned a total of nine times, and minor changes were constant.

One of the new roads was the spectacular Iron Mountain Road, planned by Senator Norbeck to accent and intensify the beauty and wonder of the Memorial. Borglum wrote that the scenic road, prototype of many throughout the country, was an indispensable part of the monument itself, and he praised the loyal and talented Senator for the "greatest partnership that has been offered the National Memorial." Borglum had walked every foot of the winding trail with Norbeck during the planning.

Lincoln Borglum once came upon a man on a scenic point of Iron Mountain Road. The man had a car and a trailer wedged by a sign proclaiming the spot to have a good view of Rushmore. He explained that his car couldn't make the grade and the turn ahead was too sharp for his trailer, that the trailer was at too steep an angle to sleep in it. "And the worst of it is," he confessed, "I just lost a 100 dollar bet." Then the man introduced himself as Senator Reynolds of North Carolina.

"I'll be glad to take you wherever you'd like to go," Lincoln offered. "And maybe we can send someone to move the car and the trailer for you."

"Leave them as they are," replied Senator Reynolds, "they can be a memorial to Senator Norbeck."

Gutzon was glad to see South Dakota making some improvements on the roads in the Black Hills. Once he had tried to get to the mountain from Rapid City after heavy rains and had to turn back before he was out of the foothills. During a wet spring, roads and valleys alike were a sea of mud. He tried again with another car. He kept trying on six successive days always landing in a slippery ditch. He finally made it. He had lost a week's work, but he knew every ditch between Rapid City and Mount Rushmore.

In the fall of 1932 Senator Norbeck succeeded in getting a windfall, an appropriation of $50,000 which was later doubled. This did not have to be matched by private funds, but there was a catch to it. It was Public Works money, to be spent only to give jobs to the unemployed, landscaping the grounds.

The financial distress on the project was at its lowest. The new workers were the unemployed from the area from all walks of life. They were to clean up and beautify Doane Mountain, construct steps, walls, walkways, and make the Memorial viewing area safe and attractive for the public. So fierce was the pride of the regular Rushmore employees, that a sort of caste system built up between those who were actually carving the mountain and those who were laboring to improve the viewing area. Those who had worked on the mountain at the hardest jobs, the drilling and the blasting, had their own seniority system, and they were intensely proud of their positions.

Up to this time there had been a number of changes on the Commission. Cullinan, the President, had resigned and Fred Sargent, President of the Chicago and Northwestern Railroad was elected to the vacancy. Borglum lamented, "I could not resign. The rock of Rushmore was riveted to my neck."

The size and personnel of the work force at Rushmore changed some from season to season. The available money regulated the number of men on the project, and the abilities of men who were available for seasonal work, decided how much and what type of work could be accomplished. Some of the men liked their work better than anything they had ever done and learned their new skills rapidly. Such men were on the job for many years. The workers got to know each other well, and were like members of the same family. Hardly a day was without its bit of excitement or sorrow, or hilarity, or suspense.

One worker was a stone mason, somewhat older than many of the Rushmore men, but with two young sons at home. One day an FBI man came up to the mountain asking Gutzon and others a lot of questions, and then calling the stone mason away from his work.

"Do you have two young sons?"

"Yes, I do."

"Do you know what they have been doing lately?"

"Well, no, I—"

"They've been busy making counterfeit money out of lead in your attic."

"Oh no!"

"Yes. Quarters and halves. Not bad either considering what they had to work with!"

"You know I sort of wondered why those kids were so quiet up in the attic!"

A popular worker from Hermosa was "Whittlin' Jack" Zazadil. Jack cheerfully did any job that was asked, and regaled his peers with tales of his far flung adventures. Like Villa, Jack had a hobby of making violins. Only he didn't call his "Strads" like Villa did, because in his opinion, his were just a little better. He also cut and polished rocks and gems from the nearby Badlands, and carved fish and flowers from gems. He would amaze visitors by his tales of petrified trees in Custer Park, standing erect with unbroken limbs cradling petrified birds' nests.

One of the foremen was Art Johnson of Keystone, who for some reason went by the name of "Whiskey" Johnson. He worked on the project for many years and acquired some rock of his own eventually, an old mine near Keystone, which produced nothing much but hopes. Another Johnson who worked on the mountain was Alfred.

A third Johnson, A. I., a mining engineer from Keystone was helping put the electric highline through the Hills, when he chanced to meet Borglum.

"That power line looks monstrous crossing those Hills," Borglum complained. "Don't you know that nature abhors a straight line?"

"Electricity doesn't follow beautiful curves like you artists make," was Johnson's answer, which seemed to mollify the artist.

Matt Reilly was a trusted worker who made the rank of foreman. Once when the Borglums had to be away for a short time, they left instructions with Matt to start removing a granite formation called the "Three Monkeys." This was a granite knob which was in a position near enough the carvings to be removed separately, thereby getting rid of the disturbing projection. Since it was not part of the carving, Matt decided to take it all off quickly in one mighty blast. He was rather proud of his idea, which seemed to him to surpass his instructions. As luck would have it, the Borglums arrived just in time to see the massive knob shoot straight out from the side of the mountain and rain down the canyon with a resounding roar. Although Matt was in some disgrace for a few days, Borglum saw the humor of the incident, and soon joined in kidding the Irishman about his "monkey business." Lincoln had known Matt as a boy in Connecticut.

Norman (Happy) Anderson was a top notch driller who went to Minnesota after the completion of the project. He was no relation to Otto (Red) Anderson who also stayed on the job some time, and was reliable and well liked by Borglums, and the men. Merle Peterson of Rapid City was thought to be one of the best men on the job, and took more than a usual interest in the work. Several other men who mastered the precision work of drilling were Miles Gardner, Eldon Gordon, and Ray Grover.

Carl Baird, for many years the night watchman at the project, had the reputation of being more or less of an outlaw in the earlier, wilder days of the Black Hills. Of course he fostered this reputation himself. To prove that he was really a "fast gun" he would shoot chipmunks off the top of the mountain with a 45, while bets were being made behind his back.

A faithful worker was Alfred Burg, an excellent man with explosives, who held the job of "powder monkey". He had a son, Ray Burg, who held another important job, that of "call boy". Ray would stand on a windy peak to relay messages from caged men hanging over the chasm below, so he was the one who got the blame if the men weren't moved to a new position fast enough to suit them.

There were numerous instances of two or more from a family working together on the Monument. Ed and Charles Halsted of Keystone were employed for some time. Charles ran the big compressor. The Jones boys, Frank and Glen, were as much remembered for their records on the baseball diamond as for their work on the job.

Gail and George Wilcox were brothers from Rapid City who made part of their career the mountain work. George operated one of the banks of winches on the peak, located on the big heads. He received unmerciful razzing from the others that since he was strenuously exercising his right arm so much in operating the winches, they could see that it was growing noticeably longer than his left arm. George later became an Air Force General. Gail, who became a Ranger at Grand Teton National Park, lost his life trying to save a tourist.

The blacksmith shop was one of the busiest places in the compound. Robert Christian and Matt Cindel were two who were proud to be blacksmiths for a mountain carving. Gus Jurisch, Scenic rancher, was a steel carrier.

A most necessary job was that of water hauler. Don Clifford hauled the daily supply of water to the workers and the project. He later became an administrator of tourist oriented businesses. Orville Worman, who held several different jobs on the mountain, became Captain of the Highway Patrol in Rapid City. John Hayes, Keystone, operated one of the hoists.

From the Indiana limestone quarries came Joe Bruner, one of the few skilled stone cutters ever employed. Nils Leden was another stone mason, but he couldn't stand hanging out in space to do his work, so he didn't stay long on the mountain. But he was an excellent workman, so Borglum hired him to do some impressive fireplaces at the Ranch. A third trained stone worker from the east was Jens Ikast. Art students often came to work at the mountain for a while as apprentices, or to help at the studio. Ivan Wellman and Arthur Cerasini were two of these.

Jobs were hard to get during the depression, even for the well educated, so many of the men at the mountain were well trained and experienced in other fields. Robert McNally had a college degree, but gladly took a job at Mount Rushmore at the bottom of the pay scale. He was a local hero though, as the capable catcher of the baseball team.

When funds ran out on the mountain, and work had to be discontinued, the men would scatter in all directions looking for other work. But at the first rumor that a Rushmore appropriation was forthcoming, almost to a man, they would drop everything and rush back to report to Gutzon.

Borglum had many friends among the wealthy and powerful. When they failed to see the magnitude of his work at Rushmore, he felt that they had let him down. In fact, many of the commissioners were chosen because of their wealth and prestige. So certain was Gutzon of the vital importance of his dream, that he felt his enthusiasm should spread like a contagion, and that everyone should see his dream as he did. There were disappointingly few gifts of any size for the Memorial. Borglum approached such friends as Owen D. Young, George Eastman and Bernard Baruch. He was incensed that Baruch intimated that his reason for not backing Mount Rushmore was that Woodrow Wilson had not been included. Perhaps politics influenced other possible donors. Or perhaps it was the remoteness of the state of South Dakota from population centers and from the homes of philanthropists. The wealthy and influential regarded South Dakota with vagueness, if not antipathy. The state was in the "dust bowl" of the arid, windy "dirty thirties" so the depression had more than a normal sting. Furthermore, it was a conservative state financially and politically, and very little was known about the land and its people. Many of the few tourists who did wander through the state, expected to see the Sioux Indians in buckskin and eagle feathers standing behind government fences.

The unspoken thought was that the money might have been easy to raise, had the mountain of granite been within a few hours drive of New York City. Borglum had once felt that the state of Illinois would happily furnish money for the Lincoln face, but this proved to be another of his unfounded, over-optimistic ideas.

When Norbeck squeezed through the Reconstruction Finance Corporation allocation, releasing $50,000 to the Mount Rushmore Commission for work on and around the mountain, South Dakota's Governor Green did not give up the specified amount until September of 1932, too late to do anything except minor work on the roads and tourist facilities. Depression bitten Dakotans felt it was their money, and they sharply criticized the use of any of it at Rushmore, but

Norbeck had intended this amount for the Memorial when he sought the money originally.

Then Norbeck wondered if perhaps the Federal windfall might be matched by the idle Rushmore appropriations for which private funds had never been raised. Again he was successful, and the bank balance for the 1933 season looked the brightest since the work began. Work started during the dry, gusty winds of March and continued until the cold blasts of December.

Even Borglum received some of his long overdue honorarium that year. Some of the money had been owed him ever since Tucker left. Lincoln Borglum, still his father's best assistant, had not yet been put on the payroll. A skilled Italian carver, Luigi del Bianco, who had previously worked with Gutzon, was hired to assist in the refinement of the faces. There were more jobs and more workers than ever before, so in spite of the drouth and depression, 1933 was seen as a banner year for the Rushmore people. Everyone felt that at last things were going well.

Tourist traffic also increased significantly that year, with people registering from 48 states and many foreign countries. Of course, the roads in the area were all dirt and gravel, but they were average for the Midwest at that time. There were rustic cabins for rent in the Hills, many with cooking facilities. Tourists were expected to bring their own dishes and linens. Most of the visitors hoped above all to get a look at Borglum, as they were convinced it would be something to tell their grandchildren.

In 1933 the first major change in administration took place. By Franklin D. Roosevelt's executive order, the project was placed with the National Park Service branch of the Department of Interior. The Park Service Director told Norbeck that he was totally opposed to the idea of a mountain being mutilated. He intimated that he didn't want anything to do with the South Dakota project, but since it had been forced on him, the Service would view it sternly and strictly. This was an added thorn in Borglum's side. Borglum was more reluctant to be controlled by the Park Service than the Park Service was to have mountain sculpture under its jurisdiction. Haughtily the Service officials pointed out that previously National Parks had been works of nature and National Monuments were of scientific, natural, or historic significance, that up to that time no National Memorial had been purposely created by man.

President Roosevelt was well acquainted with Borglum and in sympathy with the idea of the Monument, so he signed a bill eliminating the need for matching funds, for the entire amount

As Superintendent of the work, Lincoln oversaw all phases of the project. Here he inspects the compressor air hoses on top of the mountain. Workers on the top were called winchmen and call boys.

remaining of the original Rushmore appropriation, which amounted to $120,000.

One reason that it was decided to put Mount Rushmore under the Park Service was to guarantee the intergrity of the area, to preserve the balance of nature which made the site inspirational, the perfect backdrop for a national shrine. Borglum himself had long insisted that there never be campgrounds, tourist traps, or billboards close to his work.

The year 1934 which did away with all pretenses of trying to raise private financing for Rushmore, was also the year for Lincoln Borglum to finally make the payroll. He had worked long hours at his demanding and exacting job ever since 1931, and even after working so long without pay, his official status raised a few eyebrows.

If only the general public knew more about his monumental work, Gutzon complained, it would be easy to create an atmosphere which would produce all the additional funds he needed. Borglum talked with his friend William Randolph Hearst about his plans, and his infectious enthusiasm led the famous publisher to sponsor a contest in his newspaper empire for the best short statement about America, to be used as the inscription to be incised in large letters on the mountain. The inscription begun by Coolidge some years before, had long since been scrapped.

The Hearst family had been original owners of the Homestake Mine, and were interested in art and in South Dakota. Borglum agreed with Hearst that a nationwide contest might provide the public exposure necessary for continued support of the carvings.

Few contests in history commanded so much high powered publicity, or created such eager participation, as this contest for the best 600 word history of the United States. There were four divisions, adult, college, high school, and grammar school. Top cash prizes were $1,000, a large sum during the depression. There were also Regional prizes, including scholarships. But the big reason that there were 836,735 entries nationwide, is that every entrant hoped that *his* words would be the ones to become immortal, to be carved on a mountain.

All entries were judged regionally and then nationally. Oddly enough the greatest interest in the contest was in the New York City metropolitan area. Even the distinguished historian, Henry Woodhouse, published articles in New York, urging people to enter this contest.

Roosevelt himself agreed to preside over a committee of illustrious judges which included Senators Pittman, Hiram Johnson, Tom Connally, Peter Norbeck and C. L. McNary, as well as Eleanor Roosevelt, Isabella Greenway, R. G. Sproul, Fred Sargent, and J. A. Chandler. The leading American poet, Edwin Markham was a regional judge for New York. Other regional judges were distinguished professors, eminent historians, and established authors.

Borglum was at his most persuasive when he gave the first announcements of the giant contest over the C.B.S. radio network. Newspapers and radio alike found the contest a welcome relief from the grim depression and drouth stories which were daily fare.

One of the contest winners was William Burkett, whose 575 word history of his country won the national college division. The passage of time was to bring events which barred any of the winning inscriptions from being incised on the mountain as planned; however, many years later Burkett, who became a successful businessman in California, had his inscription cast in bronze at his own expense. It was duly installed on Doane Mountain on the Borglum Viewing Terrace. The biggest winner in the Hearst contest was the state of South Dakota which received nationwide front page publicity that the most lavish advertising budget could not have bought.

In 1935, the new Congressman Theodore Werner, from the western South Dakota district, determined to introduce a bill to get a clear $200,000 appropriation for the mountain. The appropriation would mean a lot to his poor district. Speaker of the House Rainey had the bill confused with another and refused to recognize Werner, until Congresswoman Isabella Greenway King, during a recess, explained to Rainey that Werner had charge of "Dear Gutzon's" bill. Werner was recognized, and the new manna from Washington was passed with little opposition. Gutzon had been in Washington, seeing the right people and wielding his considerable influence. His master lobbying had again paid off.

The physical plant at Monument headquarters now began to show some much needed improvements. For all the previous years water had been hauled to the work in 20 gallon cream cans, at the rate of 50 or more a day. But now the commission authorized the creation of a water supply with a reservoir, pumps, pipes, and modern sanitary facilities. Alternating 110 volt electric power was installed. New machinery was purchased, making it possible to put more men on the job. Things were going so well that the sculptor pushed on, and did not even shut down the work for the winter. Borglum was pleasantly surprised that the Black Hills' winter did not have the sting of Connecticut. After that, whenever there was money, work was continued in the winter.

The scaffoldings where winter work was underway were covered with tarpaulins of firm canvas, and 55 gallon oil drums were made into efficient little fireplaces, burning the plentiful pine wood. It was found that concentrated heat had to be kept at a distance from the icy rock, as the heat would cause the rock to spall off in an uncontrollable way. Although granite is a hard rock, composed of feldspar, mica, and quartz, it shatters easily when water or ice crystals are present and direct heat is applied.

Borglum remained active in many walks of American life during this time. He kept up his interest in aeronautics and was asked by Congress to chair a National Committee to recommend airway controls. He was also interested in conservation, beautification of America, music, sports, architecture, and western movies.

There were some personality clashes during the Rushmore years, which was inevitable considering that 135 workmen were involved, plus a couple of dozen commissioners, plus a number of congressmen and senators from both parties, and several government agencies, and even several Presidents of the country. But the major conflict, all the way through, was between Borglum and Boland. Borglum was a genius. He was not a practical basinessman, and had no intention of devoting his days to business routine. His work was art. Boland was a methodical and conservative Midwest businessman, who didn't comprehend that by nature the worlds of the true creative artists and the conventional businessman were poles apart. Boland was steady, plodding, rational, orderly, reliable. Borglum was creative, impulsive, spontaneous, forceful, dynamic. Borglum accused Boland of holding too tight a rein on the finances, of unfair restraints, of erecting stumbling blocks, and even of destructive interference. Boland accused Borglum of irresponsibility, of poor administration practices, of wasteful procedures, of lack of cooperation. He felt that Borglum was stubborn and egotistical, while Borglum felt Boland was unimaginative, contrary, and stodgy.

Part of Borglum's trouble was that he was an easy spender, open and generous to a fault. He didn't want to be bothered by the mundane word of finance and paperwork. Because his pay had always been so slow and irregular, he had been forced to borrow to make payments on his ranch, and when he could not make payments promptly, he lost his credit rating in the city which was to find unprecedented prosperity because of his work.

The property in Connecticut had long been heavily mortgaged. Mary had arranged to mortgage it when her genius husband was trying to keep the Stone Mountain project going. After that, the couple was always treading water financially and but for Mary, would have gone under several times. (The morgage was not paid off until after Gutzon's death, when Mary had to sell enough land to meet the final payment.)

Borglum found it hard to raise the money he needed for his ranch and to finish the home he had started to build. When he couldn't keep up with payments or taxes, and the bankers in Rapid City refused to help him, the ranch was taken from him and put up for sale at the county sheriff's sale of land with tax claims against it. From the steps of the Custer County Courthouse, the auctioneer presided. On the block was the 1120 acre Borglum Ranch. (Gutzon had been led to believe when he purchased it that there were 1500 acres, but it developed that 480 acres of School Land had been counted.)

When the Borglum Ranch was cried, bidding was at a minimum, because money was not readily available. The bids closed and the high bidder was none other than Lincoln Borglum. Thus the historic ranch of the cloverleaf brand was retained by the family, and Gutzon and Mary continued to call it home. It is little wonder that more bitterness towards the business community of South Dakota was nurtured by this incident.

A great humanitarian enterprise of the Borglums during the '30s illustrates the type of a man Gutzon was. During the depression and drouth some 8000 Indians of the Ogalala Sioux tribe were starving on the Pine Ridge Reservation, not far from the Borglum Ranch. As soon as Borglum heard of this, he swung into direct action to help his neighbors.

"The Indians are in a condition of want, unbelievable and unforgivable for us," he wrote in an open letter to South Dakota. He went on to report that the situation was so desperate that the Indians were eating their own ponies to exist. The aroused artist also wrote the Department of Interior.

Then the Borglums, father and son, set out to visit all of the West River South Dakota ranchers from Bison to White River, in an effort to get a herd of 100 cattle together to feed the Indians. Starting with 5 select steers from their own herd, the Borglums quickly received more donations from others nearby. Then they rode and they wrote, and they spoke and they pleaded. People read the message and heard the pleas,

Gutzon's historic old slaughter house studio now stands on the Borglum ranch near Hermosa.
Photo by Albert Zeitner

so when the Borglums appeared, they were ready to help. Enlisting the aid of area cattlemen, they finally covered the territory and met their goal. After much foot-dragging the government agreed to furnish trucks to transport the cattle to Reservation Agent, James McGregor, and hereditary tribal chief, Jim Red Cloud. Sheep and buffalo were next added to the list. Many of the cattle were on the thin side, but could readily be fattened on the native grass of the Reservation, where the cattle were apportioned according to need.

Simultaneously, Borglum called the public's attention to the facts that the Indians were without warm clothing and blankets for the cold, long winters and inadequate shelters. The indomitable Borglum was successful in getting surplus army clothing diverted to the Indians through the aid of Secretary Wilbur of the Department of Interior. Then he asked Governor Green of South Dakota to try to get some army blankets for the Indians. Army officials, after some haggling, granted the request, and loaned 5200 blankets to the tribe, asking for a guarantee that the blankets be returned in the spring in good condition. So Borglum protested the requirements to the chief of staff, General Douglas MacArthur, who was understanding and cut through the red tape.

Borglums were personally involved in all of this work, as busy as they were. Their reports of the plight of the tribe were not just hearsay, but the result of careful personal investigation. The help they initiated was not a mechanical dole, because the two men took part themselves as a gesture of concern and friendship. Both Borglums were made honorary members of the tribe, an honor not lightly bestowed. Gutzon became honorary chief Inyan Wamblee, (Stone Eagle) at a colorful and joyful ceremony at Pine Ridge. The sculptor was widely portrayed by the press in full regalia topped by a priceless eagle feather war bonnet, Lincoln Borglum was inducted as "Indian Leader" into the tribe at a ceremony at the reservation hamlet of Kyle, which suddenly acquired a huge tent population of deliriously grateful people. One of the multitude of spectacular features of the prolonged celebration was a buffalo hunt. The spirit of both occasions was of unrestrained exuberance.

Lincoln Borglum was becoming famous as a photographer. Through the 1930s the Eastman Company was experimenting with various kinds of film and new concepts of photography. They provided Lincoln with cameras and film, as they felt that the work at Rushmore, in the splendid scenery of the Black Hills would provide many crucial tests for their new equipment. Lincoln took a camera with him wherever he went. He took candid shots of the workmen with their jackhammers, of his father in his swing harness, hanging over the precipice of granite, of the dignified and exalted face of George Washington chiseled in gray stone against the intense blue of the summer sky, with sharp branches of green pine in the foreground. It wasn't long before some of these pictures became magazine covers for such popular periodicals as LIBERTY, THIS WEEK, CORONET, LIFE and the SATURDAY EVENING POST.

Lincoln Borglum pictures were used in newsreels, in syndicated newspapers, in Sunday supplements, in Rushmore brochures, and often in history and travel books. Exhibited in photography shows, some of Lincoln's photos took top awards. He was a winner in a National Graflex contest. His works were shown in museums, and the Witte Museum in San Antonio had a one-man show of Lincoln's best pictures. He was asked to devote more of his time to the growing art of photography, but he had to let this interest remain incidental to his real work.

Work did not occur on the mountain according to a definite prearranged schedule. That is, the plan did not call for finishing one face and then the next in sequence, with a certain amount of the budget, in time and money, being spent on each. Many, including Boland and other commissioners and the government, did not understand this. The sculptor was carving a marble statue in his own studio, but even here he would not have made an artificial schedule such as to spend one month on the face, one week on the right arm, one week on the left, etc. Mathematical and exact progression is not the way of art, large or small. Some work was done on the Lincoln face at the same time work was progressing on Jefferson. Meanwhile other workmen were clearing a space for the entablature, or starting the Hall of Records excavation. And Borglum himself might be working on the further refinement of the Washington face. As the artist and designer, Borglum had to oversee each job, because he had to know where the good stone was located in relation to the mountain and to the focal point, the face of Washington. He had to see for himself the fractures in every granite mass, and study the blocky mineral crystals which might spell disaster.

For example, a small supported fracture along the edge of a nose could be acceptable, but if the face were planned so that fracture ran through the tip of the nose, that part of the work would be doomed. Only an artist could visualize the necessary changes. Nevertheless there were many, like Boland, who attempted to force Borglum's work into their preconceived laymen's notions of how a mountain should be carved.

With crises and stumbling blocks every step of the way, the work on the Memorial was often sheer agony for the sculptor. To friend and critic alike, the tremendous responsibility he felt, the overwhelming force which drove him on and on, his complete and unqualified devotion to this carving, were almost incomprehensible. He was in his 60s. Year upon year, and day after day, he had been climbing the resistant and demanding mountain in wind and rain, heat and cold. He was always aware of being involved in a tremendous struggle.

When the atmosphere between Borglum and Boland became more charged with recriminations and mistrust, Boland went to Washington to plead with the Park Service to send a man to Rushmore to put in direct charge of the work. The Park Service acquiesced, softening their decision by notifying Borglum that the new man would be an experienced engineer, who would be able to relieve the sculptor from all except the true artistic work on the mountain.

In 1935 engineers on the mountain were earning $6.00 per day, the same as the drillers. Common laborers earned $4.00 a day. A few, such as the skilled stone carvers and the master pointer earned $12.00 a day. The pay scale was in keeping with those days, and with food and housing costs low, $6.00 a day went a long way.

After the usual struggle, the questioning of the sculptor's motives, the slurs on the meaning of his work, and slander about the pace of the progress, another monetary appropriation came through in 1936. This showed Congress's lack of faith in the whole enterprise, as it had a restriction barring the expenditure of any of this money for work on any figure not yet started. By July 7 in 1936 work was ready to resume.

The engineer the Park Service sent to the scene was Julian Spotts, a graduate of the University of Missouri. Although he was well trained and familiar with granite quarries, he had little knowledge of the work in South Dakota. But he felt ready to take over as soon as he arrived. He took out his slide rule and went through several pages of figures. Then he announced to Lincoln Borglum that according to his calculations there was adequate power to have 16 men working on the stone cliff with jackhammers.

"Is that so!" Lincoln replied. "Well, if you will just look up there for a minute you can count 30 men up there running jackhammers right now."

Prior to one of the dedications, Lincoln sent some of the workmen to the mountain top to speed up the preparations for the big moment. Spotts was furious. He said Lincoln was out of line, and had no authority to direct the men, without the previous approval of Spotts. At this point Lincoln said, "Maybe I should just resign here and now and leave you to carry out the work." This temporarily ended further opposition.

An improvement both Borglums were grateful for was the installation of an aerial tramway to transport the workers to their jobs. This saved the time and the energy of the men for work on the mountain itself.

Spotts was supposed to relieve Borglum from administrative chores, thus making it possible for the artist to devote full time to his art. In a way, this concept was impossible. The work and the administration of the work were two sides to the same coin. Administration included supervision of employees, qualifications, and terms of advancement, work assignments and daily planning. Borglum knew his men and their abilities as no one else could, certainly not Spotts. Borglum knew that work like this could not be done on the basis of work lists, quotas, timetables, and paperwork.

When Spotts told Borglum how to proceed one day, the irritated artist snapped, "Have you ever carved a mountain?"

Spotts didn't deign to reply. Borglum resisted the edicts of Spotts, because he was determined not to be undermined by government "red tape." Borglum was there to carve a mountain, not to take lessons in bureaucracy. Borglum and Spotts quickly became antagonists. It was obvious the impasse could not continue.

What bothered the Interior Department the most was that the artist did not furnish them with a complete detailed blueprint of all future operations. They wanted lots of statistics, maps, timetables. They wanted estimates of daily power requirements, inventories of supplies and descriptions of the physical plants. They wanted lists of purchase dates of machinery, and dates and types of repairs made on the machines. They wanted continually updated rosters of the workers, their hours on the job, the kind of work they did each day. They wanted reports on the numbers and positions and changes and localities of all the models, and the reasons for any changes. What it amounted to was complete control of all aspects of the project.

Spotts wanted to follow all the rules and regulations he was used to in the Park Service. Borglum thought most of them were a lot of nonsense. Both men complained loudly to Washington, so John Nagle, Superintendent of Memorials for the Park Service, came to South Dakota to investigate, and to try to resolve the difficulties.

Nagle agreed with Spotts that the Park Service should have complete control. He firmly recommended that the work should go forward on only Lincoln and Roosevelt until these two faces were exactly as far along as Washington and Jefferson. He advised a rigid schedule detailing even the number of hours to be allowed for Roosevelt's mustache. Nagle liked Borglum, however, and tried to make peace. For awhile Spotts devoted most of his thought to improving the physical plant of Rushmore and installing long needed new equipment. Then he ordered a beautification program for the surrounding area.

One reason that the cost of the project seemed forever greater than even the most careful estimates, was that it was almost impossible to guess how much stone would actually have to be removed from any one spot. And most of the overall cost for time and supplies for the carving itself was for the bulk removal of tons and tons of stone. Almost four times as much granite was eventually removed, as had been planned in the beginning. This was because cracks, fractures, rotten granite, and hard crystals were so located that the faces could not be placed where it was the cheapest, or fastest, or easiest. These things could not have been foreseen.

Between Jefferson and Lincoln was the only place for Roosevelt, since a narrow canyon borders Lincoln to the right. But for a few tense days, it did not seem that there would be enough sound rock for Roosevelt's head. Anxious workmen had to penetrate the rock of the mountain to a depth of 120 feet before finding the necessary solid granite for laying out the features of the fourth face.

When it became apparent that the carving would become a financial bonanza to South Dakota, many entrepreneurs wanted to climb on the bandwagon. Gutzon was approached by people with all sorts of schemes, commercial type ventures which would be instant successes with the Borglum name and backing. He knew he was being used, and he was heartsick when people he considered friends tried to commercialize on the monument. One of his friends came up with the idea of a resort Inn at the Keystone "Y", with the Borglum name and design and backing, and the friend in charge of the whole thing. Others wanted exclusive rights to pictures, and stories, and an assortment of tasteless souvenirs.

Thousands of people a day were now visiting the mountain, and their delight and approval were truly making the monument a National Shrine. One such visitor was the trend setting American architect Frank Lloyd Wright. He said the addition of the countenance of man to the mountain made it look "As if the mountain had responded to human prayer." Wright was so thrilled that he agreed to help his friend Gutzon plan and build the Hall of Records.

As the emphasis shifted to the fine finishing, Hugo Villa of the Jefferson fiasco reappeared on the mountain as if nothing had ever happened, and at once he was put back to work. Any rift which Borglum ever had with a friend or employee was soon mended. At times

Robinson and Norbeck had differences with the sculptor, but they always admired and respected him. They accepted him as an unusual man of rare vision and integrity.

There was no doubt but what Borglum irritated numerous people, including, at times, his best friends. To him Rushmore came first. He was working on a monument to the greatness of the country he loved. All else was secondary. He was an artist and full of self-confidence. He would sometimes try to bypass the Commission, he paid little attention to the long pages of regulations the government prepared for his work, he hated being bogged down in financial quagmires, and he was strong willed and abrupt. But such was the personality of the man, that all of his friends remained true, and no project ever had a more loyal group of workmen.

One of the artistic problems had been whether to show Abraham Lincoln with or without a beard. Borglum's magnificent head of Lincoln in the Rotunda of the Capitol was beardless. It had been so unnerving to Robert Todd Lincoln when he had seen it, that he gasped after a startled silence, "I had never hoped to see father again."

Borglum's equally revered, seated Lincoln, in Newark, depicted the more familiar bearded Lincoln. Borglum was a zealous Lincoln scholar, and had even written an article about Lincoln, in which he stated that he felt those who criticized Lincoln as being awkward, stooped, ill dressed, and ungainly were 100% wrong. He felt that Lincoln had the easy grace of an outdoor man, and that his face revealed a richness of character imparting true spiritual beauty. Lincoln was an idolized subject, and both Borglum and the son he had named for the Great Emancipator, were determined that this Lincoln of the mountain would surpass any ever done. Borglum wanted to depict Lincoln's powerful influence on the nation's life. He felt that the Lincoln Memorial in Washington, D.C. was a monstrosity, because of the formal Greek architecture, which had no relationship to the life or times of Lincoln.

Borglum finally decided on the bearded Lincoln, feeling that on a face this size the beard would add strength and contrast to the composition. He studied Lincoln's life mask and self description. He also used 6 photos of Lincoln which he felt were accurate. He decided that Lincoln's expression was determined by the right eye, and the sad mouth "which bore the hint of a remembered smile." To Borglum the complexity of the Lincoln character was apparent on the face.

Lincoln Borglum succeeded William Tallman as Superintendent of work, so he was privileged to oversee most of the work, and do much of the work himself, on his namesake. This was the face which was the real challenge to him. He watched intensely as careful work brought emotion to the brooding and powerful features. After long hours and weeks and months, it was gratifying when he heard many travellers say that their favorite head of the four was Lincoln.

One of the problems in this locality was the mineral deposits in the pegmatite dike on that part of the mountain. Besides great, pale, blocky feldspar crystals, they ran into silver and tin crystals on the side of Lincoln's face.

From a little distance, the granite faces looked impressive enough, but when the viewers saw two or three workmen hanging in front of one eye, or at work on a minor detail like a lapel, it became apparent how truly immense was the scale of the Memorial. When they could make out the details of the four carvings from the top of Iron Mountain several miles away, they couldn't help but be awed by the sheer size of the accomplishment they were witnessing.

There was a great deal of agitation among women's groups, as the four men took shape, for the inclusion of a woman on the mountain. Susan B. Anthony was the choice. Particularly insistent were the women's clubs of Minnesota. They wrote to their congressmen and to Borglum and the Park Service, and came to talk to Borglum in person. The sculptor listened patiently to the ladies, as he had an unusual regard for women, numbering many women among his oldest and closest friends. Other groups came to him with good cases for the inclusion of their hero's likeness. Even Franklin D. Roosevelt was earnestly proposed. All were told the truth, that there was not enough solid rock left on the mountain for any except the four figures then underway. Borglum did tell the ladies and the others, however, that there would be room for their favorites in the Hall of Records.

Since the dedication of the Washington figure in 1930 there had not been another dedication. So in the winter of 1936 Gutzon started making plans for another extravaganza, the dedication and unveiling of the head of Thomas Jefferson. Roosevelt was arranging a schedule to visit the depression torn Midwest that summer, so Borglum arranged to have the President as the featured guest. When the appointed day dawned, the sculptor could hardly conceal his irritation. He had scheduled the ceremony for late morning so the sun would light up the youthful Jefferson countenance to the fullest. Eleven o'clock came and went, then 11:30, and still no sign of the President. Then by noon Roosevelt had not appeared. By the time the late guest arrived, the flag draping the Jefferson face was well in the shadows. Roosevelt had expected it to be a normal, routine affair, and had rejected the opportunity to make a speech. With flags flying of Spain and France, all but dwarfed by the 70 foot flag over Jefferson, with blasts of dynamite controlled by Lincoln on the peak sending down torrents of rock, with flag-bearing parachutes released from circling planes, with a great crowd transfixed by anticipation, Roosevelt was far more impressed than he had expected to be. He was deeply moved as he saw the soul and the immensity of the mountain. He grabbed the microphone and rose to the occasion with an impromptu and eloquent speech.

"I had seen the photographs. I had seen the drawings. (Of this great work) . . . yet I had no conception, until just 10 minutes ago, of its magnitude."

"I think we can meditate a little on those Americans ten thousand years from now, when the weathering on the face of Washington and Jefferson and Lincoln shall have proceeded perhaps a depth of a tenth of an inch . . . meditate and wonder what our descendents will think about us. Let us hope that they will believe we have honestly striven every day to preserve for our descendents a decent form of government to operate under . . ."

Jefferson was entirely unlike Washington and the two faces side by side enhanced one another, accenting the individualities. Borglum had used as a guide Brower's mask of Jefferson made during his life. It showed Jefferson as a handsome young man, a patriotic idealistic man, whose youthful face was rather unfamiliar to the public.

Rushmore was beginning to attract wide acclaim. At last the doubters, who had perhaps long been influenced by the Stone Mountain days, were transformed to believers.

The work starting in the summer of 1937 was supposed to be done according to Park Service plans approved by Spotts and Nagle. The plan called for the completion of the figures in a prescribed order. Borglum resented the attempts of the Park Service to control his artistic freedom. He thought of his project as art; they thought of it as engineering. Francis Case of Custer, a long time backer of Rushmore, was now in Congress and recognized Borglum for what he was, a creative genius. Case undertook to educate the Congressional committee on the realities of mountain carving, and was able to get a small appropriation to keep work going another season.

Borglum went to Washington to attempt to get a new contract. He felt that he was being unfairly treated, and noted that public funds tended to flow in the direction from which the most noise came. Boland reiterated that Borglum was not worth any more than he was getting, because, he pointed out, Spotts was doing much of the work which Borglum had previously done. Borglum argued that he could very well do without Spotts. Boland's viewpoint was the one which was accepted.

Literally crushed, Borglum wrote, "It is a beautiful finish to ten years of work on Rushmore, giving South Dakota what I have, in monument, roads, and publicity . . . worth millions, that its own citizens have connived to successfully destroy my credit and keep from me the little money I was earning for the great asset I was creating."

The argument over money continued all summer and Borglum did not get any fee that year. Lincoln Borglum, as usual, was on the job, supervising the actual carving, seeing that everything was proceeding the same as if his father had been there. By the end of the season over 265,000 people had gazed in wonder at the recognizable stone men.

On September 17, 1937, on the 150th anniversary of the adoption of the Constitution of the United States of America, it was time for another dedication, this time the titanic, sorrowful head of Lincoln. Although the speaker was Senator Edward Burke of Nebraska, the high drama of the occasion was again left to Borglum. He emphasized that the colossal work had been accomplished without adequate power or tools, and without the hoped-for trained assistants.

Much of his talk was a forceful appeal for public support for funds to

The lifelike eyes of Lincoln were a major sculpturing achievement, as was the optical illusion of glasses across the eyes of Roosevelt. Veins of minerals and crystals were discovered while making all of the faces. Photo by S.D. Travel Division

finish the work he had started, as he knew it should be finished. The entire crowd was with him when he said, "Where greatness is promised, history and civilization never forgive its absence . . . or those responsible for its failure."

A minor flip occurred, when an N.B.C. announcer mistakenly promised that the head of *Franklin* Roosevelt would soon fill the large smooth place between Jefferson and Lincoln.

As before, an enormous flag fluttered over the face. Starting with the poignant sound of taps, from a bugle near Washington's head half a mile away, blown for Senator Norbeck who had died of cancer, and other departed friends of the mountain, and ending with the thunder of dynamite and shattered rock, the Lincoln ceremony unrolled slowly before a softly weeping crowd.

About this time Borglum decided that he would like to have his last studio where his first had been, on the golden shores of California. Borglums tried to buy a lovely home at Montecito, near Santa Barbara, and started spending their winters there. Gutzon had quit Texas with some annoyance, because most of his grand plans for the big state had been disregarded. California and the far West had always appealed to Borglum. He liked the climate, the dynamic growth, and the atmosphere which was right for creativity. He thought California afforded people an unusual opportunity to be original in unique surroundings and superb scenery.

The next season, Borglum, beleaguered by the continuing tension and impossible working conditions at the mountain, went again to Washington. He announced firmly that he would remain there until some changes were made in the administration, and he added that the changes should include payment for his previous year's work. Lincoln was in charge of the work at the mountain, which started early in May.

Borglum declared that the National Park Service had to quit telling him how to carve his masterpiece, and that Spotts, Nagle and Boland were only interfering with the completion of the work. The ensuing battle resulted in the resignation of Commission President Sargent, followed by others. Then a bill, largely composed by Gutzon himself, was introduced in Congress. Backed by Key Pittman, Francis Case, and others who had influence in Congress, the bill was to reorganize the commission and the administration of the entire Mount Rushmore project.

Case saw that the root of all the problems was that Borglum was a genius, and that Mount Rushmore was his own creation. He knew that few people understood genius. He best summed up his reasoning when he said, "No matter how many problems have arisen, no matter how many mistakes have been made, no matter how much more we might have done, had the funds been available, the indisputable fact remains that what was once an unknown mountain, has become a great, living, inspiring memorial, that will outlast any other man created thing in America."

Through Case's tireless dedication, the bill passed, restoring control of the project to its originator and sculptor, and to a hand picked commission, and allowing $300,000 for the completion of the Memorial. The expanse of the Memorial was also increased to 1,000 acres. Borglum was jubilant. At last it was *his* mountain, as it had been in the beginning. He rushed off to South Dakota with renewed vigor and hope.

Borglum now had the power to hire and fire, to advance his best men, to determine salaries, and most important of all, to decide how the work should proceed. It was a tremendous relief for him to be able to stand back and look critically at the work as an artist does, and when he saw that something needed to be done to improve a certain area, to be able to give the order which would immediately put a workman on the job.

Spotts was gone. Boland had resigned, the Interior Department regulations were no longer in force, and there was money in the till. There was almost a feeling of euphoria at the mountain. Senator Pittman was named Chairman of the new commission. Roosevelt appointed the commissioners at Borglum's recommendation. There were the well known Senators Townsend, Norris, and Bulow. Other members were Kent Keller, Russell Arundel, William Williamson, Herman Oliphant, Eugene McDonald, and L. B. Hanna. Two women were named, Isabella Greenway and Mrs. Lorine J. Spoonts. William Williamson and William Bulow were from South Dakota. Williamson, Pittman, Keller, McDonald and Arundel constituted the executive committee of the commission. Borglum was named General Manager.

Arrangements were made for the United States Treasury Department to be in charge of financial matters. They were to take care of such business as procurement, disbursement, and accounting. The headquarters for this work was set up at the Treasury State Accounts Office at Watertown, a city in the northeastern part of South Dakota. An employee from this office was also assigned to work at the mountain to certify payrolls. The Treasury Department was efficient and Borglum was glad to cooperate with them. George Storck was the man to be charged with the responsibility of the financial office.

The new system worked well and the men were on the job all year-round, with progress being more rapid and congenial than ever before.

In 1938, with plenty of workmen on the faces, and a generous working budget, Borglum began work on the Hall of Records. It was to be on the opposite side from the heads in a small canyon to their right. He had always considered this Hall an essential part of the project.

The entrance facade was to be 140 feet high with a door 12'x20'. The entrance was to have a vivid stone mosaic, rich in deep, blue lapis lazuli and shining gold. The foyer, hewn from gray granite, would lead to the great hall, a magnificent room 80'x100' drilled from the heart of a timeless peak. The gleaming walls of polished stone were to have illuminated niches of bronze, protected by glass, where all the classics of art, science, literature, and music, all the accomplishments of our civilization would be preserved for the unforseeable future. A bronze and gold bas relief frieze was to border the entire hall, depicting the discovery and ascension of the Western world. There would be carefully carved busts of the great men and women who were the acknowledged leaders of our endeavors. Placed between the recessed cabinets, the busts would commemorate our growth, our versatility, our Nation. Symbols to be used in the decorative motifs were to represent the Spanish and French explorers, the Colonial English, the early Americans, and the true natives, the Indians.

There was to be a platform near the Hall, and the graceful stone stairs were to be lined with cool seats, well placed for rest, and contemplation. Even the door was to be a work of art, ornamented with intricately modeled bronze figures from Christopher Columbus to typical Twentieth Century Americans. It was to be a Hall for Eternity, the soul of the dream.

Besides preliminary work on the Hall, the summer of '38 saw noticeable advances on the head of Roosevelt. Borglum's model had been a vigorous model of the Rough Rider he had carved during his friend's lifetime. Several onlookers noted that Teddy Roosevelt of the mountain bore a striking resemblance to the sculptor himself. Both wore mustaches and their powerful, rugged faces, the epitome of courage and determination, were not unlike. Throughout history, sculptors and artists have consciously and unconsciously used themselves as models; however, in this case the likeness is coincidence.

Borglum stated, "Roosevelt seems fairly to have leaped with life. He kidnapped energy and carried it into the Nation's home. He remains undrawn. None will engrave him. His spirit is at large, uncaptured by artist or sculptor."

The dedication of the Roosevelt face took place in conjunction with the golden anniversary of South Dakota statehood, on July 2, 1939. The evening pageantry marked a dream come true for 83-year-old South

Dakota Historian Doane Robinson. The Pine Ridge Sioux Indians in traditional brilliant costumes turned out with their leader, Chief Standing Bear, to dance to the beat of their rawhide tomtoms. Western star William S. Hart entertained the crowd of 12,000. The Governor of South Dakota, Harlan Bushfield, gave the main address. Sky rockets flamed across the night sky and aerial bombs echoed through the pine covered hills. Powerful searchlights played for the first time on four granite faces, the Nation's Shrine of Democracy.

The men who worked on Rushmore liked to be together, even in their time off. The families felt unusual comeraderie. Rushmore even had its own baseball team, organized and managed by Lincoln Borglum. The men worked together so well that the team would often beat the teams representing the largest cities in the Hills, Rapid City and Lead and Deadwood. Morale was really high at Rushmore the year its baseball team took the Black Hills tournament and went on to become runnerup in the South Dakota State Amateur Baseball Tournament in Aberdeen, losing the final game in the 16th inning. Everyone connected with the mountain was in Aberdeen shouting for that team.

Work on the mountain was done before strict National safety regulations, so hard hats and safety shoes were not required. Most of the men wore sturdy, well-mended clothes and leather boots, with soft caps or hats for headwear. Goggles and respirators were commonly used, as breathing the hard and grainy rock dust was a recognized health hazard. One of the men who worked on the mountain, died some years later, with silicosis listed as a contributing factor to his final illness. Silicosis is a lung condition caused by inhalation of rock dust and resulting in scar tissue on the lungs. Several men put in compensation claims for silicosis in later years. Most cases were not critical or disabling. Lincoln Borglum himself has considerable scar tissue in his lungs, because as superintendent, he had to move from place to place, where work was in progress, and he often had to pause to give instructions to workmen, in noisy places where it was difficult to communicate. It was almost impossible for him to keep his respirator on.

A safety precaution always enforced was to stagger the men who were at work, so that no two were ever placed one directly above another. How easy it would have been for a man to drop a hammer from his cage and have it fall on the head of a worker below.

The steel cables which suspended the men at their work were the best obtainable. They were 3/8-inch industrial cables made by the Roebling Company. Their working factor was 4000 pounds and a breaking load of 8000 pounds, a bountiful margin of safety. Each winch had more than the required amount of cable and the cables were constantly inspected. Most of the wear would occur within ten or twelve feet of the harness from which the men worked, so the weakened portion would regularly be cut away, and there could be no safety hazard in this respect.

In the early stages of the work, when a lot of heavy blasting was scheduled, all of the men were immediately removed from the blasting area, after the dynamite had been positioned. The drillers could work on the drilling of some area distant from the danger zone, so that there would be no chance of an accidental explosion of the charges. Generally there were two detonations in a day. These were scheduled just prior to the noon break and just before closing the work down for the day, or approximately 12:00 noon and 4:00 P.M.

There was a close call once, when a man was working above the charges he had drilled, and which had been filled by the powder monkey. The man was absorbed in his work and paid no attention to the darkening sky. Suddenly a summer electric storm closed in. Lightning struck the power line and the electric charge followed the cable, setting off a dynamite cap about 20 feet directly below where the worker had started a new hole. Badly frightened, the worker turned in his drill for the day, and after that work ceased when such storms approached.

One time, after the new cable car had been installed for the workmen, five men were in the car making their morning trip to the top, when a pin sheared off the mechanism controlling the ascent of the car. The car started hurtling wildly down the mountain. The witnesses stood paralyzed over the situation they could not control. An alert foreman shoved a piece of two by four into the mechanism, slowing the descent, and providing a safe landing in which no one was injured. That is no one was injured in the landing, but one nervous worker, "Happy" Anderson, had panicked and jumped to the ground before the cable car reached bottom. His was a rough landing, and he had several broken ribs to prove it. The worried Borglum rushed him 26 miles to the Rapid City hospital, and remained until doctors pronounced his injuries minor. Before long Happy was back again on the job, laughing with the rest at his lack of faith.

Outside of these two incidents, there were no accidents worth mentioning in all of the years of construction, a safety record which was studied with interest and envy by numerous firms, and was a source of justifiable pride to the Borglums.

Peace and tranquility were short lived at the mountain. Borglum had been walking on clouds since he had been given full control of his work. He could now see that he was winning his struggle with the mountain and its protective elements, wresting forth from the cold granite the very soul of democracy. But in the midst of work and elation came a terse message from Washington, D.C. that the new administration was to cease at once, and the project would be immediately returned to the National Park Service's authority.

It was a stunning blow. Borglum was heartbroken. He vociferously protested that he found working under the Park Service "intolerable". President Roosevelt, who had brought about the thunderbolt by executive edict, said his order was final, and was not subject to change. Borglum could do nothing. Things were farther confused when it was announced the Treasury Department would remain in financial charge.

Borglum fumed, "This order puts me right back where I started . . . at the mercy of unsympathetic men who have no idea how to instill life into blocks of granite." He felt the walls of stone closing in on him.

The new orders also stated that no more work was to be done on the Hall of Records. Of all the slaps Borglum had taken on this project, this one was the most cruel. To him, sending the mountain on alone to meet the future history of the world, without its inscription or Hall of Records, was like "mailing a postcard to a foreign country without a name or address, or even a signature."

Nagle came to make a report on the state of the work for the Park Service. His swift survey criticized the stairs, the buildings, the tourist facilities, and the long-range plans. Again the Department of Interior requested step-by-step multiple copies of blueprints for every anticipated move on the rest of the project. They pointed out that such voluminous paper work was normal administrative procedure, and the strict regulations must be adhered to. Nagle stopped all plans for the Hall, and Borglum accused Nagle of trying to control everything.

To Lincoln Borglum, Superintendent since 1938, his father's sorrows and frustrations were his own. Lincoln understood his father as no one else did, and he understood the work on the mountain as well. Overall morale was excellent under Lincoln. In spite of setbacks, conflicting orders from Washington, delays and layoffs, the men liked and respected Lincoln. They knew he would do anything to help accomplish his father's dream, and watching his unselfish devotion, they were ready to do anything he asked.

There had been considerable rumbling in Washington that Gutzon had been allowed to employ his son on the project. The suspicion was that the Borglums were getting rich at the South Dakota work. Lincoln had worked several summers and two full years without pay, and then as chief pointer had received less than $2,000. Even as Superintendent his salary was only $4,800.

Lincoln, by this time, was married to Louella Jones, a rancher's daughter from Beeville, Texas, the niece of Mrs. Lorine Spoonts who had long been a Rushmore commissioner. Lincoln had built a home for himself and his bride on the ranch near his parents. He was kept busy helping his father with other commissions such as the Texas Trail Drivers, and was also a successful rancher with a fine herd of Hereford cattle.

As chief fund raiser, lobbyist, and publicity chairman of Mount Rushmore, in addition to being artist and designer, Gutzon Borglum had to be away from the mountain more than he would have liked. His critics loudly noted each absence. But few realized how detailed were all the instructions he left, or how great his faith that Lincoln would carry them all out precisely right.

Here are some of the actual instructions from pages written and illustrated in detail by Borglum before leaving on one of his trips.

"I want you, in beginning the work and allotting the positions of the men, to avoid the two finished faces completely, and not touch even the hairline around the face of Washington or his chin, nor the face lines or forehead of Jefferson."

"On photograph #1 I have drawn a circle where you can locate Payne to begin drilling under what will be Washington's ear, at what is to be the left hand lapel of his coat. Put one or two men on the lapel, which I have marked #2, and two men on Washington's shoulder, and work down carefully from the top where I have marked #3."

"I have marked Lincoln's eyes. You can put two men in each of two cages. I would use Anderson on one side and Bianco on the other, Bianco by the feldspar streak and Anderson on the outside. I would then give Payne with Bianco, a position on the nose, and have them begin to take off stone from the nose, by drilling in squares and breaking off the stone to within 6 or 7 inches, so as to make a second cutting remain for all that. Have Bianco and the man you put with him cut right into within 6 inches of the finished surface, but do not try to cut the eyelid or the eyeball. Make a round mass for these. Lincoln's face at this time will probably take six more men."

"If you can put any men down on the block that I have marked #8 without any danger of tools or stone falling on them, all right. I would put about 3 men on the big crag."

For many years Borglum had refused to be beaten down by politics, bureaucracy, miserliness or jealousy. He had repeatedly fought back when things went wrong.

He told his friends, "I conceived the Memorial in all of its aspects and raised most of the money to produce it. In spite of vicious sabotage and political trickery I have carried it on to a point where those who have never given a helping hand are trying to seize the success as theirs."

With a zest and a bounce which belied his age of 73 he simply never took "No" for the final answer. But now he was heavy hearted and the mountain was taking its toll. While he prepared to go out again to win public support and to try once more to be allowed to finish his work in his way, he was doing so without his old energy and drive. In fact he was weary and almost despondent, when Mary announced that she wanted to accompany him. This made the trip acceptable. Gutzon loved to have Mary with him, and she had dropped other activities to be with him as much as possible. When he was making a speech in her presence, her expression of calm dignity and intense pride, was an inspiration to him.

A popular lecturer, Borglum had a way with words. He was forceful, direct, so brimming with enthusiasm that casual listeners soon became partisans. Although he had a booking agent, the Clark Getts Company in New York, many of his invitations to appear on platforms were because of the dramatic impact of a man carving a mountain. His personality came through well on radio. His diction and timing were of professional quality. He was constantly asked to take more platform appearances than he did. Most of those he accepted were more for promoting and publicizing his mountain than for any small profit he might make from lectures. His appearances were at colleges, service clubs, educational associations, park boards, radio interview programs . . . anyplace where he thought there might be prospects of stirring up more interest in Mount Rushmore, interest which might indirectly be converted to support and dollars for the shrine.

In 1941 things should have been looking up in South Dakota, the worst of the depression was over, highways and advertising had improved, and the mountain was truly becoming the most loved man-made wonder in the world. But the Park Service was in complete charge, and Gutzon was not one to give up. He left Lincoln on the job as before, and with his ardent listener Mary, he set out for the east.

He told Mary he thought with enough appearances and nationwide radio talks, he could swing public opinion so pressure would demand that the masterpiece should be finished as he knew it should be, with its rightful signature the Hall of Records. He strongly felt that he had to remove government apathy about the Hall, because without it the Shrine of Democracy would not be complete. What he wanted was a

A shrine convention gathers at the ampitheater of Mount Rushmore, an area where many cultural and historical programs take place during summer days and evenings.
Photo by S.D. Travel Division

new appropriation, and the restoration of his authority on the project.

As Borglum saw it, the stone faces, which would outlast western civilization, might someday be approached by men from an entirely different culture. The carvings would be a great mystery. Archeologists would look eagerly for clues. Finding no explanation, they would theorize that the four were gods or demons, or priests, or kings, or mythological figures. He pointed out how little we know about the Incas, the stone faces of Easter Island, or even the Sphinx, although these are all relatively recent in comparison to the hundreds of thousands of years Rushmore is expected to last. Borglum believed that the accomplishments of American civilization in many ways were monumental, and he wanted to leave records which would prove this.

He hoped to help make his country immortal. It was a lofty and exalted vision, a beckoning dream, but then, so too, had been the carving of four colossal faces on a once isolated granite mountain.

Lincoln saw his parents off, and as the train steamed away from the mountains he experienced a feeling that his father would never return.

A radio appearance in Chicago was on the itinerary. Gutzon arrived in Chicago early and took time to look up an old friend. Borglum had been troubled by his prostate gland for a few years, and this particular friend, who had been a classmate of his at St. Mary's in Kansas, was now a doctor at Henroten hospital.

"This is a simple matter," the doctor reported. "Why don't you just check into the hospital before continuing on your trip? We'll take care of you right away."

Borglum thought somehow he might magically regain his full strength and vigor. He consulted Mary. Although slightly apprehensive, she agreed the minor surgery should be performed. His wish was hers.

The operation was a success, but when Borglum should have been rapidly recovering, he developed a blood clot. Fear struck Mary's heart. She stayed constantly at his side, laughing and reminiscing, but feeling icy cold. Gutzon's condition grew progressively worse each day, but the doctors still assured Mary that he would soon improve. Mary went for days without sleep, trying to tell herself that she was needlessly alarmed, and trying to keep her children updated by phone and wire, without unnecessarily frightening them.

On the tenth day, Lincoln could stand it no longer. He knew that the situation was critical and he flew to Chicago to be with his parents. Only then did he recall his earlier premonition. His sister Mary Ellis flew in from her home in the west. Gutzon responded briefly to the presence of Lincoln, but the rally was short. Three days later, March 6, at the age of 74, the sculptor Gutzon Borglum was dead. Mary was numb. Suddenly the whole world seemed alien and unreal. Lincoln was filled with fear as well as with grief, for he knew that the torch had been passed to him.

Even the death of Borglum was not without controversy. Borglum had once expressed the wish to Lincoln, that when he died he would like to be buried in California, where he had gone as a youth to seek his place in the world of art. Before the distressed and sorrowing family could make any arrangements, Russell Arundel, then chairman of the Rushmore Memorial commission, proposed that the artist's final resting place should be at Mount Rushmore. Against strong opposition from the Department of Interior, a bill was introduced to authorize the burial on National Memorial property, and it was passed and immediately signed by Roosevelt. However, the bill prescribed that private funds be raised for the crypt and entombment. Borglum died in debt, and his close friends were scattered around the world, so the task of raising funds immediately looked formidable. Borglum was buried first at Chicago. Later a second futile attempt was made to get the permanent grave at the mountain. The family requested that all such efforts should cease at once. They felt Gutzon's final resting place should be in keeping with his wishes, and should not be a publicity gimmick for South Dakota. The body was moved to Forest Lawn in California, to a quiet green spot in the Court of Honor. Lincoln lovingly designed and cast a bronze tablet for that last niche.

At the mountain the Borglum name is not forgotten. The epic story is told day after day in words and in pictures, from the Visitor's Center and from the Amphitheater. There is a Borglum Memorial Highway and a Borglum Viewing Terrace, but beyond this there is the real spirit of Borglum for all to feel and marvel at, for no one can see the elemental faces without knowing an awakened pride in our land and its people, without sensing the presence of the genius who gave a soul to a mountain.

Borglum (dark suit) inspects the drilling which will further define the eye, while workers in casual safety attire take a break.

From left to right in this 1928 photo taken in the original Rushmore studio are Mrs. Jesse Tucker, Gutzon and Mary Borglum, Lincoln Borglum, Doane Robinson, and Major Jesse Tucker.

Lincoln Borglum as a boy of 12 rode a pony on the pack trip to Mt. Rushmore in 1925. Theodore Shoemaker, Ray Sanders and C. C. Gideon are in this group with Lincoln and his father.

One of the early meetings of the Rushmore Commission was held at "the Mountain" shortly after the first season of work. Gutzon is in the center. Photo by National Park Service by Bell

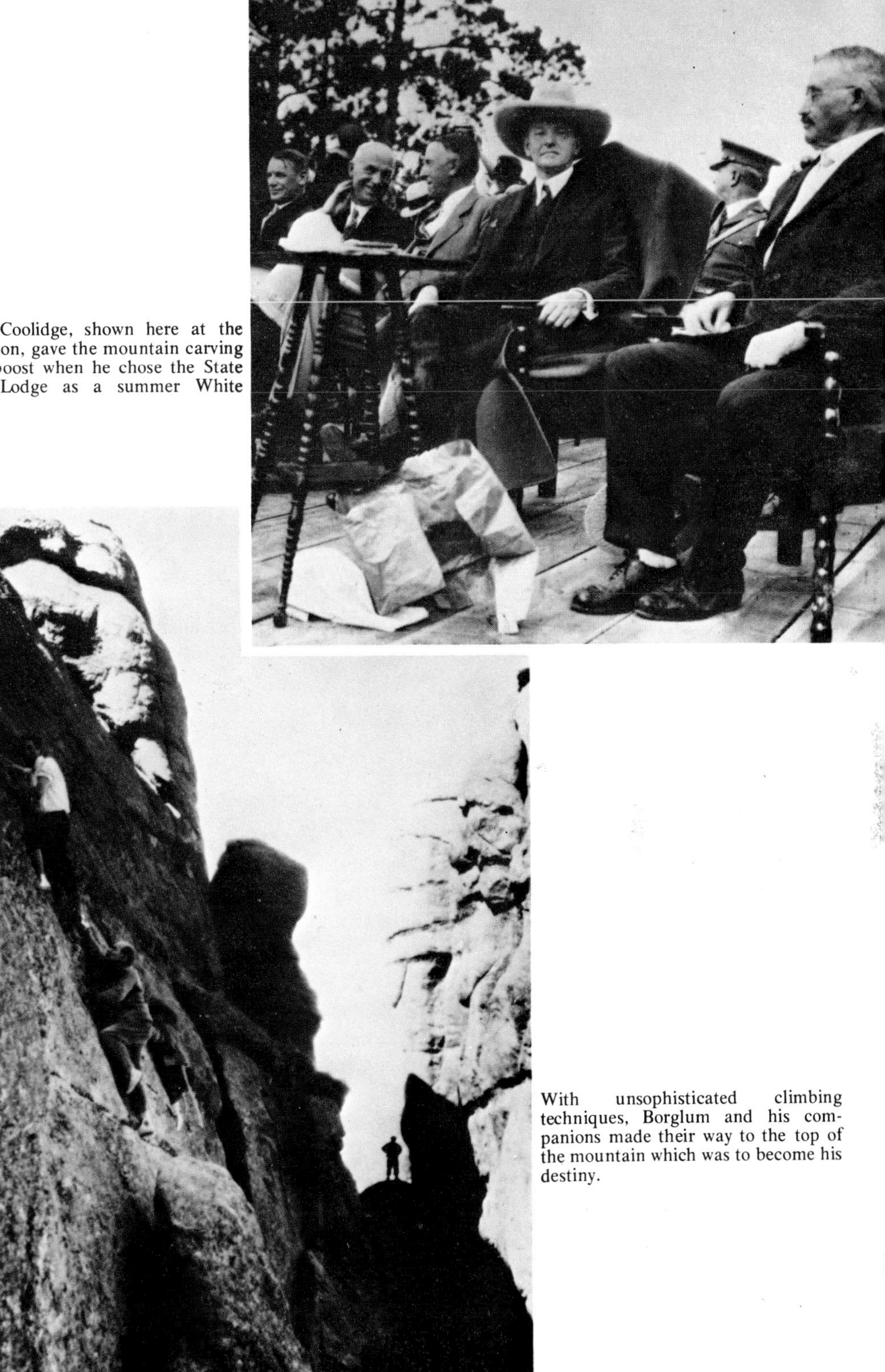

vin Coolidge, shown here at the ication, gave the mountain carving eal boost when he chose the State ne Lodge as a summer White ıse.

With unsophisticated climbing techniques, Borglum and his companions made their way to the top of the mountain which was to become his destiny.

F.D.R. had not planned on speaking when he arri late for the ceremonies at Rushmore, but swept al with the emotional impact of the Borglum dedication, reached for network microphones to praise the work saw.

To hard rock miners turned "assistant sculptors" preparing dynamite was all in a day's work

Photo by National Park Service by Bell

3

Gutzon Borglum, American Sculptor

To fully understand Mount Rushmore, is to know its context in the vigorous life of Gutzon Borglum, one of the nation's greatest sculptors. Unusual men are influenced by their times and by the personalities of the people they come to know. It is quite unlikely that a memorial to the spirit of our country could be done at present, or that our times would produce a man sufficiently motivated to accomplish such an overwhelming task. In the first place, it has not been fashionable to be a "flag waving" patriot in this part of the Twentieth Century. For another thing, at this time, people could probably not agree on what should be carved on such a memorial. Then, with the radical ecology approach exaggerated out of all proportion, perhaps the carving of any kind of shrine on any mountain would be hotly disputed, and finally would not be allowed. And a dominating factor is that the cost of this tremendous work would be prohibitive now, as the Monument was created during the rock bottom financial crisis of the Great Depression, and *inflation* was only a textbook word.

Gutzon Borglum could well have been writing about himself when he wrote in an article for the now extinct *American Magazine,* "A Giant is an ordinary person who is bigger than his world." Borglum was a talented, impelling man, a zealous participant in the life of his land and his times. He was a super patriot, a defender of human rights, a spellbinding speaker, a gifted inventor, a student of nature . . . a dreamer, a doer, and a genius.

For further insight into his character, consider the people he knew. He was a friend of General John Frémont, fearless explorer of the American West. He was a close personal friend of the rough and ready

Gutzon de la Mothe Borglum, the son of Danish immigrants, was already one of America's great sculptors at the time he first went to South Dakota to discuss carving a mountain there.

Teddy Roosevelt, of the soft words and the big stick. Paderewski, the Polish patriot and musician, was near and dear to Gutzon Borglum. Gutzon knew Woodrow Wilson, Robert Lincoln, Orville Wright, John Ruskin and Luther Burbank. The dancer Isadora Duncan, the actress Sarah Bernhardt, the singer Mary Garden, the sculptor Auguste Rodin, were all in his circle of friends. Others he knew well were Jack Dempsey, Alexander Graham Bell, Rupert Hughes, Helen Keller, William Randolph Hearst, and Frank Lloyd Wright.

Borglum had ready access to the White House from the time of Theodore Roosevelt, until the death of another Roosevelt, Franklin. The only president of those times Borglum never really became well acquainted with was Herbert Hoover. Gutzon worked actively over the years with Theodore Roosevelt, Woodrow Wilson, Calvin Coolidge and Franklin Roosevelt, and not only on projects connected with the arts. Many senators, representatives, and other political leaders were friends of Borglum's. During his London years, he received favorable comments on his work from Queen Victoria. This fact alone is a reminder that his character was molded by other times. The Civil War was barely over when Borglum was born, and he was over 21 before South Dakota even became a state, and almost 60 when the work at Rushmore began.

When Borglum was a struggling, young artist, he did not have the ultimate goal of creating the world's greatest stone memorial, but he did have exactly the right background to enable him to embrace the opportunity when it came. He had the natural talent, the hard won training, and the luminous vision, which were necessary to convert a dream into reality.

During the formative years of Borglum's career, there were many changes in this nation, but by and large, these were the growing and the flowering years of our country. The United States was becoming aware of its own greatness, and its potential, and the arts were beginning to find a home in this land, to acknowledge a real American Heritage.

The James Borglum family was only one of the thousands of families migrating from northern Europe to the land of freedom and opportunity, attracted by the call of the West. Such families and their children never tired of praising their adopted land. These were people who were proud to be Americans.

Another thing that readied Borglum for his great task was his fondness of outdoor life, a trait common to many western pioneers and their families. He loved horses and riding. He loved action. He translated his feeling for nature in his vibrant and stirring interpretations in oil of the golden days of California in the 1890s.

Borglum kept careful notes of the birds and trees, the ferns, the flowers and insects and grasses of his Connecticut estate, Borgland. He loved the sea, the rocks, the mountains and the prairies, the sweep of the plains, and the promise of the desert.

Things which seemed larger than life, greater than average, or stronger than normal, always interested Borglum. He liked his studios to be mammoth, with massive fireplaces and soaring ceilings. He admired enormous canvases and huge statues. He had already created an immense Lincoln head, and the heroic sized *Wars of America* monument for Newark, and sculpted General Lee on Stone Mountain, when the Rushmore plan was set before him.

Gutzon de la Mothe Borglum was born in 1867 in St. Charles near Bear Lake, Idaho, the first son of James Borglum and his wife. The James Borglums had crossed the Atlantic from their native Denmark. Mormon converts, they had joined a caravan of 126 wagons and walked across the continent to their promised land. A plaque in the town square gives Gutzon's birth date as 1871, but family records and later Borglum's passport, prove that the 1867 date is correct.

Soon Gutzon's brother, Solon, was born in Ogden, Utah, when it became apparent that Utah would be the most thriving of the Mormon settlements. Perhaps the industrious James would have stayed in Utah, had it not been for the loss of his wife. The brave young mother who had left her homeland and joined one of the world's most arduous treks, either died, or disappeared quite unexpectedly, when her sons were both tiny. Records are not clear on this, but at any rate she left a grief-stricken husband and two solemn, puzzled little boys.

Alone, as he had never been in his life, the young immigrant father knew that his sons needed a mother, so he soon married Ida, his wife's sister. They decided to make a clean break with the past. Although James had been a woodcutter in Denmark, he set his goal at a professional career. Interested in medicine, he moved his family to St. Louis, Missouri, where he won his medical degree. With his growing family, he moved next to Fremont, Nebraska, where he started his first practice in a thriving frontier town surrounded by fertile farmlands. In due time Gutzon had 7 half brothers and half sisters. Young Gutzon did not fully accept his stepmother, Ida, and his father was a very busy doctor. However, there were things he liked about Nebraska . . . the wide spaces, the fleet horses, and the Indians. At a tender age he was sent to a good boarding school, St. Mary's, a Catholic School, in Kansas. His greatest accomplishment at school was demonstrating a remarkable native skill for drawing, particularly graceful and spirited horses.

The James Borglum family moved to Omaha, where Gutzon briefly took a job in a machine shop, and dreamed of "running away" to California, which was then the magic land of "milk and honey."

He left Nebraska as planned, to go West to seek his fortune in the arts, but the rest of the family also moved to California, fired by Gutzon's enthusiasm. Gutzon found a job as an apprentice to a lithographer and at last was in his true element, but the elder Borglums, discouraged by life in Los Angeles, returned to Omaha. Gutzon, then only 18, already recording his first California experiences on canvas, remained in his new home, and set up his first studio.

With his career as a painter beginning to prosper, Gutzon received his first major break when the gracious Jessie Benton Frémont, wife of General John C. Frémont, recognized his great talent. In addition to commissioning the young man to do a portrait of the general, she saw to it that her wide circle of wealthy and important friends became aware of the name and work of young Gutzon. With Borglum's magnetic personality, he won this following with ease.

After marrying Lisa Putnam, an art teacher and painter, somewhat older than he was, Borglum, encouraged by Mrs. Frémont, went to Paris. In Paris, to the delight of his bride and his sponsor, he was soon accepted as a member of the prestigious National Society of Beaux Arts.

Gutzon was beginning to be interested in the power of sculpture, when he met one of the giants, Auguste Rodin, who took a liking to the young American, and exerted a strong influence on him. Borglum comprehended that few artists showed the courage of the great sculptors. To him, expression could be more true and meaningful in three dimensions. He had found his field.

Borglum did not study in Italy, because he felt that the overpowering style of early Italian sculpture might prevent him from developing his own originality. He later said in an interview for the New York Tribune, that he considered contemporary Italian art non-existent, and that any attempts at new art for that nation had failed because of the Italians' dedication to mass produced religious works, mainly copies of their glorious past.

Borglum was, however, tempted to work in England. He praised the English art of his day, as he liked the way the conservative English painters and sculptors plodded along with pictures which looked like what they were supposed to represent, and statues which needed no interpreters, for at this time radical changes were taking place in art concepts and styles in France.

So, after a short stay in Spain, Gutzon and his wife moved to London, a city which Lisa did not like. Gutzon was soon invited to become a member of the Royal Academy, where his work came to the attention of Queen Victoria. When the Queen invited him to show his works at the palace, the young artist did not realize it was a *command performance,* and that he should have accompanied the one-man showing. The Queen, nevertheless, was generous in her praise of the paintings he sent for her examination. Lisa was homesick for America, and perhaps tired of being in her young husband's shadow, so she sailed for America, while Gutzon continued to make a name for himself in England.

Commissions were pouring in after that from both the Continent and America, so Borglum made frequent trips across the Atlantic. Around the turn of the century, he was on a research expedition to New York, when he got word of the high stakes competition for General Grant's Memorial. He determined to enter it. A fluke ruling called his work ineligible on the ground that it was too good to be the work of an American.

One of Gutzon's competitors for the Grant Commission had been his brother Solon, who had married a French girl and was living in France. Gutzon claimed that the horse for the winning design of Henry Shrady, was created by Solon. Gutzon regretted entering the competition, but by the time it was over he was comfortably established in New York and was determined that he would try to help build an American school of art.

Solon had always been Gutzon's favorite, as both were involved in art and sculpture; however, he was also close to his half brother Auguste, who had studied music in England while he was living there. Auguste also married a French woman. As a boy he had not been particularly fond of his stepmother, or his stepsisters or stepbrothers, but when his career began to bloom, he grew less resentful, and eventually grew close to all the members of his family. Once, while in an expansive mood, he had sent tickets to Europe to his stepmother and half sister Harriett, and had proudly guided them on a grand tour.

Wanting to show his love and admiration for his father, Gutzon also borrowed money to give his father the trip to his homeland Denmark, for which he had yearned for so many years. Confirmed Americans, the Borglums also esteemed the homeland from which the family came.

While Gutzon was working in New York, his father died quite suddenly. Dr. James Borglum had been thrown from a horse. Gutzon hurried to Omaha and was of great comfort to his stepmother. He had loved and admired his father more than anyone, except perhaps Solon, so he felt a deep personal loss when his father was gone. The devoted Gutzon saw to it that the widow, Ida, was never in need for anything, until she too died in 1911.

Later Solon Borglum's death was entirely unexpected. Solon, a gifted and popular sculptor, died of a ruptured appendix. This was a major blow to Gutzon, and the ensuing heartache left a hole in his life which was never quite filled.

Gutzon and Lisa had grown apart. Gutzon was tireless, eager to meet life head on. As the crescendo of his popularity and his work increased, Lisa felt no longer needed. Gutzon yearned for children with whom he could share his zest for life. Lisa was tired of traveling, tired of trying to keep up with her highly charged, younger husband, as he moved from one triumph to the next. She was weary of a succession of rustic flats and elegant suites. Life with Gutzon was unpredictable, all mountain tops or canyon bottoms, with no gentle valleys in between. What Lisa wanted was a quiet, orderly routine, a measured and peaceful progression of her days. Lisa had left London for California, with the understanding that Gutzon would soon follow. But when he settled in New York, both knew that their lives had taken on different meanings, and that their days together were over. After much correspondence, they agreed to a separation.

Gutzon set up a studio in New York, which seemed to him to be the center of the world. He soon met all the most prominent people, the doers and the thinkers. One of the students who worked under him, helping in his studio, was Marion Bell, daughter of Alexander Graham Bell. Alice Hill was another protégé. But his most welcome visitor was young Mary Montgomery, whom he had met on a transatlantic voyage. He was fascinated by the charming and brilliant Mary. Besides being the first woman to graduate from the University of Berlin, the young lady had an excellent job with a publishing company. She was fluent in 6 languages. A witty conversationalist, she was also an intense listener. She was completely entranced by the sculptor.

Gutzon's studio became an international salon of bright and successful young Americans. Mary offered spontaneously to be a part-time secretary for the busy, but slightly disorganized, sculptor, and Gutzon, who hated paper work anyway, gladly accepted her offer. So Mary's warmth became part of the magnetism which drew the wealthy and famous to the Borglum studio.

In 1902 Gutzon had received an important commission for some large mural paintings for the Midland Railway's Manchester Hotel in England. He designed the murals in his New York studio, then sailed to England to get them approved. The designs were readily accepted so Gutzon hurried back to New York to get the work underway. He was pushing himself too hard. With a high, mysterious fever, he was taken to a New York hospital, where for some time it was touch and go. The malady was tentatively diagnosed as typhoid. It was a long fight, and the recovery period was slow. When at last he finished the murals, he decided never to accept commissions for oil paintings again. His restored energy would all be exerted on the challenge of sculpture.

Gutzon did not like competitions as a means of selecting a sculptor for a specific commission. He thought that the people who wanted a statue should familiarize themselves with the work of the various artists, and on that basis, select the one they wanted, and then work with the man of their choice on the plans until there was mutual agreement. He thought it was unfair to expect talented people to devote weeks and months of thought and time, just to see if their work happened to please a panel of judges. To him the selection of a sculptor should be the same as the selection of a doctor or lawyer, and the relationship should be based on trust and understanding.

Gutzon prepared a forceful statuary group for the Saint Louis World's Fair of 1904, not in the spirit of competition, but as a way of contributing his say in the American arts. It had been predicted that he would ride to fame on horseback, and sure enough, his spirited horses of "The Mares of Diomedes" won him a gold medal. He had at last achieved the recognition in his own country that he had abroad.

He then made a sensitive statue of John Ruskin, whom he had known in England. Soon commissioned by Bell, he caught the fervent gratitude of America, as he built a likeness of James Smithson, English benefactor of the Smithsonian Institution. (The model mysteriously disappeared and was found many years later by Lincoln in a bag of broken pieces in the South Dakota Studio. Lincoln restored and cast it, and it is now in the Smithsonian.)

Borglum received a major commission when he was charged with creating the angels and saints for the Belmont Chapel of the Cathedral of St. John the Divine in New York City. Mary loved to watch him work, and came often to help and advise him. She fervently sided with him when his angels erupted into a nationwide controversy. The crux of the situation was that the ecclesiastical hierarchy rejected the models of the angels, on the grounds that they appeared too feminine. "Angels," they

The spirited horses of the "Mares of Diomedes" won a gold medal for Gutzon at the St. Louis World's Fair and established his reputation as an American Sculptor.

Photo by The Metropolitan Museum of Art, Gift of James Stillman, 1906 declared, "are masculine."

Borglum was dramatic, original, and self assured . . . a natural subject for the press. The *New York Times* seemed to delight in reporting that Borglum, in a "fit of rage" had destroyed the angels. The truth is, that the artist had very carefully sliced off the clay faces of the offending angels and cast them in silver for himself. Then patiently, he created the required new masculine faces for the Chapel angels, which were subsequently accepted.

In addition to his many commissions, Borglum found time for a variety of civic and political activities. At the turn of the century his greatest new enthusiasm was flying machines. This was something which captured his imagination. He witnessed some of Orville Wright's first flights at Fort Myer, near Washington, D. C. Soon he became a prominent member of the *Aeronautical Club of America,* and his studio was crowded with precision scale replicas of planes, many with changes he visualized and invented himself. Encouraged by air minded friends, he perfected an improved propeller and a streamlined fuselage, among other things.

Another field to which he began to devote much time was writing. His style was brisk, descriptive, and lucid, predating by many years the utterly candid journalism we now take for granted. He felt qualified to write on almost any subject . . . from aeronautics to flood control, from French Art to American Politics. Magazines and papers snatched everything he wrote.

Some of Borglum's works done during the early 1900s were Isadora Duncan, General Sheridan, Nero, North Wind, and John Mackay. These were climaxed by the large inspired head of Lincoln he did in marble out of respect and devotion, and which was purchased for the Rotunda of the Capitol.

His justifiable elation was shared by Mary Montgomery, who was by then his secretary, advisor, and critic. About this time Lisa finally divorced Gutzon. The artist felt sad for the past, but at the same time freer than he had been since he was a youth in California. The divorce settlement awarded Gutzon's paintings to Lisa. (Many of these works of art have never been found.)

In 1909 Gutzon asked Mary to be his wife. Mary did not hesitate. She was a successful career woman. She had been an official of a publishing company. She had written for the Encyclopedia Brittanica. A graduate of Wellesley, she moved with ease in the highest social groups. She had a Master's degree from the University of Berlin. Instead of following the social whirl of the traditional debutante, she became involved with the arts and sciences, with translating Sanskrit and

Cunieform. In spite of all this, Mary was Biblical in her willingness to give up her life style for the man she loved.

Mary Montgomery Borglum was a petite lady, about 5 feet tall in her stocking feet. Her eyes were a lively blue, widely spaced and deeply set, revealing a vivacious personality. She had long, brown, extremely fine hair, which she wore in a bun, sometimes carefully waved around her oval face.

Although her features were not delicate enough for classic beauty, Mary was graceful and charming, and easily stood out in a group. Her true love and concern for family and friends made them think of her as beautiful.

Especially devoted to hats, Mary dressed in feminine styles which were becoming to her, but not extreme. She made no effort to be a fashion leader, putting comfort and neatness ahead of style.

Pictures of Mary point up her modesty and selflessness, for she always let others stand in the center or the foreground, and she seldom looked directly into the camera.

Since Mary was a fluent linguist, her English was perfect and distinct. Her well modulated voice had no hint of the affected accent preferred by social register graduates of Eastern girls' schools at the time. A sparkling and witty conversationalist, Mary kept up with the affairs of the nation and the world, and most of all, of the people involved in all the arts. But perhaps she was most often sought out for her ability to empathize and to listen.

Mary had a positive influence on Gutzon's career. While the sculptor was quixotic and impulsive, Mary was calm and steady. Gutzon despised such details as keeping track of finances. The hours he spent on a commission, the cost of his supplies, or travels, on a commission to him were all incidental. He was quick to loan or give away his money, and was equally magnanimous with time and talent. He wanted to wipe the words debt, pay, and finance from his vocabulary. Mary was precise, accurate, organized and efficient. Gutzon was dynamic, electric, sensitive. He wanted to embrace the whole wide, wonderful world and all of mankind at once. His Mary had the qualities most needed for those privileged to live their lives with genius . . . patience, understanding, faith and love. Like Ruth in the Old Testament Mary said to Gutzon, "I am ready to go wherever and whenever you go."

Gentle, selfless, and modest, Mary was to become the perfect balance for the strong willed, intense Gutzon. By keeping his home life happy and serene, by being a gracious hostess to his incredible assortment of friends, by being an instinctively accurate critic, Mary inspired Gutzon to even greater accomplishments. His pet name for her was "Peggy", and she called him "Dane". Although history has not given Mary the credit she earned, it is significant that Gutzon had a far greater admiration and respect for women as *people* than most men of his time. He wrote, "I find in women all that is fine and wonderful."

Gutzon's first look at the Black Hills of South Dakota was when the newlyweds stopped on their honeymoon to visit with Mary's brother Marshall, who had become a minister in the booming gold town of Lead. While that was his introduction to South Dakota, he was already in love with the unspoiled beauty of the West and its majestic mountains.

The joy of the sculptor was supreme in 1912 when he became the father of a son, Lincoln. Among stacks of telegrams of congratulations was one from T. Channing Moore, a family friend, suggesting the name *Lincoln.* The birth of the Borglum heir was greeted by the famous and powerful of the world. A few years later a daughter, Mary Ellis, was born to the exultant father and grateful mother.

Gutzon was a proud and exemplary father, and Mary a wise and loving mother. The close knit family were to make the word "home" a reality to the sculptor in such farflung places as Stamford, Connecticut; Atlanta, Georgia; San Antonio, Texas; Montecito, California and Hermosa, South Dakota. No father and son team in America were closer than Gutzon and Lincoln.

Now the sculptor's work had even more feeling and depth. His statue of Abraham Lincoln sitting on a bench, created for the city of Newark, was the epitome of the emotional appeal of his work. The sorrowful, kindly Lincoln looked human and approachable, and little children loved to climb upon the bench to sit by his cradling arms. "Rabboni", a statue of the trusting Mary Magdalene, which now stands in Rock Creek, Maryland, was another profound work. It was partially paid for with a magnificent Gobelin tapestry, now in the Borglum studio.

Borglum was one of nine eminent American sculptors chosen to do the carvings for the new Pan American Union Building in Washington. During this time he became well acquainted with Washington society. He did statues of Henry Ward Beecher, Henry Lawson Wyatt, Zebulon Baird Vance, during this period.

Borglums found a home they loved, an impressive estate near Stamford, Connecticut, and it was here that Gutzon built the first distinctive studio of his own design, which was increasingly flooded with commissions in all stages. *Borgland,* as they named the estate, was a haven of beauty and quiet, the perfect counterbalance for the hectic professional life.

An arresting piece of work during this period was another shocker to conservatives. It was the statue of Atlas bearing the weight of the world. Surprisingly "Atlas" turned out to be a woman. Delighting in the controversy, the sculptor explained that only *woman* has the strength and endurance for such a weight.

Borglum's commissions had great variety. There was a small commemorative medal for the American Red Cross, and then there was the enormous fountain at Bridgeport, Connecticut. Part of the intricate fountain was a 14-foot horse trough. The face of the infant Lincoln Borglum adorned the main part of the fountain in cherubic fashion. At one time a modern freeway was scheduled to eradicate the fountain, but Bridgeport preserved it and is proud to have it near the center of the city.

Borglum's statues were becoming known all over the world for their accuracy and beauty, but most of all for their force and emotion. He studied each of his subjects thoroughly until his mind was saturated with information about everything which went into making this individual unique. Then he would select a climactic moment of the subject's life to portray in stone or bronze. He did not feel that a statue should be a generalized portrait, a composite of personality traits. He felt that the statue should be specific, showing the humanity of the person at an explicit and eloquent moment. The viewer should be able to recognize without being told, Borglum felt, whether the subject was sad, or proud, or fearful or happy. Because he researched his subjects so carefully, he won a growing reputation for the portrayal of true life in three dimensions. Even his headless, armless "Torso of a Dancer" proclaims action, grace, and the constant striving of the human spirit.

Although he was a contemporary of those who started new schools of art, such as *surrealism* and *cubism,* and had known the *impressionists* in Europe, he chose to stay with *realism,* as he felt that the great qualities of mankind could only be presented by staying as close to the truth as was possible. He was sometimes severely criticized by artist friends for his somewhat "old-fashioned" approach to art. His work was so authentic that he even acquired a remarkable collection of Civil War swords, while trying to find exactly the correct one for a period statue. Borglum's acceptance by the majority of his peers, attests to the success of his philosophy of art.

Gutzon Borglum was a man of a little over medium height for that time. A stocky build, and exceptionally broad shoulders made him appear somewhat shorter than he was. He had brown hair and piercing blue eyes, rather widely spaced and topped with close wiry brows. His cheeks were broad, his jaw square, and his chin determined. His hands were extraordinarily expressive. He was seldom seen without a brisk felt hat, which covered his balding head, the result of the mysterious fever early in his career. He would often wear a richly colored silk scarf around his neck. His clothing was somewhat of a hybrid between that of an imaginative artist and a western bank president. His countenance was mobile, with lightning changes from gentleness to ferocity, from cynicism to rapture. In later years he wore a pince nez and his forehead became lined like one who had looked upwards into the brilliant sky for a long, long time. His voice was resonant, his diction precise, his words, colorful. He spoke rapidly and with feeling, accenting his words with appropriate gestures.

He was easily dominant in almost any group, as he radiated energy and knowledge and vitality.

A life member of the *Fencers Club,* Gutzon Borglum thought everyone should develop their bodies, minds, and talents to the fullest. Boxing was another abiding interest of Borglum's. So was riding. He especially championed participant and amateur sports.

Added to his list of accomplishments was public speaking. He was in great demand for talks on all sorts of subjects, and was considered an authority on such biographical topics as President Lincoln. His talks were lively, dramatic, and full of surprise. He was an influential political leader in Stamford, and active in the Bull Moose party. Once urged to become the candidate for Lieutenant Governor of Connecticut, he turned it down because of his true commitment to art.

The fruitful Connecticut years were abruptly halted when Borglum went to Atlanta in 1915, at the request of the President of the United Daughters of the Confederacy, Helen Plane. The ladies had an earth shaking proposition. They wanted the sculptor to carve the likeness of Robert E. Lee on Stone Mountain, a great exfoliated dome of granite near the city. The idea captured Borglum's imagination, but he gave one look at the sheer, naked expanse of rock and told the ladies that a portrait of Lee on the small area they had reserved would be like "putting a postage stamp on a barn."

Instead of turning the whole thing down, he went to the owner, Sam Venable, and asked permission to suggest to the ladies that the entire mountainside be carved into a memorial depicting the heroic story of the Confederacy. The patriotic daughters of the defeated cause were ecstatic. The idea was so magnetic to Borglum, who was attracted by the stupendous, that he accepted the commission. He could visualize the most tragic days of America immortalized on the mountainside, and was eager to make this his masterpiece.

Stone Mountain, shaped like a huge gray whale, was a tantalizing challenge.

He didn't know exactly how to go about carving his vision of the noble Lee and his fiercely loyal, still proud, but ragged army, on the granite wall, but then neither did anyone else in the entire world. Borglum found that he had to accept the responsibility for everything in the project. He was expected to design the sculpture, plan the physical processes for getting it on the mountain, find the necessary help, and worst of all, even to take charge of raising all of the funds.

He became an admiring Lee scholar, finding himself almost as ardent about the Civil War General as he was about the Civil War President, Lincoln. World War I intervened, but after the War, his carefully sculptured 20 foot head was unveiled to a stunned crowd, who cried in unison, "It *is* Lee." The eventual success of the project seemed inevitable. By then Borglum not only agreed it should be done, but he knew how to do it.

Other commissions were completed during the Stone Mountain period. These included Governor Aycock of North Carolina, Governor William Hoard of Wisconsin, and King Christian of Denmark. His largest work of the period was his *Wars of America* memorial for Newark. It was apparent that his art took precedence over everything else, when he spent more money having this impressive group cast in bronze in Italy, than he had received for the entire commission. It was the largest sculptured group in America at that time, and it met with the approval of both public and peers. And it left the artist in debt, which was not unusual.

Gutzon's sculpted people looked like people. They had wrinkles, moles, and windblown hair, and they also had strong character, as to him, art did not show ugliness, hate, or evil. He believed in the spiritual and warm qualities of our citizens and our leaders, but he thought these could be depicted with truth and not through glorified exaggeration.

Perhaps it was this dedication to truth that brought about his misunderstanding with the Stone Mountain Association. They rejected the idea of a ragged or defeated army. They saw Lee's followers decked out in heroes finery, marching as if they were the victors. Much of the bitterness centered around finances, which was prophetic. A commemorative Stone Mountain 50 cents piece, designed by Gutzon, was authorized to be struck. There were to be two and a half million of these silver coins, to be sold to collectors at $1.00 each. This idea had been Gutzon's and that it ever bore fruit was only because of his countless trips to Washington to exert political pressure. However, the Stone Mountain group wanted to start using the money for other purposes than finishing the Memorial according to Gutzon's plan, and because the sculptor had spent so much time raising funds, the Georgians complained that the work was going too slowly. There was constant tension, bitterness and uncertainty, often exploding into vehement quarrels. The recriminations made Gutzon feel that he was in the eye of a storm.

The Stone Mountain experience was not without its bright spots. Borglum was excited to find that there were ways to make gigantic sculptures look true to life. He liked working outside. With young Lincoln following his Dad all over the project, Gutzon believed the work would be completed. The people from Atlanta found they could not dictate to the sculptor, so while he was in Washington on business connected with the project, they attempted to negotiate a deal with one of his associates to take over and finish the job. Gutzon rushed back to find that the Association had voted to terminate its contract with him. He immediately destroyed his clay models, as any sculptor would have done, for they were his personal property, and after many changes, would have been of little use to anyone else. The Association raised a furious cry, and demanded the immediate arrest of the fleeing sculptor. Borglum escaped into North Carolina with the law of Georgia hot on his heels. North Carolina's Governor McLean proclaimed he would call out the militia to protect the sculptor. Georgia's try for extradition failed. This was all eagerly reported by the nation's press.

Many of Borglum's difficulties throughout his life involved finances, a lot of them stemming from the mortgaging of the Connecticut estate in order to help finance Stone Mountain. Borglum was an impulsive spender, though not reckless. He did not feel that thrift, or strict budgets, or bookkeeping were necessary parts of his life. Many times his commission barely paid for the cost of his supplies, and often he would donate an important work, or turn part of his money back to the organization which had commissioned him. He really wanted to finish the Stone Mountain job, just as he later wanted to finish Mount Rushmore, and if it were only money which kept a project from completion, his own needs were forgotten. It was Mary who endeavored to keep the family finances straight. Mary tried to protect Gutzon and the children from financial troubles. Quiet and businesslike, she solved many problems, knowing that her husband's compelling genius was of prime importance. She felt that if she could keep finances from imposing on his time, somehow sufficient funds would flow their way.

Borglum loved music as well as the graphic arts. He played the violin with skill and verve. Another art form he admired was the cinema. He saw that it had a great opportunity for education in America and promotion of the arts. His favorite movies were westerns, as he was an

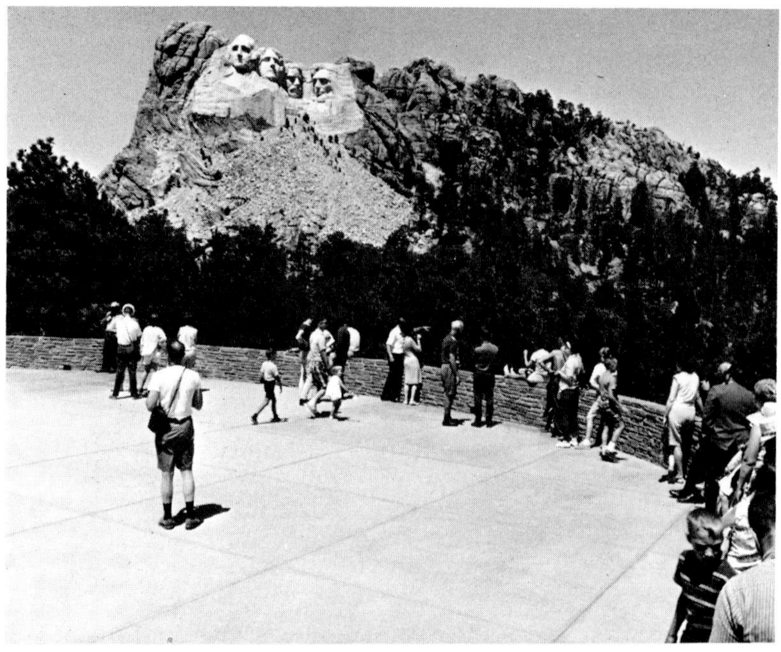

The Borglum Terrace of the Visitor's Center on Doane Mountain has an exceptional view of the carvings, which look the best in the morning light. An interpretive program can be heard from the terrace. Photo by S.D. Travel Division

admirer of all things western, particularly the fiery horses which galloped across the early silver screen, reminding him of his boyhood and youth in the West.

During World War I Borglum was occupied by many activities besides his art. He made an investigation for President Wilson of the inefficiencies and frauds connected with our infant aircraft industry. Having become an acknowledged expert on aerodynamics, both designing and engineering, he saw that the country was off to a bad start. His detailed and thorough report was slow to come out, as he pulled no punches. It was instrumental in the removal of General Squires from office, but the two later became friends. Borglum told the nation in 1918 that aeronautics would assume great importance in the world and that this nation should start at once to set aside large tracts of land for safe airports and to plan the use of the airways.

Also during the War, after meeting Czechoslovakian leader, Thomas Masaryk, Borglum set up on his estate, a camp for training volunteers willing to fight for the independence of the "Czechs."

Aside from the Stone Mountain group, the individuals and committees who commissioned Borglum were highly satisfied with his work. Many of his commissions were repeats, or were won through recommendations from proud clients. This grateful acceptance of his work was in evidence from the time of his early benefactress, Jessie Frémont, to the unprecedented national admiration for Mount Rushmore, long years after his death.

Borglum's home was always an informal center for anyone who entered the Borglum sphere. Mary was almost a mother to the young art students befriended by Gutzon. Workers and assistants who helped in any way were welcome at Borglums. Mary would keep track of the families of those who worked for her husband, too. She knew when the babies had fevers, and when the children's pets got lost, and when a birthday party was planned for "Grandma." Wherever they lived, Borglums were also visited by wealthy patrons of the arts, by painters, politicians, singers, dancers, and athletes . . . the successful in every field. Borgland, in Connecticut, the Menger Hotel Suite in San Antonio, and later the ranch house near Hermosa, South Dakota, provided the cultural background on which the sculptor thrived.

Borglum's "terrible temper" and "artistic temperament" were mostly myth. Probably the legend started because great artists were expected to be temperamental, and then, as now, the press loved to pounce on a minor incident and expand it into fat, black headlines. Borglum had a personality which was always good for a story, and the incidents in which he was involved were easy to exaggerate. His work often involved large groups of people and controversial subjects, so there was always room to dig and find some sort of disagreement. He certainly did not destroy the angels' faces. Nor did he destroy any property belonging to the Stone Mountain Association. The presidents with whom he is supposed to have had violent disagreements, Theodore Roosevelt (over the nomination of General Leonard Wood), Coolidge (over the Rushmore inscription), and Wilson (about his Airplane Investigation report) were soon reconciled with Borglum and on friendly terms with him until their deaths. Most of Borglum's friends were close to him throughout his life, and those who worked with him usually remained as long as there was work.

A sincere love of nature was apparent from the start of Borglum's career, when as a boy he had sketched the fleet horses of the Lucky Baldwin Ranch in California. Borglum later became Chairman of Central Park in New York, and used his influence to keeping this park an oasis in the midst of a forest of steel and concrete. He spent much thought helping the Latin flavored San Antonio keep its historic Missions, and its unique meandering river, with a touch of the tropics. He helped plan a dazzling water front for Corpus Christi. Suitable landscape design and correct placement of his sculpture, went with every commission for outdoor work.

He criticized many American cities for their garishness and commercialism and their mediocrity. Without being asked, he gave many cities excellent advice about beautifying themselves. For example, he told the city of Chicago that Lake Michigan should be the focal point for scenic walkways and parks, for islands of adventure and learning, instead of a vast, dirty, commercial harbor for industry and trade. Later, he worked out an ambitious plan to beautify the entire state of Texas.

Even such economically important projects as the hydroelectric plant on the Osage River for which the *Lake of Ozarks* was created, drew his wrath. He wasn't against dams or power projects per se, but he did feel that they should be planned with an eye for the total ecology and not just economics with a dollar sign. He knew progress and beauty could be compatible.

Borglum was a believer in American art. He was a prime mover in the encouragement and promulgation of the arts in the schools of the nation. A strong speech which he gave before the first *National Arts Committee,* urged the government to promote a cultural consciousness in America. He felt that the government department should scout out potential artists, encourage and nurture talent, and provide forums for the arts, but that the government should never try to guide or mold the arts.

"Don't tell anyone what wine to like, what songs to sing, what time of the day or night heaven is at its loveliest . . . help them to find their wine, their voice, their heaven . . . not yours, nor mine."

"We should institute art festivals all over America. We should have 9 or 10 larger cultural centers in America selected to help with regional festivities, music and drama, painting and sculpture and dancing." These were his plans for the arts.

Borglum was advisor to this National Committee and it is clear his word was heeded. The National Arts program was given a start during the depression days and the government never did try to diminish the freedom of the arts. Many of the local art fairs and festivals recommended by his report are still seen each year in all parts of the country and this nation is conscious of its culture and the products of individual genius as never before.

Many articles were written about Borglum during his life for magazines such as *Scribners* and *Reader's Digest.* He was the subject of speeches at women's clubs and orations at schools. His work was discussed on radio programs. He was better known than most of the artists of his day, and his following was a cross section of American life. His is still the first name millions of Americans will mention when suddenly asked to name a sculptor.

With his vigorous personality and enthusiastic involvement in many fields, Borglum was a superb subject for interviews. Wherever he went to lecture, to unveil a statue, to discuss a commission, there were reporters on hand to ask his opinions on a scrambled variety of subjects. They knew his answer would never be "no comment," and that their story would probably get at least a 2 bank 24 point headline. They asked him his opinion of the Lindbergh kidnapping . . . *he decried it as a national blot;* his preference in the Baer Carnera fight . . . *he hoped Baer would win;* his opinion of Europe . . . *America is better;* how he felt about Western Civilization . . . *"because the acquisition of money amounts to madness, civilization has failed."*

In his letters, and essays, and speeches, Borglum wrote volumes. His favorite writing materials were the backs of standard size, yellow Western Union telegram blanks. Borglum's plan for world peace was one of 20 selected for the Edward Bok *American Peace Award* for writers. It was included in a book published by *Scribners.* He wrote short articles for many periodicals. Often his subject was art, but just as often it was roads or parks, or politics, or the plight of our cities.

His "Letters to the Editor" were the delight of editors from coast to coast. They were well written, to the point, attention getting, and presented the unknown side of controversial issues. When he was working in South Dakota, the *Rapid City Journal* was a special recipient of pungent Borglum letters.

Some of the letters reported the progress of work on the mountain, but often he wrote berating Rapid City for its shortcomings, or prodding the conservative South Dakotans into action on many fronts. Once he wrote, "South Dakota has the worst roads of any first, second, third, or fourth class state in the Union, and is thoroughly at home with them."

He also was constantly inundated by correspondence. He received hundreds of letters from all over the world. Many were from children. Both children and adults often asked for autographs and pictures, yet few contained the courtesy of an envelope or a stamp.

He wrote long letters to friends, to family, to politicians, to committee members, to bureaucrats, and to artists. In addition there was a great volume of mail about proposed commissions. Sculpture was a popular form of art in American cities at their zenith. An unimaginable variety of ideas for statues was advanced. There were reams of letters to answer. People in Kansas City were considering a Pioneer monument and wanted his suggestions. St. Louis was thinking about an Indian monument. A Colorado committee inquired about the possibility of a statue to Buffalo Bill Cody. El Paso wrote about a tribute to Coronado. Corpus Christi corresponded about a Christ for their waterfront.

There were no fees connected with these letters. All Borglum got from most of these proposals were hours of work and heavy files. But all inquiries, no matter how casual, indefinite, or inconsequential, received careful consideration and complete answers. Mary was an immense help to Gutzon in all this obligatory letter writing.

Gutzon, like most great men, was far ahead of his time. He was on the *National Highway Commission* and carefully planned a complete system of cross country highways long before any of our present freeways were envisioned. His highway plans were the predecessors of the *Interstates,* but would have had major differences. They were planned not merely to make travel easier, but to make travel more interesting and beautiful. If his plans had been used, the roadsides never would have become lanes of blazing billboards, and gardens of beer cans and facial tissues. He foresaw these possibilities and wanted

One of Borglum's best works is the North Carolina monument of Gettysburg National Battlefield. Reminiscent of the pose of the flag raising on Iwo Jima, this is one of Gettysburg's most photographed statues. Photo by Albert Zeitner

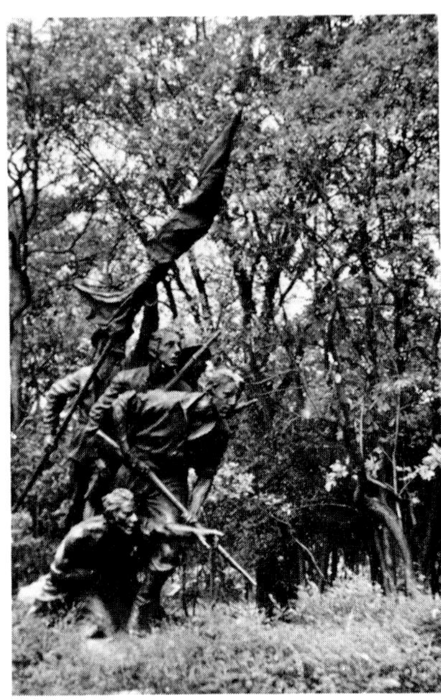

to keep the highways like parks. Where was the money to come from? The Borglum highways would have been self sufficient. The government was to purchase enough land along the highways, so that land could be leased for filling stations, motels, restaurants, acceptable road signs, and suitable businesses. The money from the leases would be enough to keep the highways up, and landscape and patrol the parks. Uses of roadside land for garbage dumps, old car graveyards, and tourist traps would have been prohibited. Borglum called his roads the *Federated Transcontinental Military Highways.*

He thought the park-like rest stops should be living museums of native American trees and flowers, and birds and insects, heightened with true American architecture. The highways were to be a virtual vacation in themselves. He advanced these ideas in the early years of the century while times were good and the country was expanding. His plans were read, talked about, and then ignored.

The *energy* shortage was familiar to Borglum. He could see it coming. He could also see how serious the *flooding* problems would become on the Mississippi and other major rivers, and he knew of the millions of dollars of loss which could come from drowned crops and water logged property. He also knew about the terrible troubles that *drouth* could bring. And for *all* of these he had a plan.

He worked out in meticulous detail a massive plan for mid-America, which would save lives and crops and property and dollars, and would provide energy far into the future, which would pay for the well conceived plan. He wanted to prevent disastrous floods by cutting a canal flowing straight south through the dry heartlands of the country. He said measures to prevent disaster must be on a scale as near as possible to the forces which created such havoc. His canal would start in South Dakota. All the major tributaries to the Missouri-Mississippi drainage basin were to be dammed so that the flow of water would be controlled. The canal and lakes resulting from the dams were to be used to irrigate the fertile but dry lands of Nebraska, Oklahoma, Kansas and Texas, assuring a plentiful food supply for a growing population. The water rates and the hydroelectric power rates would provide money for the maintenance of the system.

In this way the Missouri River would be changed to a minor river, and the man built canal would be the major waterway straight down through the center of the nation, hoarding and using all of the precious, fresh water. With faith that the work of man should be beautiful, besides being useful and good, Borglum would have landscaped the canal, so that every mile of it would be a tranquil picture.

No one paid much attention to Borglum's plan, and those who did,

This is a model for one of Gutzon's first large marbles, the head of Lincoln in the Rotunda of the Capital. Photo by National Park Service

said it was too expensive; however, floods, drouth, and power shortages, since then, have cost many times more than his bold proposal.

It was in 1924 while Borglum was still working on the figures of Jefferson Davis and Stonewall Jackson for Stone Mountain, that he got his first letter from Doane Robinson, the imaginative State Historian of South Dakota, about the possibility of carving some kind of monument, possibly Western, on some granite pinnacles in the mountains of South Dakota. The first interchange of letters between the two was to set the future pattern of Borglum's life. Although he continued to create smaller sculptures the rest of his life, it was the gigantic ones which took precedence.

Borglum had worked in Raleigh, North Carolina, for some time after leaving Stone Mountain, and then he decided he would like to settle in Texas. He was enchanted by San Antonio, and liked Texas for its bigness, and its atmosphere of the old Southwest. He moved his family to an elegant hotel suite, enrolled his children in San Antonio schools, and fixed up a succession of three studios during his years there. He was active in state and civic affairs and in the arts, so the Borglums became well known and well loved in Texas.

Art critics have not all accepted Borglum's work as great. Some criticize his realism, and others have never been able to see beyond the sheer mass of mountain carving. Borglum thought that great ideas should be loudly heralded and that great monuments should be on a colossal scale. When someone leveled the charge that bigness is not necessarily art, he assented and went on to point out that bigness was an important asset to historic art. He said that the pyramids of Egypt, the heads on Easter Island, the ruins at Ankhor and the Wall of China, might never had attained world recognition had they been on a small scale. He felt that the immense project at Rushmore was in the best American tradition. It was to be a memorial on the scale of the vast ranches of the West, the cloud piercing skyscrapers of the East, the daring of industry, the thick volumes of American writers, and the flowering of our agriculture.

Rushmore became Gutzon's final masterpiece, one of the top tourist attractions of the world. It was no accident that it was chosen as the background for the first *Telstar* broadcast. With the Mormon Tabernacle Choir singing "The Battle Hymn of the Republic," with the flag flying, and the sun emerging from the clouds, the great faces on Rushmore projected to the world, the very image of America.

It is tragic that Gutzon did not live to see that day, but he did know before he died, that he had given a spirit to the mountain, and that the name of that spirit was *Democracy.*

When Borglum died quite unexpectedly towards the end of the Rushmore years, leaving his son Lincoln, to finish his important work, thousands mourned his death. "It was too soon. He had so much to contribute," were the words so often used. But examining doctors told Lincoln and Mary that had Gutzon not died when he did, the condition which caused the blood clot would have prohibited him from ever scaling the heights of *his* mountain again; that his life would have been almost that of an invalid. To the man who had so loved life, that he had lived every waking moment to the fullest, that would have been harder to take than death itself. Lincoln knew, more than anyone else, that destiny had spoken with a greater wisdom.

Lincoln Borglum, standing near the old studio at the foot of Doane Mountain, hopes that the work at Rushmore will someday be completed by the addition of the Hall of Records, which had been started across the ravine from the faces.

Although the perch on the side of the sheer cli looks precarious for Lincoln, the safety harness were so good that there was never a serious ac cident in all of the Rushmore years.

Lincoln Borglum accepts the praise of Goverr Kneip for the bas-relief portrait of his father the historic marker for the Borglum Memor Highway. Behind Governor Kneip are Harv Wickware, Les Helgeland, and Hoadley Dea

Lincoln Borglum addresses the South Dakota Bicentennial Commission after Mou Rushmore was designated a National focal point. His wife, Mary Anne Borglum, si to the left. Hoadley Dean, president of the Mount Rushmore Memorial Society, lool on.

Crumbling old mine buildings throughout the Black Hills are constant reminders of the gold and mineral "rushes" which started most of the communities.
Photo by Rapid City Journal

The towering granite spires of the Harney Range represent the solid core of a mountain range which was once much higher, the oldest mountains in the nation. Photo by S.D. Travel Division

Towards the end of the project work could be seen proceeding in different stages on all four faces simultaneously

Theodore Roosevelt's glasses prompt many questions. They are mostly optical illusion created by skillful use of lights and shadows.

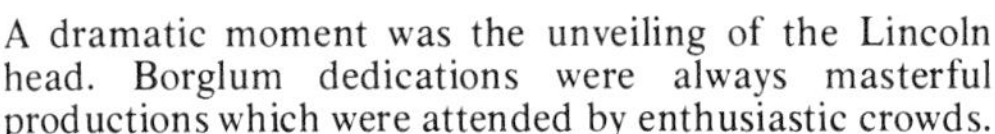

A dramatic moment was the unveiling of the Lincoln head. Borglum dedications were always masterful productions which were attended by enthusiastic crowds.

› many, Borglum's Washington is
› best existing likeness of the first
›esident.

Little did Gutzon know, when he planted the stars and stripes on top of the granite knob that he would toil here for the rest of his life.

It is apparent from this workman's face that to him this is not just another job, but an immortal work of art.

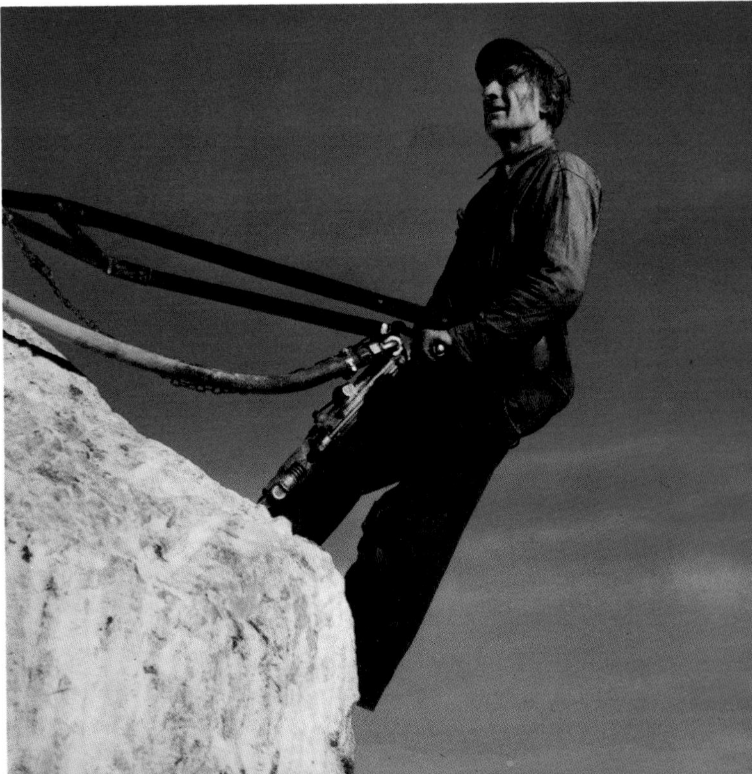

The Lincoln face, is thought by many to be the best face on the mountain, and one of the best Lincoln likeness anywhere. Herb Conn inspects the face each year to prevent weather deterioration.

ɔst of the time the buffalo herds of Custer State Park and Wind Cave National Park, are oblivious to the strangers
ıo delight in watching them. Photo by S.D. Travel Division

ail rides are a popular diversion in the Black
lls during most of the summer and fall. Many
ectacular trails lead into meadows and canyons
r from highways. Photo by S.D. Travel Division

he goat that couldn't read . . . or maybe he
rected the sign, as he lives in the little ravine
ehind the giant faces.
Photo by S.D. Travel Division

Campers at Sylvan Lake in Custer State Park enjoy unpolluted air, unsurpassed scenery, good fishing, invigoratin hikes, and cold swims.

Photo by S.D. Travel Divisic

unt Rushmore, as a National morial, is under the supervision of the ional Park Service of the Department nterior. Photo by S.D. Travel Division

Fall is a peaceful time in the Black Hills, with warm sunny days, frosty nights, and spectacular scenery.

Sioux Indians called the Black Hills **Paha a.** Although a few live in the Hills, most dwell he large Reservations near the Hills in western th Dakota. Photo by S.D. Travel Division

The surprising Badlands are not dead and forbidding at all, but a haven for a wonderful variety of flora and fauna of the West. Photo by S.D. Travel Division

The Pasque, South Dakota's State Flower, is one of the first flowers to be seen in the spring in the Black Hills.
Photo by S.D. Travel Division

Like giant Ming Trees, graceful junipers guard desolate stretches of Badlands and foothills. Photo by S.D. Travel Division

Traffic jams, distracting roadside signs, wandering pedestrians, commercial horsedrawn vehicles, and "trail rid are only a few of the problems of the Keystone area being studied by long-range planners. Photo by Rapid City Jou

In the frosty autumn days the aspens turn to gold, and wild asters and goldenrod with red poison ivy paint meadows with gypsy tones. Photo by S.D. Travel Div

South Dakota's governor Tom Berry and F. D. R. listened spellbound as Gutzon elaborated on his plan for Mount Rushmore. Photo by Rapid City Journal

Gutzon Borglum in his safety harness was the designer, the chief engineer, and the fund-raiser for Mount Rushmore, but never asked a worker to do something he would not do himself. Photo by S.D. Travel Division

The dramatic windows of the Visitors Center, which w recently broken by a vandal's bomb blast, reflect countenances of four great American leaders and travelers who have come to pay them homage.
Photo by S.D. Travel Divis

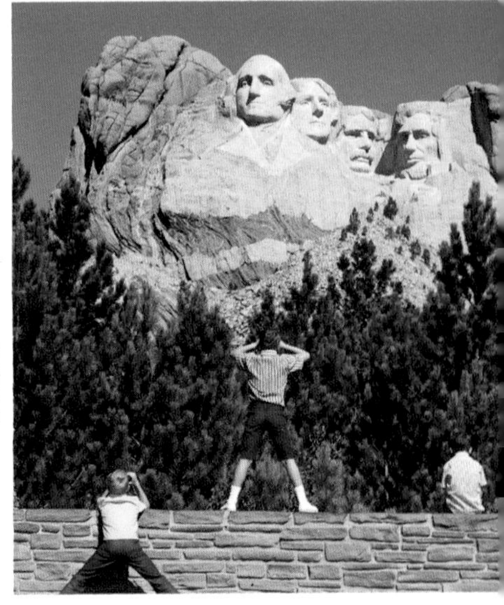

Children, sometimes to the surprise of their parents, love Mount Rushmore. Naturally attracted to things done on a big scale, they also like to look for mountain goats and deer, take pictures, and climb the wide stone steps, and what is more, they catch the spirit of the Memorial.

The rain suddenly cleared as the Mormon Tabernacle Choir, standing at the foot of Rushmore, sang for the Telstar broadcast seen around the world.
Photo by S.D. Travel Div

A large bronze plaque at the Viewing Terrace gives a concise history. At one time Borglum planned on carving an inscription on the mountain itself.

The author stands at the entrance to the Hall of Records, the great part of Borglum's unfinished dream, located in a ravine across from the carvings. Photo by Albert Zeitner.

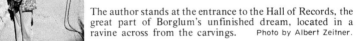

ld" burros in Custer State Park are friendly beggars, but often cause traffic jams on the busy highway, US 16A.

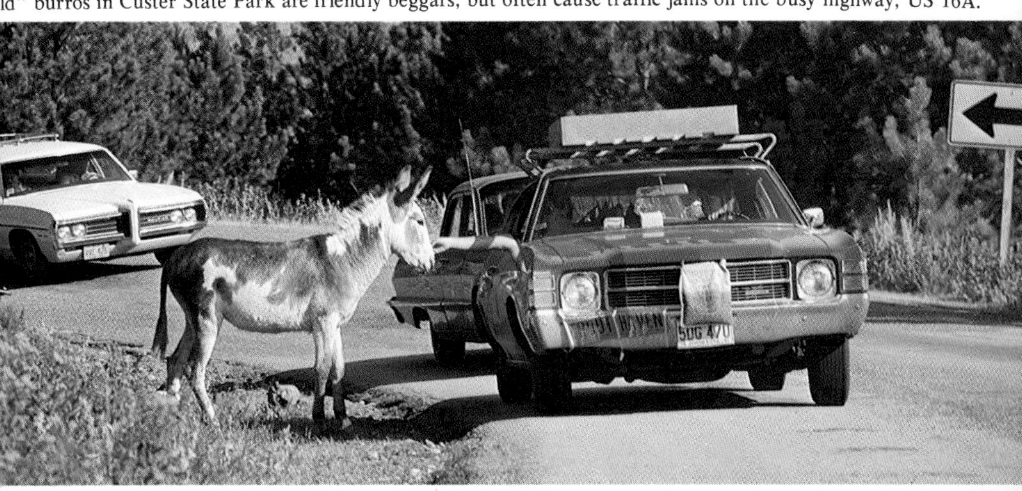

; bust of Gutzon Borglum at the Borglum Viewing ·ace across from the faces, is the work of Lincoln glum.

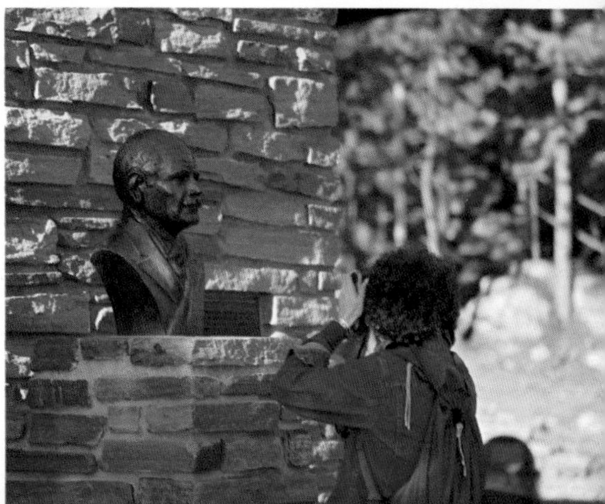

Engineers say that the famous pigtail bridges will need replacing before long. There are already load limits on bridges. Tunnels on this route have by-passes for trailers and motorhomes. Photo by S.D. Travel Div

An early picture of the Washington face shows the winch house on top from which the workmen were raised and lowered to their work. Jefferson's face was first started on the left of Washington.
Photo by S.D. Travel Division

The cable car carrying men and materials to work was a big improvement over the arduous daily climb.
Photo by National Park Service by Bert Bell

The Arts and Crafts Room of the concession building is famous for handmade silver and turquoise jewelry made by Indians of the Southwest. Photo by S.D. Travel Division

Concretions like this one being attacked by an eager "pebble pup" often contain fossils or exciting crystals. There is no bag limit for hunting South Dakota gems. Photo by S.D. Travel Division

From a huge window in the studio at the foot of Doane Mountain, Borglum plans one of the many cha
necessitated by the mountain itself.

4

Lincoln Inherits A Mountain

Lincoln Borglum was immediately put in charge of completing the Memorial. His father had called him the only thoroughly trained and experienced help, the only always reliable aid, who had been at the Monument the whole time. Lincoln alone could carry out the work as it had been planned by his father.

In accepting the assignment, it was doubly difficult for Lincoln. He was grieving for his father who had been the life of the project, and he knew that the federal bureaucracy would never allow him to finish the whole dream as his will and conscience desired.

Lincoln and Louella were living at the ranch. There were still men in the area glad to work on the mountain, although the worst of the depression was by now over.

Only a month after his father's death, Lincoln became the father of his first child, a daughter, Robin. Mary was a delighted grandmother.

Mount Rushmore wasn't the only work that Lincoln inherited. There were several other commissions in one stage or another at the studio on the ranch, including a bust his father had just started of Congressman Reed for Washington, D.C.

Gutzon's models for Mount Rushmore were for figures continued to the waists. Hands were to add additional expressiveness to Washington and Lincoln, and details of period clothing were to distinguish the centuries of our culture, the 18th, 19th and 20th. Lincoln was fully ready in every way to carry this out, but he knew that funds were low, and that with talk of war, new funds would be impossible to raise. He decided to use the rest of the funds on the faces alone.

Lincoln Borglum is seen in his safety harness descending to his work on one of the faces. He worked on the mountain for several years without pay.

There was considerable work to be done on Roosevelt, as well as the refining of Lincoln's face. After doing as much as he possibly could with the remaining funds, Lincoln made his final report to the Commission. He recommended the removal of the debris, and he pointed out the vital need for a Hall of Records, but he said the figures themselves should be left as they were. He thought the four faces were exactly as his father envisioned them. On the last of October in 1941 he turned over the Borglum Commission of the mountain to the eternal charge of the National Park Service. As far as was possible the mighty job was done. Five weeks later the nation was at war.

The government didn't pay Lincoln for his work any more rapidly than they had Gutzon. Lincoln signed his final invoice in the summer of 1941, but it was the winter of '42 before payment was made. His money for the statue he finished of Thomas Brackett Reed, Speaker of the House, from Maine, which was placed in the Capital, was also slow in coming. Lincoln had to beg the government to pay Mary the rest of the fees due Gutzon at his death.

Although his father's dream was never finished, Lincoln Borglum turned the Memorial over to the Park Service in 1941, with the great faces so nearly complete he felt no more details necessary. Photo by National Park Service

Mount Rushmore had cost $989,992.32, most of the amount from the government. Some had been raised by the four brochures Gutzon had published, and some was privately subscribed. Only about $25,000 came from the citizens of the Black Hills who were to reap millions of dollars in financial benefits. Custer, which was to become one of the primary beneficiaries, gave less than Sioux City, Iowa.

Much of the money had been spent on buildings, equipment, supplies, and a big slice for wages and salaries. The work had covered a span of 16 years of the sculptor's life from his first rendezvous with destiny to his death, but the actual work was expanded over 13 years from the time of the first drilling. Counting the many shutdowns because of lack of funds, and the winters when work was at a standstill, and subtracting that from the total, reveals that the actual working time was only about six and one-half years or 78 months. In all about 450,000 tons of granite were removed, 90% of them by dynamite. This works out to around $2.00 per ton. If the Monument would have been made of concrete, the hauling of the sand alone would have cost 3.5 million dollars.

Over two million people a year see the Monument, which is open to all the year around. If each person over the past five years would have given one dime, the amount would have paid for the entire Memorial.

After the war, 1947, Senator Case, backed by John Boland, made a genuine effort to get a new appropriation to finish the entire Mount Rushmore project according to the artist's plans, and under the direction of Lincoln, who was ready to carry those plans out. To finance it, Case proposed a specially minted Mount Rushmore half dollar. It was thought that commemorative coins would raise funds for removal of the debris, added parking space, and the Hall of Records. Nothing came of this attempt.

Lincoln was asked to become the first Superintendent of Mount Rushmore National Memorial, under the Park Service branch of the Department of Interior. It was rather an anachronism, as he had spent so many years as an unhappy victim of Park Service policy. After thinking it over, he accepted, and as administrator, set the pattern for continued growth of interest in the greatest memorial of its kind in the world. He was also actively managing his ranch at Hermosa, and working in the studio there. Lincoln remained with the Park Service for several years. In 1949 he decided to sell most of his ranch to a neighbor, Dick Mieners. He moved with his family to Connecticut, where he hoped to help his mother develop the property at Borgland as a Gutzon Borglum Studio. Louella Borglum did not like the east. She became increasingly unhappy about her life, so to try to restore family peace, Lincoln and his family returned to South Dakota.

Louella was no happier there, so after a short time Lincoln decided that his wife might be better off if she were near her family and roots in Texas, and in 1951 they moved to Beeville. The following year on October 7, a son, Jimmy (James Gutzon) was born. Lincoln became prominent in civic affairs in Beeville. He went into ranching since Beeville is located in some of the finest Texas ranch country, and ranching is a field that Lincoln knew well. He was popular with the ranchers of the region, and was soon involved in the leadership of statewide activities concerned with ranching.

Lincoln's mother, Mary Borglum, after her husband's death, had devoted much time trying to settle Gutzon's complicated financial affairs. After a struggle, she received the rest of Gutzon's Mount Rushmore honorarium. Mary estimated that Gutzon had put about 40% of his commission during the years, right back into the mountain. She continued doing what she had been doing for so long, promoting the story of the National Memorial, and of the man who had given the best years of his career to its creation. She kept close track of family, and of friends, which numbered in the hundreds. Most of all, Mary longed to write a definitive book on all of the Rushmore years. She was deeply disappointed when publishers turned down her story of Rushmore written for her granddaughter, Robin. There was some talk of collaborating with Rupert Hughes, a family friend, but finally she worked with Robert Casey on a Borglum biography, "Give The Man Room."

Mary was used to traveling, so she was ever on the move. Perhaps she was unconsciously avoiding having to call any place "home" without Gutzon. Without him, no place was right.

She liked Mexico City as a place to spend part of the winter, for the bright gaiety of the Mexican Capital could bring a smile to her thoughtful face. She went to California, where Gutzon had dreamed of moving, and to South Dakota. She went to New York, where she had been Gutzon's volunteer secretary, and to Connecticut, where she had lived as a bride. She went to Washington where her husband had battled for his dreams, and where many of his works were on display.

Mary was interested in trying to keep the Mount Rushmore environment the way she knew Gutzon would have wanted it. She followed in his footsteps in making speeches, in writing letters, and in lobbying for art.

The increasing commercialism at Mount Rushmore annoyed Mary, and she led a dedicated but losing fight to turn the trend around. She didn't like every hamburger hut using the name *Rushmore,* nor every ceramic factory portraying the Monument on futuristic ash trays, Greek vases, and Colonial turkey platters. She enlisted support and a strenuous effort was made in both Pierre and Washington, to see if there were not some way to stop the dilution of the Rushmore name. All was to no avail.

When the Rushmore Memorial Society hired Gilbert Fite to write the Rushmore story while so many of the principals were still alive, Mary graciously allowed Fite to go through stacks and stacks of Gutzon's personal files, letters, and papers. She gave him his choice of pictures. She herself spent many hours telling him of her vivid and accurate recollections of the long adventure filled years of Rushmore. But when Fite's book *Mount Rushmore* came out she was desolate and unconsolable. She felt the book emphasized all the wrong things. She felt it was biased in favor of those who had often made Gutzon's life miserable. According to her view the Fite book made Gutzon the villain in all the financial troubles of Rushmore, and she knew this was not true. She thought the book unduly critical of Gutzon, and she said that she believed that since Gutzon was no longer there to give his side of the

The countenance of the Great Emancipator emerges slowly from the ancient rock. Lincoln Borglum did much of the work on the president for whom he was named.
Photo by National Park Service from Rise Studio

story, Fite had been inclined to accept the exaggerated tales of the people who had crossed Gutzon's path, while he fought to preserve the integrity of his work.

After reading Fite's book, Mary wrote, "The Bible says 'By their works ye shall know them.' And in this case, since the work was so great, I had hoped that the record would be. I soon found Fite wanted to include every swear word the workers used to each other when they were worried, irritated, hungry or tired. I told Fite I didn't think that necessary. They all ended up as friends, loving each other, and that was all that was important.

"There is no seamy side to Mount Rushmore and its story, and I don't want anyone to invent one to please the public."

The plans of the Borglums to buy the estate at Montecito, in California, were never completed because the land and home were part of a jumbled estate in litigation. So Mary took some time from her busy schedule to visit her two children whenever possible. In the winter of 1955 she stopped in Beeville for a few weeks, to visit with Lincoln and

Louella before going to Mexico City for a holiday visit. She went to the local beauty parlor to have her hair done. When she was ready, she phoned Lincoln to come and pick her up. It was a pleasant day, almost like spring, so she decided instead of waiting inside, to walk around in the large yard for a few minutes, until Lincoln came. She had barely started her leisurely stroll, when a friendly, big collie, glad to have some company, jumped towards her in eager play. She fell to the ground, breaking her hip in the fall. When the horrified Lincoln arrived seconds later, he rushed his mother to Corpus Christi, only 60 miles away.

Doctors at the hospital set the hip, put in a pin, and assured Lincoln that Mary would not be seriously incapacitated. Nothing to worry about, they said. Lincoln felt that he had been through this before. Instead of improving, Mary continued to grow weaker, and failed to respond to therapy. Baffled, the doctors ordered complete tests, which revealed that Mary had advanced cancer. For six months the hospital staff tried everything to help the tiny, gallant woman, but realizing that there was nothing more they could do, they gave in to her plea to be allowed to go to a family guest house near Lincoln. Here for three months she received tender care and love, spending long hours rich in bittersweet memories. After three months, Mary died. She was buried in Forest Lawn, California, beside the man to whom she had given her lifelong devotion. Perhaps she knew that it would be said of her, "If there would have been no Mary, there would have been no Rushmore."

Mary's death was a blow to Lincoln and to his sister, Mary Ellis. Lincoln was involved in problems with his own family, but he realized that some day he would have to return to South Dakota and the problems of Mount Rushmore, to keep faith with the efforts of his mother, as well as with the work of his father.

Lincoln was left with memories of the devotion of his parents to each other, and to Gutzon's work. And he was also left with boxes and boxes full of clippings and notes, of memos and telegrams, of letters, and half finished manuscripts. Carefully he saved everything of Mary's as he had of Gutzon's sure that some day he would find the proper place for them.

Along with his other activities in Texas, Lincoln maintained his interest in sculpture, and several towns and ranches in that part of the state have Lincoln Borglum originals. Beeville was quite delighted to have a resident sculptor.

As a sculptor, Lincoln was plagued by the same types of groups who had often made Gutzon miserable. The indecision, and the bickering and lack of understanding by political groups and citizens' committees, have always been the bane of creative artists. The City Council of

Corpus Christi decided not to accept Gutzon's statue of Christ which they had asked for, and which was partly done at the time of his death. Then the city fathers of Spearfish, South Dakota, decided they wanted a "Christ on the Mountain" overlooking the site of the Black Hills Passion Play. They asked Lincoln if he would use the head modeled by Gutzon and finish the statue for them. Lincoln accepted the assignment.

The head had been modeled to show Christ bidding the wind and the waves to be still, and Lincoln pointed out that the features should be modified and softened to show a teacher standing for his gentle "Sermon on the Mount." The committee opposed any change. So Lincoln built the body to scale and the model was 17 feet tall. However, radical ecologists of Spearfish loudly deplored the idea of such an addition to their community. They said Spearfish did not need the type of progress that this new attraction would bring to the community. The *Sierra Club* joined in the protest, saying that the beautiful scenery surrounding Spearfish should be left unmolested. Since the complaints and insults of the few were so noisy and continuous, the Spearfish leaders reneged on the deal they had made with Lincoln.

Another example of the way people are inclined to treat artists is seen in a long and strange series of letters from a Professor Wilson at Chadron, Nebraska, who wanted Lincoln to create a Sioux Indian Memorial on the college campus there. At first he seemed to think Lincoln was Gutzon's grandson. He had Lincoln make trips to Chadron several times to talk about the proposed commission. Lincoln spent many hours on this project without a cent of pay, and nothing more was ever heard of the whole idea.

A perfect instance of the way the Borglum family was imposed on for more than half a century, resulted in a big file of letters from a man in the east. The writer said he was an author and was compiling information for a book about famous people from New England. He begged Lincoln for all kinds of detailed information about his father. Lincoln generously provided a biography of his father, some pertinent letters and papers, and a description of Mount Rushmore. Then the writer wanted pictures of the Borglums and the Connecticut Estate. Lincoln provided these, too. He patiently answered reams of questions and requests. After a lengthy period, Lincoln received a copy of a small volume in the mail, and with it a bill requesting the prompt payment of $2.00.

Such items would have been front page news during Gutzon's day, but Lincoln's temperament is so different from his father's, that the press does not follow him around for stories.

Several men could work simultaneously on different parts of a head. Here two men have plenty of space as they work on Lincoln's eye. Photo by National Park Service

Several intriguing foreign offers have come to Lincoln. One was from Guanajuato, Mexico, asking for a heroic sized statue of Hildalgo. A tentative model was submitted. Then there was a violent change of political leadership in the Latin city, but the offer was never formally withdrawn. Later a South American committee asked Lincoln to come to carve a monument on a large rock landmark near the Amazon River. They stated that money was no object.

Lincoln began working on smaller items, such as miniature carvings. He did models of 4-H children proudly showing their prize winning animals. Lifelike sculptures of valuable Texas cattle were commissioned by successful ranchers. Bas relief scenes of Texas ranch life were carved with feeling by Lincoln.

One of his interesting assignments was to be the technical advisor of four miniature busts of American presidents, which were carved out of gem sapphires for the Kazanjian foundation of California. These are now in the Smithsonian.

Some of Lincoln's finest small scale work was for jewelry. Primarily done in a technique called "lost wax", the sculptures were cast in gold. Lincoln's larger commissions are discussed in the Studio chapter.

Louella Borglum continued to be plagued by poor health and emotional problems, so she was really not any more content in Beeville than she had been in South Dakota or Connecticut. Lincoln realized that there was no way he could make her happy, as she had lost interest in everything around her. The tension and worry were too much for Lincoln. He became seriously ill. His doctor told him that he had suffered a heart attack and that he could not recover unless he found a place to rest in complete peace and quiet away from any possible turmoil. So in 1962 Lincoln and his son Jimmy returned to South Dakota to live on the Borglum Ranch.

When he began to recover, he was invited to a party at Ellsworth Air Force Base near Rapid City. His dinner partner was Mary Anne Ellsworth, widow of General Richard Ellsworth for whom the base was named. Mary Anne and Lincoln discovered that they shared an uncle by marriage and countless friends in Texas and in South Dakota. The evening was delightful to both of them, and Lincoln soon felt better than he had in years.

Mary Anne Thornton Ellsworth, a Texan by birth, and a member of a prominent old San Antonio family, had by that time been a resident of South Dakota for many years. Her husband had been in command of the large South Dakota SAC air base when his plane had been caught up in an unexpected, turbulent storm and crashed, killing the pilot and all the crew. Mary Anne was left alone with three small sons. Dwight Eisenhower dedicated the base as Ellsworth Air Force Base, shortly after the accident.

Mary Anne's world had suddenly been turned upside down. Everything seemed pointless to her, as she struggled to pull herself out of her grief and shock, and to make a new life for herself and her family. Neither travel nor the social whirl was the answer, so she plunged herself into work and community service. As the manager of the *Villa Ranchero* shopping center, she demonstrated astute business ability. An active member of the Air Force Wives, she was made an honorary life member. Helping Rapid City and the Air Base in many ways, she also found time for ceramics, decorating and art. Mary Anne and her fine sons were popular and busy in Rapid City, and had adjusted to their loss; still there were many times during her eleven years of widowhood, that she felt quite alone.

Mary Anne, dainty, slim, and blonde, was, and is, a beautiful woman. Her long hair is sometimes dramatic and sophisticated, and sometimes becomingly casual. Her finely chiseled features and lovely skin are accented by clear, blue eyes. She moves with the natural grace of one who keeps fit by gardening and swimming. She has a flair, perhaps accentuated by years of military life, for always dressing exactly right and for putting other people at ease.

Lincoln continued his sculpting, and was again a leader in Rushmore affairs. He saw Mary Anne often, since they had so much in common. The vibrant, witty, Mary Anne soon erased the mood of despair with which Lincoln had left Texas. As devoted friends, the two quickly realized their companionship had changed their lives.

Still disillusioned with life, Louella Borglum died in Texas in 1963. She had been wealthy, socially prominent, the wife of a well known, highly respected artist, the mother of two lovely children, but she never found happiness or contentment. This restlessness and dissatisfaction had caused some sad times for Lincoln.

On April 9, 1964, Lincoln and Mary Anne were married in the tiny church in Custer State Park. They had the blessing of all their children, and the well wishes of all their friends. It was his birthday, and Lincoln knew that he had found the greatest gift of all, true love.

Mary Anne's sons and Lincoln's daughter Robin, were all young adults at the time of the wedding, but Jimmy Borglum was only ten at the time, and had been only eight when he was separated from his mother, so he was especially happy to be part of a family again. The whole family became remarkably close and loyal. The newlyweds made their home on the South Dakota Ranch, where Lincoln had retained some of the land and all of the buildings. Jimmy went to the little, one-room county school across from the ranch. The teacher, Mrs. Anne Mieners, was a gifted instructor as well as a family friend. It was her husband who had purchased much of the Borglum land.

Mary Anne, like Gutzon's Mary, has since devoted her energies to smoothing the way to her talented husband. She keeps the gracious Texas home running calmly and beautifully. Her garden provides bright bouquets and seasonal delicacies and attracts rare birds. She is a brilliant hostess, a clever decorator, a gourmet cook. She works with equal skill and enthusiasm at the Borglum Ranch and Studio in South Dakota, where Borglums often go for summer visits and for special events.

Lincoln and Mary Anne chose the Rio Grande Valley for their permanent home for several reasons. The warm climate is good for Lincoln. They had both lived in Texas previously and had relatives and friends in Texas, and had liked the places they had lived. They agreed that "The Valley" had a comfortable pace of life and was a unique combination of a rural area with the cultural advantages of progressive small cities interested in the arts.

The Borglum home is surrounded by citrus trees (ruby red grapefruit) palms, mesquites, bougainvillia, and a wonderful variety of tropical plants. Spanish in style, every room in the house is individual and charming. The setting is in the country, but the small town of La Feria is a few miles west, and Harlingen, a major Valley city, is a few miles east.

Lincoln has a studio in the big home, where he works on commissions. There is also a casita (guest house) on the property. The big green lawn, kept so by irrigation, is tended by Lincoln on a riding mower. The swimming pool is piped to sound like water rippling over the rocks of a mountain stream. With surroundings of beauty and quiet, the Borglums are nevertheless constantly busy. Widely recognized when they travel, few Valley residents are aware of the Borglum's presence.

Perhaps Lincoln Borglum will soon get the commission he has been waiting for over thirty years, the chance to finish his father's dream—The Hall of Records for the nation's Shrine of Democracy.

5

The Problems of Rushmore Today and Tommorrow

It is summer. The sky is infinitely wide and blue. Fleecy clouds evaporate on sight. The traffic is a solid ribbon of color winding its way through deep cuts in the schist and the slate through the tall, green Ponderosa forest. Many of the cars are from across the continent, or across the seas. All eyes are on the high granite peaks, suddenly perceiving in the distance Mount Rushmore, gleaming in the morning sun. Most people gasp in awe, savoring the moment, glad at last, that they have made the pilgrimage.

Pictures and movies do not prepare visitors for the reality. Few comprehend the immensity and the profound impact until they stand there in person. The incomparable setting, the magnificent carving, the grandeur of the Memorial bring a quickened pulse even to the urbane, sophisticated traveler. Many admit to breathing a silent prayer upon their first view of this foremost man-made wonder of the New World. People stand wordless as they gaze at the embodiment of a dream, a portrait of the nation's soul.

If the sculptor, Gutzon Borglum, could hear the comments of viewers, he would know that he had won his battle. It seems impossible enough to make rough, gray granite look like human skin and hair and eyes, like glasses and cloth, but it is a greater mystery to realize that the artist did not portray just four men, but succeeded in capturing the spirit that made this Nation great.

There is a feeling of happiness on the mountain. Strangers speak warmly to each other. People smile and relax. They hold doors open, make room on a bench for someone else, give up their place in line. They seem overjoyed to be part of this time and place. They seem to

New Keystone, or "The Strip" was devastated by the flood, but has since been rebuilt much as it was before. Battle Creek and Grizzly Creek come together here.
Photo by Juell Johnson, S.D. Highway Department

take pride, in an old-fashioned way, in America and all that it stands for.

Mount Rushmore Memorial is open to the public free of charge all the year around, but summer and fall are the best times to visit. Many tourist attractions and accommodations in the area are closed in the winter, although for those traveling on a limited budget, winter rates are lower at the places which do remain open. Spring, sometimes delightful, often brings heavy, wet snows, strong winds, or dark, dreary days. Winters are not as cold in the Black Hills as popularly imagined. Daytime temperatures are often in the 50s. Summers are somewhat hotter than people expect for a mountain area, but nights require blankets. Humidity is low so the heat is not cloying or sticky. Most bright, summer days are exactly what summer should be.

Tornadoes are rare, but flash floods are feared, as they are in all mountain regions. But all the inclement weather most tourists see will be an occasional quick thundershower. And once in awhile low clouds will bathe the mountain tops, providing a rare thrill to those who see the fog rapidly lift to reveal the monumental sculpture blazing in the sun.

When the visitor arrives at Mount Rushmore, a Ranger will direct him to a parking space. There are several large, paved parking areas, which are also free. Wide walkways lead through the quiet woods to the spacious stone and glass Visitor's Center. Here again an intangible feeling of idealism, of dedication, and timelessness, permeates the atmosphere. Visitors wander out onto the curved stone patio to view the tremendous panorama, and to listen to the fluent and stirring story which tells of the challenge and how it was met, of how the spirit of America came to be depicted on a stone mountain in the heart of America. This is a moment people share with fervent pride, and only those who have actually experienced this will understand.

At the start of the '70s about 2 million visitors a year made their way to this shrine. A disastrous flood in Rapid City and vicinity in June of 1972 resulted in a sharp cutback on the number of visitors, but the next year the count was near 2 million again. Bicentennial plans brought an increase. The future projection is for 6 to 8 million visitors a year. It will maintain its status as one of the most visited National Parks or Monuments or Memorials.

Many people return to Mount Rushmore year after year, and to these it is still an important highlight of their summer. Said Mrs. Alvin Hubbell of Ohio, "We vacation at Sylvan Lake each summer, but we never feel that our trip is complete until we again spend a day at Mount Rushmore."

Some, who saw Mount Rushmore in the building stage during the depression years, return later only once. To them it is a pilgrimage to mecca. The emotion aroused in those who were part of the scene in the early days is overwhelming.

William Tallman had been close to the Borglum family as a boy in Connecticut, and his parents had been Borglum family friends. Tallman had grown up and married on the Rushmore job, but had left prior to Gutzon's death. Recently he returned to see the Memorial in the heart of the tourist season. He walked around among the thousands of visitors like a man in a daze. He saw as many people in the viewing area in one day as formerly visited the mountain in a whole summer. He watched the streamlined charter buses, the limousines, the campers and trailers, the Volkswagons and Cadillacs. From the top of Doane Mountain he looked across the rocky ravine where a warm sun lit every granite feature, while a white thunderhead built up in the distance. He could hardly speak. All of his memories of the Rushmore years were warm and happy, all his thoughts of the Borglums were of love.

He said that Rushmore was too great a part of his life for him even to try to recapture what was gone. He had yearned to see the Memorial once more in his life, but the experience was shattering. Although

Lincoln Borglum was only miles away at that time, he couldn't even bring himself to call Lincoln.

Tallman's grateful boss Gutzon, had once said of him, "He had a refinement of judgment, and, as Superintendent, appreciated the need for constant vigilance. He also had great patience." As he stood there wordlessly looking upwards at the countenances on the mountain, it was clear what Tallman thought of his boss.

The Rangers at the Visitor's Center orient strangers to the area, hand out literature, and answer thousands of questions ranging from locations of restrooms to, "How did they know where to dig for the figures on the mountain?" The Center also houses the office of the Superintendent. There are interesting pictures, interpretive movies, and displays. The view from the terrace is excellent for pictures. The morning sun is best, and the three dimensional perspective which photographers desire is easily achieved by focusing through the pines surrounding the terrace.

There are numerous places to walk on the mountain; to the amphitheater, or the Borglum Terrace, or to the concession building. The wide walkways are lighted at night. Climbing Mount Rushmore itself is strictly off limits, and this is enforced because of the dangers involved. Superintendent Wickware now allows scheduled groups accompanied by Rangers.

There are several highways leading to Mount Rushmore. By far the most exciting is Iron Mountain Road, alternate U. S. Highway 16, which was designed by Senator Norbeck to make the approach to the Memorial a memorable and moving experience. This is not a fast route, and may have been one of the first roads in the nation to put scenic grandeur above all else. Stone tunnels frame the carvings, one way lanes wind through aspens and pines, and spectacular curves and bridges afford unmatched views of the granite Hills and the plains beyond. The highway starts at the Keystone "Y" and goes to Custer, and is the access route to Highway 36 which goes to the Borglum Museum and Studio, to Route 87 which is the Needles Highway, and to the Memorial approach from the east.

Most of the traffic approaches Mount Rushmore from Rapid City on U.S. 16, a divided highway as far as the Keystone "Y". Here there is a choice of 16A which turns left and is marked as the "Mount Rushmore" turn, or following U.S. 16 to the right, to Highways 87 and 244, a newer route to the Memorial.

Formerly called the "back road" to Rushmore, Highway 87, also numbered 244, has been resurfaced and dedicated as the Gutzon Borglum Memorial Highway. Near the entrance to the National

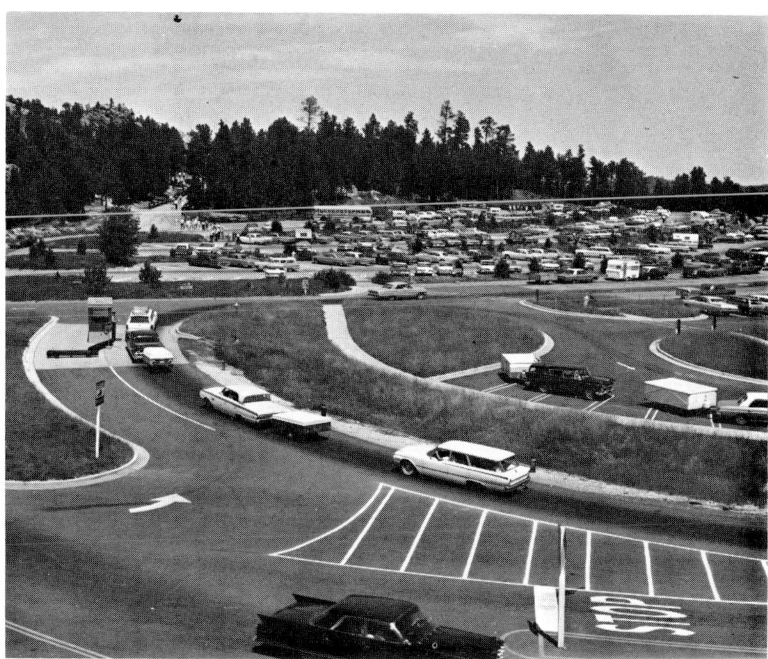

Entrances and exits to the often crowded parking areas form a confusing merge to the visitor who is suddenly under the hypnotic influence of the Memorial.
Photo by National Park Service

Memorial a bronze marker was unveiled in June 1973, with a remarkable likeness of the sculptor done by his son, and an appropriate quotation by Rupert Hughes. This route leaves Highway 16 just south of Hill City. It is one of the most scenic drives in the Hills, and is just as fast or faster than going through Keystone.

Much of the money for the highways leading to Rushmore was appropriated by the South Dakota legislature. There has always been a certain amount of resentment in some parts of the state that so large a percentage of the highway budget has been allotted to the Mount Rushmore area. Another problem which has caused the Highway Department much concern has been the traffic "bottleneck" caused by the narrow, congested streets of nearby Keystone, which have recently been widened. Even if there are unusual traffic hazards in the region, the accident rate is not high, as people driving in a scenic, mountain region tend to drive more carefully.

Four lane highway access to Mount Rushmore has been a subject of great controversy in South Dakota for some time, and the eventual outcome is in doubt. Adversaries and protagonists are the Park Service, the State Highway Department, landowners, and environmentalists. The Park Service is faced by a mammoth parking problem which is greater every season. The Highway Department has the duty of seeing that roads leading to the Memorial are adequate and safe for all vehicles. When a Master Plan was revealed in 1973, for a shuttle bus system to take visitors to Rushmore from tremendous staging areas at Elkhorn Springs and near Keystone, there was an immediate battle.

The Park Service and Highway Department wanted to have problems solved before the Bicentennial, but loud opposition prevented any drastic change in time for that big event. The environmentalists formed a "Save the Hills" Committee. Their argument was that any new highways would destroy scenic areas. Vociferous at public hearings were businessmen owning tourist oriented businesses along existing routes. The businessmen feared their operations would be by-passed by a new route. Landowners were afraid of losing land and privacy. The landowners accused the Park Service of wanting to acquire private land for the staging areas instead of some of the thousands of acres already under government control. Some influential people pointed out that the staging areas would be the fairest way to see that everyone has a place to park and a chance to get to the Memorial. Emotions were full of electricity on the subject. Hearings were held and the decision postponed until it became too late to get any major plan in action for the year 1976, for which Rushmore has been designated a *National Focal Point.*

The staging concept also met with the opposition of some of the tourists, who voiced their opinion that they wanted to drive their own cars to the National Monument. Some travelers have old people, invalids, or babies in their cars, for whom they have made special provisions, and they don't relish the idea of unloading everything and everyone into a bus, and going off to a spot without their own "headquarters."

Lincoln Borglum, who worked for the National Park Service for a long time, admits to having a great antipathy for the term "Master Plan" in regard to Mount Rushmore. "They already have enough 'Master Plans' to pave the road from the mountain to Washington, D.C." he stated.

When past Superintendent Wally McCaw proposed a radical plan, Lincoln agreed that it is a very good one, if it could be implemented. (McCaw was one of the best of Rushmore Superintendents.) McCaw's plan, which had a deep grasp of all the problems, was to plan for the removal of all of the buildings from their present sites. With the

One of the big problems facing the administration of Mount Rushmore is parking. Sometimes it appears that half of the cars have houses on wheels with them.
Photo by S.D. Travel Division

Headquarters, Concession, and Dormitories, all moved to an area near Keystone, still on the Rushmore preserve, the environment of the carvings could be restored to a spacious, cathedral-like forest. In this plan also, visitors would be transported by bus.

One proposal often aired, is to prohibit all vehicles except family cars in the present parking lots. It is true that a TravelAll with a trailer takes up the space of about 6 cars. Lincoln Borglum is against the banning of trailers and campers though. He said it would be no more right to bar a family in a motor home than a family with a foreign car or farm workers in a truck.

Double deck parking space has been suggested to alleviate the problem. This would make Doane Mountain resemble downtown Los Angeles, say opponents. To level off more of Doane Mountain for increased parking would destroy the scenic beauty of the viewing area.

If busing were used, perhaps Doane Mountain could again become a mountain park of rocks and pines, of chipmunks and bluebirds, of penstemon and shooting stars. A place where people could walk through the tall trees and sit on the cool granite, and enjoy the tremendous view of Rushmore and its world. Where all would have time to meditate and feel the quiet peace which pervaded this spot in its original solitude. Where instead of a hectic, crowded rush, they could see the pristine forested highlands, accentuated by the work of man. Lincoln Borglum devoutly wishes everyone could see the Rushmore surroundings the way he saw them from horseback on that memorable trip with his father in 1925.

The drawback of this plan is its cost. It would take a long time to move the buildings and restore the area. The cost would be greater than the Monument itself. And in view of the changes which have come about in the administration of Rushmore in the past, even an ideal solution like this, might not really be permanent.

There have been many plans and many attempts to solve the Rushmore dilemma for the future, and it would seem that the eventual outcome would be that the right of the people would prevail. That right is to come to their National Shrine over wide, scenic, safe roads, to find convenient parking for all vehicles, and to enjoy and find renewal in the wonderful world of Rushmore.

Rushmore problems go beyond the Memorial and its immediate vicinity. The development of Rapid City, other Hills cities, and the roadsides of the entire area, are all related, because most of the tourist businesses are situated there by grace of Mount Rushmore.

Gutzon Borglum wanted very much for the Rapid City area to have other attractions for travelers, which would be authentic and worthwhile, and which would remind them of the heritage of the Old West and of America. He wanted Rapid City to be unique, proud of its western tradition, a city of parks, a gateway to a shrine. It remained for his son Lincoln to create a plan which was in line with his father's far-seeing, uncannily accurate vision. Lincoln wrote to the Rapid City Journal that the Rapid River from Cleghorn Canyon through the city should be a green belt, a long and marvelous park. He wanted the old, unattractive buildings cleared out, and a wide area on each side of the river to belong to the city. In those days the federal government would have paid three-fourths of the costs. Lincoln thought a replica of a mining town of the Old West, on one side of the stream, would provide atmosphere and recreational opportunities for families.

The majority of residents didn't care much about Lincoln's plan, one way or another. Those who owned the old buildings, or homes near the river were against it, and the rest weren't really interested at all. Some prominent citizens accepted the plan and tried for a time to promote it. They pointed out that it would make the city more pleasant for residents as well as visitors, that it would keep tourists in the area longer, that it would give their city a reputation for beauty and progress.

The Borglum plan was turned down. Had it been accepted, a great tragedy could have been averted. In 1972 a violent flood swept through Rapid City, destroying everything in its path and claiming over 200 lives. Whole blocks were ravaged. Many families lost everything they had. Now once again the city is talking of the "green belt" plan, or the wide, long park Lincoln had advocated, but this time the talk is serious, and land along the stream has now been condemned.

The old gold town of Rockerville on the Mount Rushmore Highway may have grown from the Borglum idea of bringing a little of the Old West to the Rushmore Region. Not many miles from Rapid City, the saloons and mellodramas of the turn of the century, are joined by rustic shops, and stores, and museums. A divided highway splits here and encircles this tourist attraction.

Many of the businesses which have grown up along the roads to

Herb Conn of Custer is Rushmore's "dermatologist". Here, swinging over the surface of the faces for annual repair, he inspects fractures he had previously sealed with white lead and granite dust. Photo by Rapid City Journal

Rushmore have been tourist traps, and many have come and gone. At one time there were seven of the "gravity-illusions" enterprises between Rapid City and the Keystone "Y".

County wide zoning laws in Pennington County, and careful planning by developers, is upgrading the type of attraction and the type of buildings to border the Rushmore Highway. Only the best of travel oriented businesses survive. With high land prices and high building costs, the type of shoestring enterprise which was previously common, is no longer feasible.

The appearance of the faces on Mount Rushmore changes from dawn to dusk, and from summer to winter. The mountain is spectacular in the winter, but the freezes and thaws of the cold months are enemies of the carvings. Water gets into the tiny cracks and then freezes. It expands when it freezes, thus enlarging any little cracks, and causing bits of granite to break off.

To protect the carvings from this form of erosion, the Borglums devised an adaptation of an ancient method of repairing sculpture, rock dust mixed with white lead. The rock, in this case, the actual Rushmore granite, is pulverized, mixed with white lead, and used to fill every small crack that is a potential hazard. Each summer a workman is hired by the Park Service to be lowered in a harness over the four faces to carefully examine and repair each fracture. In recent years the work has been done by Herb Conn of Custer, who one year plucked a boutonniere from the First President's lapel. It was a tiny Ponderosa pine which had taken root in the rock.

Over the years, other methods have been suggested for protecting the faces. One is silicone. Another is epoxy resin. A salesman a few years back, tried to sell Lincoln on the idea of purchasing a commercial product to coat the faces. He insisted that if applied to the whole mountain, it would give perfect protection from the weather. His clincher was, "It might last as long as thirty years."

Lincoln replied, "In other words you don't really know how long the product would last or how effective it would be? According to geologists this rock wears away at the rate of an inch every 100,000 years. Can you do better than that?" At this point the salesman gave up.

Some people who have studied the mountain with binoculars or telescopes are concerned about some of the rusty and dark appearing streaks on the surface of the carvings. These distracting streaks are partly the result of rains, melting snows, and the interaction of water with the minerals in the mountain. Another reason for the streaks is that there are pieces of steel left in the mountain. These pieces of steel are the remnants of the hooks, or anchors which were used to hold work cages or to pull the workmen to the correct positions in their bosun's chairs. Liquid sulphur was used to hold the metal hooks in place. The pieces which are left are quite small, but do contribute to the rust. The original plan had been to finish all of the faces to a depth just below the bits of metal, but funds were not sufficient.

Lincoln thinks that since the winches are already in place for the annual inspection, it would not be too expensive to have a man with a portable sand blaster operated from a small compressor, eradicate the streaks at the time the cracks are filled each fall.

No one should leave Mount Rushmore without seeing it with the night lighting. If the view in the morning is thrilling, the view at night is unforgettable. The lights are turned on nightly during the most of the tourist season and schedules for programs and ceremonies are available at the Visitor's Center. The outdoor amphitheater, looking towards the carvings, is the scene of a nightly summer presentation, giving the history of Mount Rushmore, the statistics, and the philosophy. This is a full-color, sound movie which makes excellent use of irreplaceable film clips from the past. At the end of the program the well placed flood lamps light up the four faces on the mountainside. It is an impressive moment. There is usually a collective "Oh" as the audience focuses complete attention on the reality of the living granite. The surrounding rocks, the rubble pile, the pine forests, all vanish. Only the faces are real. There is more force and more meaning than ever before, and the attainment of the dream seems more of a miracle.

You can see the lighted mountain for many miles. While in the day time you glory in the setting of Rushmore, at night you only marvel at the accomplishments of the minds, and souls, and hands of men. A particularly startling view is the floodlit profile of George Washington seen to the right of Highway 87, driving towards Hill City. The splendid isolation of this view is enough to make even flag burners pause for a moment's contemplation.

Lincoln Borglum was dissatisfied with the lighting, as he knows his father would have been. The mountain was designed to be viewed from below, but lighted from above. Artificial lights placed below cause the shadows of the face to be distorted, altering the expressions somewhat, since lights and shadows are the elements which define the sculpture. There are no colors or outlines to show details or accents. Subtle nuances of shadows are missing at night, but Lincoln feels that the new automatic lights installed in 1975 will give a better view of the mountain to those who come when the sun is not right.

In a similar vein, Lincoln comments that in the 1930s no one thought that so many people would visit South Dakota by plane, or that

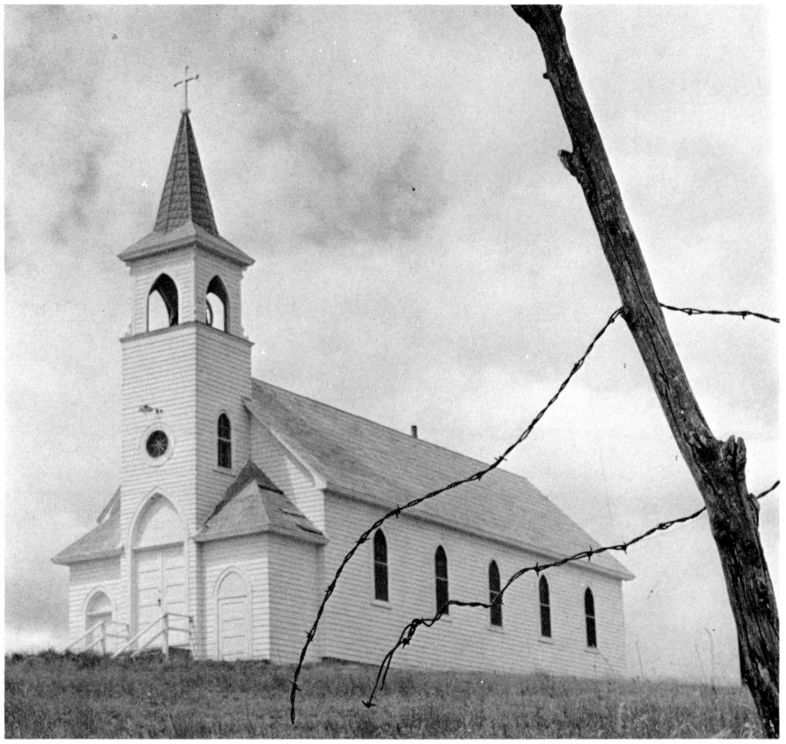

The church at Wounded Knee, an Indian community not far from the Borglum Ranch, was burned down during the recent seige of Wounded Knee by AIM leaders.
Photo by S.D. Travel Division

helicopters would make daily trips around the mountain, so the view from the top was not seriously considered. All studies of the ultimate effect were made from below, where all people came for the view in the 1930s. If there were money enough another refinement could be accomplished, which would be the finishing of the sculpture so that the view from a plane would present the same aesthetic picture as the view from Doane Mountain.

There is another problem which threatens the mountain. That is vandalism. Increasingly radicals are committing wild and violent acts to get attention, and they are choosing famous places for their soapbox. There is a strict *no climbing* rule at Mount Rushmore, and the rule is enforced. The security at the mountain is heavy, and Rangers are always alert, but for the most part those who try to climb do not mean any harm. Some may try on a dare, others may not have noticed the signs forbidding the climb. Climbers who are suspicious, or refuse to answer, or who are carrying explosives are arrested. Another type of vandalism is the writing or painting of names or slogans on the rocks or buildings or trees. This too, is sternly dealt with.

An ever present problem in western South Dakota is the Indian problem, which is sometimes dramatized by events such as the occupation of Wounded Knee or a pow-wow at Rushmore. There is a large Sioux population in Rapid City and three large Reservations are close. The whole of the Black Hills area is claimed by the Sioux, and to publicize their cause, a group of Indians camped on Mount Rushmore one summer. The frightened Department of Interior ordered a "hands-off" policy. The claim to the Hills seems mostly for the purpose of treaty renegotiation and monetary reimbursement. Most of the Sioux *prefer* the Reservation system, and they regard any threats to terminate this system with intense hatred and fear. The Sioux did not live in the Hills, so the Hills was not really theirs, any more than Lake Superior could be considered as the homeland of the tribes who lived near it.

Rapid City churches and Reservation churches do many things for

Ceremonial and tribal dances of the Sioux are still performed on special occasions. Authentic Sioux handcrafts are sold in Black Hills gift shops.
Photo by S.D. Travel Division

Huge concrete lodgepoles at rest areas off the Interstate near the Black Hills, are unique reminders of the proud culture of this area. Photo by S.D. Travel Division

the Indians. Rapid City has a modern Sioux hospital. Some Indians have done very well in business, the arts, and politics in South Dakota. The reverse of prejudice is true, in the pride the white community has in Indian leaders such as former Congressman Ben Reifel, civic leaders Harold Shunk and Art La Croix, and Bishop Harold Jones. There is a Sioux fashion industry, a Sioux moccasin factory, a Sioux pottery company. Rapid City has a historic collection of Sioux treasures in a picturesque stone building in a flower filled park on West Boulevard. It is open to the public.

Recent violence on the part of the Indians was mostly caused by out-of-state agitators and organizers, many of them neither Sioux nor Indian. Had the offensive actions been for a less "in" cause, instigators would now be serving time. Their activities were designed to attract public attention to the ideas of a minority of the South Dakota Indians, and their demonstrations hurt the native Indians as much as they did other South Dakota residents. Mistrust of the Indians has led many travelers to avoid the Reservations. Actually the roads through the Reservations are good, the pace is peaceful, and the countryside more interesting and photographic than along the Interstate.

Fishing or hunting are not allowed on the Reservations without special Tribal permits. Some of the Indian communities welcome tourists and have attempted to share in the tourist economy by building campgrounds and sending out ads and brochures. Tourist activities such as pageants, art exhibits, and rodeos quite naturally include Indians. Radical groups accuse some predominantly white towns of prejudice, but this has not been proven. Bias is more on the basis of drunkenness versus sobriety, industry versus laziness, violence versus peace, than on the basis of red versus white. The Indians in South Dakota enjoy privileges other citizens of the state do not have such as free medical care, special educational helps, and freedom from taxes. Polite and friendly people should not hesitate to travel on the Reservations or to talk with the Indians in the Hills.

The little town of Keystone is involved in several controversies concerned with its proximity to Rushmore. When Mount Rushmore was still a lonesome rock, Keystone was a typical mining town. First a roaring gold camp, it was dignified by the addition of a stamp mill in 1880. The *Holy Terror Gold Mine* produced the highest quality gold quartz, and proved to be rich in other minerals as well. Later tin and spodumene ores were the "Pay dirt" from the *Etta Mine.* The legendary *Robert Ingersoll Mine* furnished tungsten, pitchblende and beryl, and was a veritable gallery for mineralogists, who came to study its unprecedented variety.

At an elevation of over 4,000 feet the *old* town stretched along the usually placid Battle Creek, in a narrow valley with pine clad mountains rising abruptly above the three, more or less horizontal streets. Besides the mines, the town boasted several saloons, a hotel, a stable, two general stores, a bank, a big frame schoolhouse, and several churches. Parts of the old town were much the same as they had been for 50 years, until the flood of 1972. The economy of the community was bolstered by cattle ranches to the east and by occasional fishermen or hunters. There were summer camps for young people in the Hills. There were sawmills not far away. The little town had no electricity for many years, and water was from individual wells. A volunteer fire department was always alert for the first wisp of smoke.

The Borglum family stayed briefly in the Keystone Hotel at the start of the Rushmore work. The permanent population of the old town is less now than it was then. There are still not many improvements, although there will soon be a city water-sewer system; there are still two general stores. The fire department is volunteer. Gone are the bank and the hotel. Crowded against the narrow paved road are the expansive dumps of the Holy Terror Mine, and proudly on the hill stands the wooden $10,000 school, which now serves only a few grades. In spite of all this "Old Keystone" is an attractive little Western community surrounded by cathedral-like rocky cliffs and pine covered mountains.

What most tourists see is not the Old Keystone. What happened, when the Monument began drawing thousands of tourists each summer, is that investors bought up all the available land on both sides of Highway 16A near Keystone and referred to their mushrooming conglomerate of tourist businesses as *Keystone.* Indeed, the Post Office has been moved from the old town to a congested highway corner. Most of the people who operate the assorted quick food stands and souvenir shops, do not even live in Keystone, except perhaps in the summer.

This portion of Keystone, sometimes called *New* Keystone, which is on 16A, is a summer carnival. It is a traffic hazard, as the roads are too narrow for the parked cars, the oblivious pedestrians, and the steady stream of impatient vehicles headed for the Memorial. The highway is treated like a sidewalk, to the dismay of the bumper to bumper drivers. By 1976 the widening will be completed. All businesses on the east side are being moved back. Some of the souvenir shops on the west are backed up to the solid rock wall of the mountains, which confines the area. Although the general impression is of old western buildings, practically the whole "new town" had to be rebuilt or moved after the flood of '72. Logs and native unfinished lumber are the most common building materials.

For some years the situation was even worse, when the "1880 Train" pulled across Main Street twice a day and discharged hundreds of passengers to roam the streets in a holiday mood. The traffic jams at times like this were incredible for a town of 300 in a remote mountain valley. When the flood washed out the bridges and tracks, the train, based at Hill City, was forced to close the famous run. The new route of the train takes it to the larger town of Custer, which is a better route for the steam train buffs and alleviates at least one Keystone problem. Why the state or county still allow a commercial horse drawn stagecoach replica in the midst of this dangerous traffic on a federal highway is beyond comprehension.

Shops in Keystone cater mostly to impulse buyers, to curio hunters, and to tourists who have never been West before. Some of the merchandise, to be sure, is authentic, well selected, high in quality (and in price). Much is imitation, tawdry, low in quality (and still high in price). A few excellent buys are locally handcrafted items, such as jewelry and pottery. Other good buys are framed photographs, colored slides, regional art, and books. A simple, inexpensive, and authentic reminder of the trip is a piece of polished or unpolished native stone, available almost anywhere in the Hills.

The food dispensaries' specialties range from taffy and caramel corn to char-broiled steaks. To see hundreds of humans crowding these shops on a hot day clutching picture cards, drippy ice cream cones, and Japanese made Indian beads, is to see a typical carnival or amusement park.

Indians, in costumes such as they never wore, and prospectors who don't know gold from pyrite, wander around posing for pictures for a tip, and if the tip is generous, they even throw in a few yarns. One of them, a few years ago, had thousands of people believing he had fought with Custer.

Borglum hated anything artificial. His concept of the Shrine of Democracy was so elevated that he would have been appalled at the blatant commercialization of his dream. He would have resented Keystone, and South Dakota, too. There are Mount Rushmore flower pots, salt shakers, ash trays and book ends. Mount Rushmore belts, tee shirts, scarves and handkerchiefs. Imitation may be the sincerest form of flattery, but Borglum would have decried these shoddy imitations. What would he have thought had he seen the Japanese made models of Rushmore which all the shops had a few years ago, with all four presidents possessing *Oriental* eyes?

Besides fake Rushmore models and poor pictures of the Memorial, the Rushmore name has been polluted by Rushmore slaughter houses, Rushmore "burgers", Rushmore motels, Rushmore apartments. Then there are Rushmore seeds, and flours, and cattle feeds, and inevitably, Rushmore bars. Perhaps the Rushmore "hot dogs" are the least outlandish, since the Keystone slaughter house served as the first Borglum studio here.

A highly rated attraction near Keystone is the wax museum, which is billed in its ads as a Shrine *TO* Democracy instead of a Shrine *OF* Democracy. The museum now stands where the baseball diamond of the Rushmore home team once echoed with cheers for the men who drilled granite by day, and in the evening took their turns at bat, within sight of their work.

There are several large motels in Keystone with comfortable accommodations. A long range look at the mountain is their drawing card. Campgrounds are located on Grizzly Creek in new Keystone, and on Battle Creek in the old town.

Can the misuse of the Rushmore name and image be controlled? Lincoln does not think so, though he says with a smile that his Dad's and his own biggest mistake was not carving an encircled "C" at the base, for *Copyrighted.*

Gutzon Borglum was so disturbed by some of the hideous posters, drawings, and reproductions of Mount Rushmore, which began appearing as soon as the Monument began to take shape, that he wrote an *Open Letter* protesting the abortions of the true character of the Memorial. He pointed out that as Chairman of the Federal Commission charged with design and publicity, and as creator of the Memorial, he had an obligation to maintain the character and the quality of all aspects of the work, including reproduction. He even offered to help any committee personally with any Rushmore reproduction or picture they were preparing, so the public would be protected against misrepresentations.

Lincoln Borglum, too, deplores the way the National Memorial has been used for all kinds of commercialism and advertisements. But he realizes that like the Statue of Liberty, the sculpture has become *public domain* as a symbol. He understands that symbols are not always used wisely and well. As long as the public will buy dishtowels, hot plates, and hanging baskets with inaccurate portrayals of the carvings, there will be someone to manufacture and peddle them. Lincoln does feel that there is a gradual trend to a better type of travel memento. But when stone miniature reproductions of the mountain were ordered, it was a New York artist who got the commission, and when Rushmore was acknowledged with a U. S. postage stamp, it was drawn by a Californian.

For the most part South Dakota leaders are aware of the impact of Mount Rushmore to the state, but some continue to think of it in monetary terms only. The four faces are often seen in national press releases, on television news programs and commercials, on highway billboards, in Sunday supplements, and even in comic strips and cartoons. Every big promotion in the State for any reason, is sure to prompt someone to suggest a Rushmore tie-in. Visionary citizens successfully advanced the Rushmore case for designation as a primary Bicentennial focal point. Now that the Federal Reserve Board is considering reviving the $2.00 bill, active proponents are working to have a likeness of the Memorial on this denomination.

Mount Rushmore has also been used as a movie location. The Doane Mountain buildings have been used for historical symposia and educational seminars. Concerts and other special events crowd the Rushmore calendar. The final anachronism is that pictures of the mountain are frequently used to promote *conservation* of the local ecology, the very thing Borglum was once accused of destroying. Mount Rushmore now ranks with motherhood, Boy Scouts, and apple pie.

Such little dissidence as there is, rises from the fact that some of the communities east of the Missouri River in South Dakota feel that the constant accent on Rushmore has taken too much of the state's money and attention to the Black Hills area, to the detriment of their own. Nevertheless, every political candidate wants to be seen at Rushmore. Every important visitor to the state wants to see Rushmore, and even the poor farmer with 10 children saves to take them all to the mountain, which he feels all South Dakotans must see.

Although the entire area caters to tourists, the most convenient accommodations near Mount Rushmore are those located in the National Forest (Norbeck Wildlife Refuge) and Custer State Park. The Refuge surrounds the National Memorial grounds and Custer Park lies immediately south. One of the oldest of large scale State Parks in the nation, Custer Park has 72,000 acres, with facilities for every need. Well planned campgrounds are increasingly demanded by the public, and the state of South Dakota has been responsive to this trend.

The campgrounds of this region are situated on rushing streams once panned for gold, and beside clear lakes, well stocked with trout. Then there are picnic grounds with rustic tables and fireplaces, and plenty of places to pull off the road and take a walk in the wilderness. There are three campgrounds on Iron Mountain Road near the pigtail bridges. Then within the Park boundaries, there are campgrounds at Sylvan Lake, Center Lake, Game Lodge, Stockade Lake, and Blue Bell. All of the campgrounds have pure, spring water, and are surrounded by the towering rocks and pines unique to this area. In addition, near some of the camps there are such attractions as a summer theater, a zoo, a museum, riding trails, and historic sites.

Most of the lodges are complete family vacation resorts. There are housekeeping cabins, hotel rooms, snack shops, and huge rustic dining rooms, famous for native cuisine, for instance buffalo steak or mountain trout.

Most famous of these state supervised lodges is the luxurious resort, *Game Lodge,* which was the summer White House of President Coolidge in 1927, was visited by Eisenhower in 1953, and was frequented by Gutzon Borglum and his friends in government and the arts. The main lodge is a striking great building of native stone and dark rich wood, with motel, hotel, or private cabin accommodations. Visitors enjoy the hiking trails, the trout fishing, horseback riding, and camera trips to view one of the largest herds of American bison in existence. *Coolidge Inn,* near the Game Lodge, has a cafeteria, soda fountain, and groceries for campers.

Equally famous is *Sylvan Lake Resort.* The turn-of-the-century type white frame hotel, which for years was Dakota's pride, burned to the ground in 1933, and has been replaced by a structure of logs and stone, crowning a forested cliff above the lake. Guest cottages and modest housekeeping cottages are available, as well as luxury rooms. The Sioux-motif decorated dining room is accented by an unusual fireplace of precision cut, native, banded sandstone. The proximity to Harney Peak is another plus for this resort. Sylvan Lake itself, one of the oldest lakes in the Hills, is enhanced by strange, jointed granite rocks, which it surrounds, magnifies, and reflects.

Other resorts are at Legion Lake, Stockade Lake, and Blue Bell. The lodges must all be run according to state specifications, and the state derives revenue from the concessions on a percentage basis. Additional money goes to the state for timber sales and rentals from summer sites. The most unique source of state revenue is the sale of buffalo. With these various income sources carefully supervised, Custer State Park may stand alone among such parks, in being entirely self supporting. A "user's fee" sometimes charged at park entrances, has been the source of some controversy in South Dakota, chiefly by residents who object to being charged because the main route is a federal highway, or because they feel the park is theirs anyway, or just on general principles. The fee is only for park *users,* not for commuters who are merely driving through.

The Needles Highway is part of the Park. Another great accomplishment of Senator Norbeck, this road was planned to offer the best possible views of the vertical topography of the Harney Range. Majestic Cathedral Spires, the Needle's Eye, and other dramatic pinnacles of timeless rock, dwarf the pines below. It was these rock pinnacles that Doane Robinson first sought to turn into the likenesses of men. His original idea was that these tall, straight rocks could easily be carved into appropriate likenesses of western heroes such as Carson, Bridger, or Colter. But after seeing the Needles, with eminent geologists O'Hara and Connally, Borglum agreed that nature had done all the sculpting necessary here. And although Borglum was a true admirer of the West, his dream covered a bigger span.

A short distance west of the Memorial boundary in the Black Hills National Forest is Horsethief Lake, the nearest lake to Mount Rushmore. A National campground is located here. There are also campgrounds on Battle Creek and Grizzly Creek east and north of the Memorial. Both of these streams sometimes go on a rampage, as in the flood of June 9th of 1972. All streams in the area drain into the Cheyenne River which cuts through the Pierre Shale formation west of the White River Badlands.

The Memorial is surrounded by the Norbeck Wildlife Preserve, which adjoins Custer State Park, which in turn adjoins Wind Cave National Park. Because the State and Nation hold such tremendous lands for the people, the natural wonders of Mount Rushmore's environment are being carefully preserved.

In addition to the government and state owned campgrounds and lodges, there are motels and cabins in all directions from the mountain. There are rustic log cabins, and lavish air conditioned high rise motels, with colored T.V., carpeted floors and swimming pools. Some of the motels are rural and feature pine scented air and rooms with a view, and others are on the busy thoroughfares of Rapid City. Accommodations in Rapid City have long been criticized for being too high in price, compared to similar areas. This may be one of the reasons that an increasing number of Black Hills visitors prefer camping. Various organizations such as the *Chamber of Commerce* and *Automobile Club* are helpful in finding rooms for visitors.

Restaurants range from the quick food pizza, hamburger, or chicken chains to the luxurious Black Forest Inn, with its continental cuisine. Some places, Rockerville, for example, feature western chuck wagon foods. From pancake houses to supper clubs, the food establishments cater to tourists. Liquor may be purchased both off and on sale, and numerous bars and lounges serve zingy cocktails named for such Black Hills characters as Calamity Jane or Wild Bill.

A criticism of many of the restaurants and motels in the Hills has been that they are open for too short a season. Many do not open until Decoration Day and close after Labor Day. Those which do stay open before and after the season have reduced rates for rooms. The principal reason for the shortness of the season is that the area depends heavily on college students for help, so sufficient help for large establishments is not available during the school year. But some of the restaurants still close for one day a week, even during the height of the season, which would be all right, if they didn't complain so loudly about the few days of good business available to them.

Some of the activities of an area like this are eventually self policing. The truly phony ones, the superfluous and over-priced ones, inevitably drop out. Those which survive for many years, for instance Reptile Gardens, and the Antique Auto Museum, or Cosmos, or the 1880 Train, obviously must be giving the public something for their money. The "me too" copies, which often spring up near a successful business, do not last long as a rule.

Also some of the construction of the "hangers-on" type of tourist business is shoddy. The buildings don't look good long, and are easy prey for fire, storms, or vandals. On the other hand, some of these buildings which look as if they had been built in hopes that they would last the season, have contents which are surprising, hand made silver jewelry, pioneer antiques, and clusters of golden barite crystals.

Only a minor amount of land is obtainable for tourist oriented businesses. Often this land is surrounded by Forest Service land which may regulate such things as access roads, water, and drainage.

Although some tourists are "turned off" by the commercialism, the truth is that there are more *free* sights and events here than in most similar areas. Rushmore itself is free, and there are many unforgettable spectacles, far from the main roads. There are free hobby pursuits like rock hunting. There are free museums and parks. Many compare Wall Drug to a museum. And almost every weekend all summer long, there are celebrations in the major cities with parades, dramas, rodeos, fireworks, logging contests, gold panning demonstrations, and almost any kind of an event promoters can dream up. In truth, good planning should make every visitor to the Hills happy. Satisfaction is evidenced in the high percentage of repeat visits.

6

The Mount Rushmore Concession Building

The nearest building to Mount Rushmore is the enormous stone concession building which is situated on the rocky precipice of Doane Mountain about a quarter of a mile across the ravine from the carvings. Looking as if it had grown to be a part of the mountain scene, the stone and glass building houses an art shop, a camera store, a book store, a jewelry store, a gift shop, a "quick lunch" room, and a gourmet restaurant, all rolled into one. With the enviable reputation of being one of the finest concession operations in the nation, the Rushmore concession is headed by Miss Kay Riordon and Mr. Jack Riordon of the Ponderosa-Nevada Company, formerly The Mountain Company.

The well planned building, like other similar buildings in National Parks and Monuments, is operated under the supervision and guidelines of the U. S. Park Service, a division of the Department of Interior. The Visitor's Center and Ranger's headquarters are nearby. The concession is let for a long term, and is obtained by bid, with preference being given to the bid of the current successful concessionaire, all other things being equal. The concessionaire builds, enlarges, improves, decorates, and maintains the building, with government approval and direction. In addition to administrating the varied activities of the concession area, the management must provide accommodations for a large number of employees, many of whom are college students.

When the visitor enters the concession building at Mount Rushmore, after a short scenic walk from the parking lots, the first impression will be of the spectacular view of the sculptures from the high glass wall across the ravine. No matter where one goes in the building, the

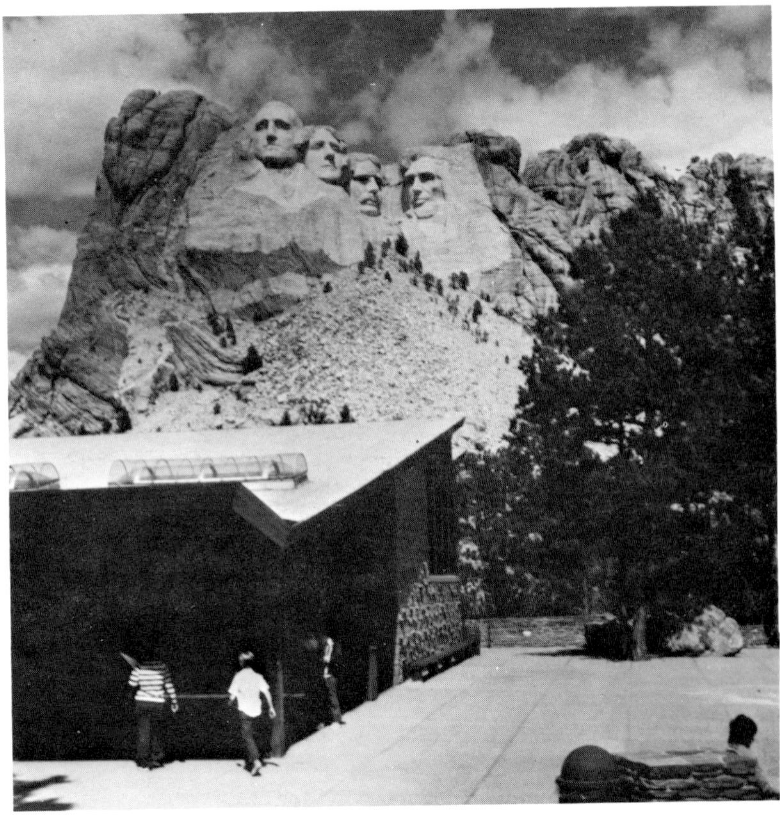

The beautiful stone concession building on the crest of Doane Mountain, affords a spectacular view of the four faces. Kay Riordan and Jack Riordan head the concession company.
Photo by S.D. Travel Division

presence of the Shrine of Democracy is felt.

One entrance is through the *Jet Room* where the tempting aroma of home cooked foods, and the convenience of self service, invite people to linger for a snack. Or they may enter through the big gift shop where they can purchase anything from a postcard to a jade necklace. Whoever enters is struck by the efficiency and courtesy of the employees, and by the cleanliness and orderliness of the counters and shelves. The light tile floors, the high beamed ceilings, along with the excellent lighting, create a feeling of spaciousness appropriate to the inspiring view.

There are glass cases and shelves, open counters, tiered racks and small departmentalized sections, but an integrity of planning gives

The Presidential Gallery is a popular new section of the concession building. Since Mount Rushmore is framed by windows in this section, film is one of the fastest sellers here. Over 100 young people are usually employed in the concession building in the summer. Photo by Jack Riordan.

unity to the whole. Most visitors enjoy taking their time shopping, eating, watching other people, or simply looking out the windows. The average visitor stays in the building 32 minutes. Most people come in family groups, and most enter with cameras in their hands. Often there are large tour groups. One can stand or sit on the comfortable benches and hear comments from residents of all parts of the nation, and often, comments in languages from other lands.

The wide variety of gift lines for children and adults is chosen by the concessionaires and key supervisors. Although there are unusual items from Israel, Spain, Japan, and Russia, the emphasis is on items made in the United States, the West, and South Dakota. Gifts are chosen to represent the arts and crafts of the area from which they come, so they are not just copies of the cultures of others. For example, an Oriental vase will be *Oriental* and not imitation Indian. Particularly interesting in this room, are the jewelry counters with authentic American and regional jewelry, such as Black Hills gold and Wyoming jade. There are elegant selections of glassware lending a spectrum of color to the windows, and distinguished collections of china, ceramics, metalware, and stoneware, and several sections for toys and gifts for the younger crowd.

Many of the unusual items are exclusive here, being made for Mount Rushmore in South Dakota, or by companies with custom manufacturing departments. Artists and craftsmen of the Black Hills find a ready market for their best works at Mount Rushmore, as the management has encouraged local arts for many years. Company President Kay Riordon is a native South Dakotan, and active in many fields in the promotion and prosperity of her home state.

Film is a big seller in this photographic haven, so the well stocked camera shop has plenty of equipment and information for the amateur or advanced shutter-bug. In addition, this part of the building, called the *Presidential Gallery,* has many items of historic interest, things which pertain directly to Mount Rushmore or to the four presidents, or to American history. There are medals, statues, stamps, wall hangings and plates. There are pictures, posters and plaques, all with patriotic themes. Handsome bronze eagles, exotic specimens of native rocks or minerals, and exciting books are well displayed. A new attraction, this gallery will add other highlights from year to year.

The real star in the Concession galaxy is the *Arts and Crafts room.* The unique room is much appreciated by discriminating visitors, because it is often difficult to find personal mementos of a wonderful trip, which are truly artistic, of intrinsic value, and appropriately American or Western.

The colorful arts of the Lakota Sioux and other American Indian tribes are in this room. Sioux pottery and Sioux bead work are noted for their precise geometric patterns in bold primary colors. There are also Indian and Western paintings and books. The crafts in this room are authentic, and the Indians or other artists have been paid fair prices for their work. Retail prices, here and throughout the concession building, are in line with those of similar establishments anywhere.

Among the crafts of other tribes, turquoise and sterling jewelry from the Southwest, play a leading role. There is a comprehensive display of the best handmade jewelry of several tribes, including the Navajo and Zuni work, and featuring turquoise from the best American localities, the classic blue-stone mines of Nevada, Arizona, New Mexico, and Colorado. The jewelry can be found in the traditional squash blossom designs, or in contemporary styling. Some of the jewelry is "pawn" which means that the Indian originally made it for his own family, but then decided to use it as collateral at a trading post. Old and good Indian jewelry is increasingly hard to find. The turquoise mines are playing out as the demand increases, and the price of silver has skyrocketed. New industries in Indian country pay better than old time hand craftsmanship, so the supply of authentic merchandise in this room, is a special treat for the connoisseur of Western art.

The books in this room have been carefully chosen so that there are not any fake Western or Indian books, such as are sometimes published. There are new books, wonderfully illustrated in full color, and reprints of classic old treasures. Fiction, science, art, anthropology, and history are some of the subjects well covered here. Among the most popular, as would be expected, are books about Mount Rushmore, Gutzon Borglum, and the Black Hills.

Near the entrance of the *Buffalo Dining Room* is a magnificent large mural, *The Buffalo Hunt,* by David Humphreys Miller, showing a hunt which could have taken place in this same part of South Dakota 200 years ago.

The Buffalo Dining Room is one of the finest in the state or in the West. Meals are served cafeteria style, three times a day. Cheerful students from M.I.T. or Southern California, or Black Hills State carry your tray and find your table. Roast prime rib au jus is the specialty of the house, and South Dakota beef is tender and delicious. Also featured are fresh salads, homemade breads, pastries, and desserts. Wherever the guests sit they can see Mount Rushmore. Original paintings and photographs decorate the walls. Coffee cups are always full, and dining is leisurely in the incomparable atmosphere.

The huge kitchen beyond the dining room is presided over by an experienced chef with a skilled staff of supervisors and college helpers. The workday here starts early in the morning with the meat cutting and baking, and the students for this shift arriving at dawn for steaming coffee and hearty breakfasts in their own dining room.

Running a National Park Concession provides unusual problems for the management. Employees who are seasonal must be housed and fed, and the students need advisors, recreation areas and a Chaplain, as well as rooms, food, and laundry facilities. Then sometimes there are special problems, morals or ethics, or health. In a way it is like a small campus. Some of the adult supervisors have apartments near the students' quarters in a scenic and secluded area behind the main concession building. With about 150 employees, Mount Rushmore's concession company ranks with the largest businesses in South Dakota, where "Tourism" as an industry is second only to agriculture.

The employees' buildings are designed to blend with the rocky forested hillside on which they are built. The peaceful decks overlook a panorama of granite boulders, Ponderosa pine, lichen covered cliffs, and vivid wild flowers. Here there is a feeling of being in the wilderness, although it is only a short distance to the great concession teeming with people.

The day starts early in the Buffalo Dining Room, as breakfast at Mount Rushmore is becoming a popular tradition. Photo by Jack Riordan.

There is a television lobby with a big color set where the young people can watch folk heroes and sports, or play cards, or just visit. There is a phone booth for those long calls home, and in the basement, a big recreation room. Swimming and fishing are available at Horsethief Lake a short distance away. Students are not as strictly supervised as in the college dorms of yesterday, but they do have rules to abide by, and their supervisors have had much experience guiding and motivating young people.

These Rushmore students come from all over. The applications are sent to the personnel director of the concession company, and they are chosen strictly according to their qualifications. There is no discrimination. The visitor is as likely to be waited on by a black student from Nigeria, an American Indian from a nearby Reservation, an apartment dweller from Manhattan, or a blonde farm girl from Minnesota. One of the main requirements is that the student come to work as near to Decoration Day as possible, and remain on the job until Labor Day.

Students are paid according to current wages for similar work in like facilities, and for those who fulfill their contract there is a handsome bonus. In addition, they have nourishing food, well furnished rooms, and a chance to spend a memorable summer with their peers. More than one summer romance has culminated in marriage, and many

All through the concession building, visitors are reminded of history, of the Old West, and of sculpture as a leading American art. Photo by Jack Riordan

lifelong friendships have developed. Some students come back all four of their college years, and some have gone on to join the tourist industry for their careers.

The top of Doane Mountain is almost a little city. There is postal service, package delivery, garbage service, and linen service. There are phones and lights, intercommunication systems, parking areas, furnace rooms, air conditioners, store rooms, supply rooms, offices. There have to be maintenance men for the machines, clean up workers, bookkeepers, stockroom boys, and inevitably people to do "K.P." duty. The little city has to have its own water and sewage system. (Incidentally the water is wonderful, pure, cold, and natural, with no need of chemical additives or treatment.)

Since much of the work is not at all glamorous, how does Mount Rushmore manage to maintain such a splendid staff? It is managed efficiently by people who have a real concern for each member of this community. The personnel manager selects students who are highly recommended and eager to make good. And finally, in talking with employees, it is obvious that there is a definite feeling of dedication and responsibility, a true pride in being part of this inspirational National Memorial.

7

The Flora and Fauna of Rushmore

When the Borglums first saw Mount Rushmore it was a primitive wilderness, virtually unexplored, except by a few miners who may have prospected for gold in streams below the peak. In fact, the great stony crag was so remote, that although Borglum knew immediately that this was his mountain, Norbeck and the others voiced a strong dissent.

The vast loneliness of this towering granite peak, the calm beauty of its virgin forest, and the spectacular panorama of rocky pinnacles, were partially responsible for Borglum's swift decision about the future of this mountain. Borglum loved all of nature. At one time he had even wanted to become a horticulturist. He had used his talents as a landscape designer, and the remarkable beauty of his estate, *Borgland,* was the result of his brilliant planning.

He visualized the green forests and the gray, lichen-coated rocks as being a perfect backdrop for his sculpture, and he really would have preferred leaving all the surroundings as natural, as untouched, and awesome, as they were that first moment he saw this scene. And today, in spite of the many changes wrought by hordes of people, and by highways, cars, and the rest of the signs of our times, much of the Rushmore ecology is very similar to what it was way back in the late '20s.

The dominant tree of the Rushmore forest is the hardy Pinus ponderosa, a tall, dark green pine, which has adapted itself to harsh conditions such as poor soil, rocky cliffs, and lack of moisture. Thick forests of pines are stretched like ponchos across the hills, with angular, gray rocks thrust up through slits. Sometimes the entire ground is naked, solid rock. Or again, it may be thin soil blanketed with brown, slippery needles and oval, golden cones. The long, straight trunks of the

Ponderosa lift the uppermost branches to well over 100 feet. Rich brown in color, the trunks have distinctive scaly plates. Needles grow in bundles of twos and threes to form stiff, graceful tufts at the ends of the branches. The stout, spreading branches do not vary greatly in size from bottom to top. Vigorous beauty is not the only asset of the pine forest, for it shelters an amazing variety of life, and the pine scented air, cool and brisk at dusk and at dawn, is an asset in itself.

At higher elevations in the dark, narrow canyons, and near the running streams, are the shapely Black Hills spruce. Among the most elegant of trees the tall, deep green spruce trees are symmetrical and tapered, truly the traditional Christmas tree. In fact, one of these trees has been the National Christmas tree. Spruce twigs and branches are crowded with short, stiff needles growing singly all around the circumference. The cylindrical cones are flexible and pendant. A subspecies of white spruce, the Black Hills spruce likes moist soil, and can endure extreme cold. It is, fittingly, the South Dakota state tree.

The third common evergreen in the area is the native juniper, a shrubby and prickly tree which is trimmed with misty blue berries which the birds find delectable. It seems to thrive in the hostile badlands, in arid foothills, and on windy, rocky precipices.

Among all the evergreens (gymnosperms) are groves of quaking aspen, birch, willows, and oaks (angiosperms). The aspens are the most prominent contrast to the dark green of the pines in the spring when their peridot colored leaves are like fluorescent lace, and in the fall, when their yellow glow is like a new source of light. In the Keystone area there are dense groves of slender, silver-barked aspen with shimmering, heart-shaped leaves. Sometimes confused with the aspen, are the rarer birches with their papery bark. The birch trees are more likely to be in narrow, moist canyons with the spruce.

Bur oak is widespread in the Hills. Although the tree can resist drouth and poor soil, it is slow growing, and often quite scrubby here. The round acorns are favorites of the red squirrels.

Prevalent, too, is the shiny-leaved cottonwood, a large and shady tree, beloved by western pioneers. A graceful, hardwood tree is the horn-beam, which has seeds enclosed in hop-like bags, and deeply veined leaves, which are clear yellow in the fall. There are also American elms, green ash, and boxelder.

The undergrowth in the Black Hills is not dense, since the ponderosa forest tends to be park-like. But in some areas, particularly along streams or in sheltered canyons, there are plentiful native shrubs. These shrubs offer springtime beauty and fragrance, and autumnal harvests of fruits and nuts for birds, animals, and man. There are the small, red pin cherries. Then there are the chokecherry trees with their clusters of dark, puckery berries, which proponents claim make the world's best jam. Buffalo berry trees are found on some creek banks, where they are easily spotted in September by their clusters of bright, red berries. Another shrub is bearberry which the Sioux call kinnikinnik, and which they burn in their pipes. Elderberry, gooseberry and serviceberry are three more native shrubby fruits. Near Iron Mountain there are wild filberts. Black walnut trees are also native, but are now extremely scarce.

In lower elevation the plum brush is showy and aromatic in the dark forest in the spring. Here, too, birds feast on the fruit of the handsome hackberry tree. Wild grapevines cling to tall trees along the wider streams. While hardly in the class of shrubs, wild red raspberries are plentiful on shaly banks most of the summer. Wild strawberry plants are common on high meadows, but seldom bear fruit.

The sole touch of scarlet in the fall, save for the wild rosebushes and a few vines, are the masses of gnarled, dwarfed, sumac trees with vibrant, fernlike foliage. The fall color in the area seems the more intense, because it is so short lived. Snow falls early in the high elevations.

Soon after leaving the eastern boundary of Custer State Park, visitors are on the open prairie. The Borglum Ranch, on the edge of the Hills, is a typical meeting place of Black Hills and prairie vegetation. Trees, except for cedar and cottonwoods, become scarce on the prairie, but there is still an abundance of wild fruit, and the prairie, which looks deceptively barren in the heat of July, is covered with rich, native grasses. Prickly pear cactus, spiny soapweed or yucca, and gumbo lilies join the transitional plants of the region. Frosty appearing leaves of sagebrush contrast with the greens and browns.

This region, so near the Shrine of Democracy, is an excellent place to study the plants of the mountains and prairies, because in a short distance the elevation, the soil, the temperature, and the moisture, change so dramatically that often each portion of a mile will bring a complete change of dominant flora. Some plants, like the freeform lichen cling to bare rocks. Others, like leafy watercress grow in the streams. Plants such as moss live in deep shade, and plants like sunflowers thrive in the brightest light. The raspberries live on loose shaley soil, and the poison vetch lives where the soil is alkaline.

The variation in the rocks and minerals in the soil makes a variation in plant life, which can be traced by such plants as the vetch, which is indicative of selenium in the soil. A sudden absence of trees on a rocky hillside may be a good reason to prospect for alabaster, a variety of gypsum. A field of evening primroses will lead to a bed of sticky clay.

Native grasses include shortstem and longstem grass plus buffalo grass, and all of the crossroads plants of the botanical world which accompany them. Grassy meadows in the Black Hills feed Hereford and Angus cattle as well as elk and deer, or are mowed for winter food for animals. The Park Service sees to it that the food supply for the wild animals is in proportion to the sizes of the herds.

The hills and the meadows which surround Rushmore are a patchwork quilt of flowers from the earliest thaw until the killing frosts of late fall. Some botanists estimate that there are about 2000 species of native flowering plants in the Black Hills and the plains nearest the Hills. Extremes of temperature and rainfall help account for the wonderful native garden. Other factors are the type of soil, of rock, available sunshine, and what position the plant holds in the ecology of the area.

One of the earliest of flowers is the South Dakota State Flower, the pasque, a member of the buttercup family which peaks through the late spring snow attired in a soft, gray, fur coat. Pale lavender in color, with cheery yellow centers, the tulip-shaped petals are actually enlarged and tinted sepals. Blue violets grow in sheltered places in the spring, and the meadows are yellow with members of the mustard family. Pale blue iris blooms on rigid stems beside cold streams, and pink phlox and lavender verbena border the roads.

Among the showiest genus of spring flowers is a penstemon. Sky blue dwarf penstemon, like miniature snapdragons, cover sandy areas. Later the blue beard-tongue and lilac shell-leaf penstemon decorate open, sunny spaces. Indian paintbrush is another colorful member of the snapdragon family.

In wet meadows are the cerise-colored shooting stars, which belong to the primroses. The mertensia or bell flower can be found in the spruce groves. Members of the pea family are a riot of color in early summer. These include golden banner, purple vetch, lavender prairie pea, blue lupine, and several colors of clover.

June and July bring wild roses, daisies, black eyed susans, thistles, and purple coneflowers. Milkweed, fireweed and bee plant are bright in July. The brilliant, red-orange wood lily lights up many forest coves. A rare and lovely flower is the creamy sego lily, which appears to have only 3 petals. The pale evening primrose, a fragile flower, grows in dry sandy spots. The red mallow is a bold flower of the foothills, while the equally vivid crimson wings, a member of the dock family, grows in arid, sandy soil.

August brings rose twinflowers, a species of honeysuckle, and tall blue lobelias, which belong to the bluebells. There are several species of showy wild asters which create patches of purple from August to October. Early fall trails are glorified by the cheerful goldenrod, cerise gayfeather, and lavender wild bergamot.

There are several poisonous plants in the Rushmore environs. The locoweed, crazyweed, yellow flax, and grassy deathcamus are poisonous to cattle and other animals. An innocent and attractive looking green and white spurge, called snow-on-the-mountain produces allergic reactions on the skins of some people. The leaves of purple nettles also produce contact dermatitis on susceptible individuals. The white berried sumac is poisonous to the touch, while the red is not. Then, of couse, there is the familiar 3 leafed bane of summer, poison ivy, which thrives in many Hills locations.

These same plants which attract the attention of the visitor now, were known and used by the Sioux Indians and other tribes, long before the coming of the white man. A purple spiked flower adorns the staple prairie turnip of the Indian. They also used a wild plantain similar to a potato, and the bulbs of a wild onion. Brown broomrape, white blossomed arrowhead, western snowberry, the fritillary lily, the hawthorn, the bee plant, and the purple spiderwort all provided food.

The leaves of bearberry were dried as "Indian tobacco." Chewing gum came from globemallow stems. Many native plants were used as herbs or medicines. Burdock was thought to be good for pleurisy, while the rush skeleton-plant was used as an eye-bath. Snowberries were valued as a laxative. Wounds were washed with anemone, and yarrow was used as a treatment for earaches. A fever was said to yield to the blazing star. For sore throats, the strong textile onion was prescribed, and even now folk medicine considers onions a specific for colds. Gumweed was used for asthma, bitter dogweed for headaches, and silktop for colic. Several plants, among them coneflowers and violets, were used for beverages, either with or without medicinal purposes. The common wild mustard was used as a seasoning.

Among the most useful food plants were those used for making the Indian's ingenious all purpose food, pemmican. Wild fruits, chokecherry, currants, and others were crushed and ground with stone grinders and mixed with dehydrated meat for a nourishing food. The Indians predated cholesterol consciousness by using sunflower seed oil in their cooking.

Sumac branches and birch bark were used in making containers. Rabbitbush, sage, goldenrod, and other plants were used as dyes or paints. Indian flutes, peculiarly melodious instruments, were carefully carved from ash. From selected oak, long pipestems were fashioned for ceremonial pipes of catlinite or shale. Brooms were made of bundles of clover.

At present, little use is made of the native plants except for several craftsmen who make novelty gift lines from driftwood, pine cones, and walnut. Local artists have met with success using pine and cedar for carvings.

It is illegal to destroy, pick, or dig up native plants in the limits of the Memorial. This also applies to Wind Cave National Park, Jewel Cave National Monument, and to the Badlands National Monument. The Park Service only removes trees when they are diseased or are too dense for proper growth.

Of course, it is also illegal to destroy plants on private property, and there is much private property near Mount Rushmore. For taking a close look at the many beautiful species of plants in the region, there are thousands of acres of National Forest land and State Park land, where one can roam at will. The best way to preserve such memories and the plants is with a camera. Since picture taking is one of the most popular of visitor's activities, there are many places in each community to get the most expert advice. The hope is that the ecology of the region may be so well preserved that future generations may be able to see the mini-world of Rushmore, just as the Borglums did in 1925.

With all these plants, there are naturally a variety of insects in the Hills. Although houseflies and mosquitoes are not as common as most places, the horseflies and deerflies are remote area pests. Grasshoppers are abundant in dry years. At present the worst insect pest is the tussock moth which threatens whole sections of pine forest with its blight. Not all insects are pests though, for there are also honeybees, ladybugs, and butterflies.

Most of the birds of the Black Hills are migratory. The merganser, junco, goshawk, bald eagle and redpoll are winter residents which join the permanent residents, owls, sparrows, wild turkeys, downy woodpeckers, bluejays, golden eagles, and nuthatches. Sometimes a few robins and meadowlarks will try to brave the life of the winter wonderland. The Mount Rushmore environment provides plentiful food for winter birds of prey and seed eaters.

In the summer the many trees and plants provide food and shelter for over one hundred species of birds, with another hundred counted as rare visitors. Robins are common, and the very pale ones of the Keystone area seem almost a sub-species. Mountain bluebirds, which match the sky above the mountain, are seen everywhere in the Hills, and occasionally, too, their rosy-breasted eastern cousins.

Anyone who has a picnic in the National or State picnic grounds will

A fisherman in the Black Hills seldom goes home without a creel full of rainbow trout. Photo by S.D. Travel Division

notice the jays . . . gray jays, bluejays and pinon jays. The busy little chipping sparrows and swallows are abundant, too. Among the best singers are the brown thrashers, the catbirds and the wrens. Not so musical are the grackles and crows. At night, the nighthawk makes a shrill sound, and the darkness is also pierced by owls. The yellow breasted chat is known to sing at night. Companions of the birds of night are thousands of bats.

Among the most colorful birds are the yellow and orange western tanager, the goldfinch, the yellow and black evening grosbeak, the russet orchard oriole, and the incredibly blue lazuli buntings. The magpie is a handsome bird in black and white. Larger birds include grouse, ducks, herons, cranes, and now and then, wild swans. A most peculiar bird sometimes seen near the Black Hills lakes or streams is the dipper or water ouzel, which walks along the bottoms of streams sometimes completely covered with water.

The confident shrike impales his prey on the thorny wild fruit trees, while the nervy cowbird lays her eggs in another species' nest. The noisy kingbird seems to be constantly waging war, and the sapsucker drums his message to the woodlands.

Shy species of birds will not be observed along the major highways and public walkways, or in the crowded tourist centers. These species have simply moved back away from civilization, as their natural foods, water supply, and nesting areas, have not been disturbed to any great extent. A quiet walk in a pathless part of the forest, with long, motionless, rest stops, will reveal a wonderful aerial parade of beautiful birds which have inhabited this lofty land for countless generations.

Lakes and streams near Rushmore offer some of the best fishing anywhere. South Dakota has a trout hatchery at Rapid City, and the clear lakes and tumbling streams are generously stocked with rainbow trout, brown trout, brook trout, lake trout, and several other species. Some of the lakes have pike and bass. Fly fishing on a lonesome stretch of stream in the pine forest is popular, but so, too, is slow trolling from a motor boat, or casting from a sandy point.

No one asks about the animals of the Black Hills without a hesitant question about snakes. Yes, the Black Hills does have rattlesnakes, though they are far more common on the prairies. The rattlesnake is the only poison snake in South Dakota. Those in the Hills are usually confined to more remote canyons, and to arid foothills. Rattlers hide when possible, and announce their presence with an angry buzz, when cornered. Tourists are not likely to see snakes in the Rushmore area, as the snakes do not like civilization. They are truly as fearful of people as people are of them. Even in the wilderness, a snake will glide silently away if he hears approaching noises. However, it does pay to be cautious. Walkers exploring strange country should walk slowly and make enough noise to alert snakes of their presence.

There are more wild animals in the Black Hills now than ever before, with a very few exceptions. One of the exceptions is bears. There are no native bears, although the earliest white men did come upon these furry

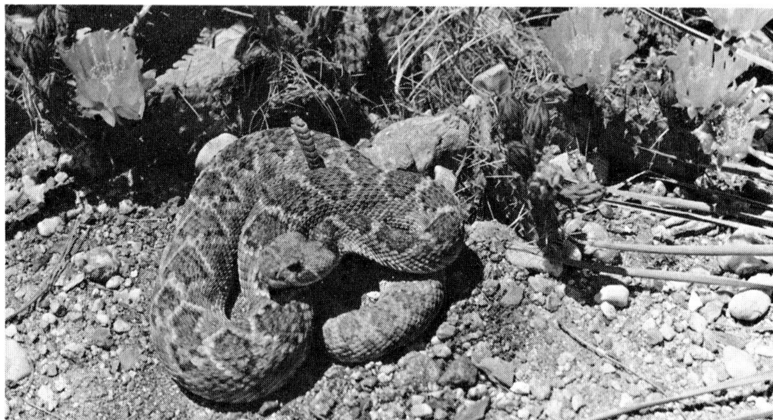

Rattlesnakes are not common in the Black Hills, but there is always a chance to run across one in a remote area. Photo by S.D. Travel Division

West of Mount Rushmore, incredibly fleet pronghorn, commonly called antelope, graze on the rich mountain grasses.

beasts. The bison herd of Custer State Park is one of the three largest in the world. To suddenly come upon a herd of the huge, shaggy "buffalo" silently grazing on a grassy hillside, is a memorable experience . . . exciting, or frightening, strange or wonderful, depending on the background of the viewer. Cars can drive close to the wild animals, with no fence in between, but although the brown, hump-shouldered bison appear to be an exotic breed of milk cows, they really are *wild* animals. Frequent signs announce this. The animals should not be offered snacks, should not be petted, and it is folly to try to get some action for a memorable picture. The size of the herd is carefully controlled. That is why local eating establishments are able to offer buffalo steaks, buffalo burgers and buffalo "stroganoff"!

Even more thrilling than the site of the historic bison, is a glimpse of some of the wild Rocky Mountain goats, acquired many years ago from the Colorado Rockies in a trade, although they were once native to the region. The graceful small white goats live in the steep crags of the Harney Range, and are sometimes seen on the top of Mount Rushmore itself. With incredible sure-footed balance, and all the confidence of ballerinas, they can be seen on some of the most rugged pinnacles of the entire area. It is prophetic that the ancient Borglum Coat of Arms featured a goat.

There are also more deer than ever before, and the hunting season in the Black Hills each fall draws hunters from many states. The white tail

Coyotes are numerous in western South Dakota and are considered a menace by ranchers who lease National Grasslands and Forest Ranges.

deer are more numerous, and the black tail are larger. In the summer, deer are likely to be seen, in the evening, cautiously grazing in the meadows or drinking from cool streams in higher elevations. Spotted twin fawns are frequently glimpsed near Deerfield. Many deer are accidentally killed at night by speeding drivers.

There are also elk in the Black Hills, though it is unusual to catch a brief view of them. Big, rather ungainly looking animals with immense horns, they are immediately recognizable. There are no moose, and no records that moose were ever native.

Antelope, seen in Custer and Wind Cave Parks, are pretty animals. A warm, tawny color with contrasting patches of white on the rear, they are really not antelope at all, but pronghorn. Their speed, surpassing all other American game animals, is matched by their curiosity. They keep their distance, but guard their right to know. In spite of being fleet and well coordinated they get down on their knees to crawl under a fence, while a deer floats smoothly over the obstacle.

Once in a while a mountain lion is reported. Ranchers come upon bobcats frequently in remote places. Quite common are the spiny porcupines, which because of their slow pace and lack of fear, are dangerous on the highways at night. Other night prowlers are skunks and raccoons. Beavers build homes in high marshes. Squirrels store up acorns from the bur oak. Cottontail rabbits nibble at the succulent grasses. Children especially like to watch the swift little chipmunks which scamper over the rocks, with their cheek pouches bulging with tidbits.

There are no wolves in the Hills, but on moonlit nights the yowl of coyotes can often be heard. Foxes find shelter and food in this region, too. A popular native animal for sightseers is the prairie dog. These little rodents live in colonies, and build vast underground cities, over which they stand guard. They can destroy great sections of valuable grasslands, so are considered a nuisance, although it is fun to watch them standing erect by their holes, and toppling in, when they suspect danger.

Other mammals include ground squirrels, field mice, gophers, and mink. Each animal finds its favorite habitat in this ecological system, because of the great variance of altitude, climate, soil, and vegetation. It is perhaps more likely that today's visitor to Rushmore will have a better chance to see more kinds of wildlife than the visitor of a generation ago. The balance of nature is being well guarded in the Rushmore world.

Depicted as the Declaration of Independence was announced, Jefferson is the only one of the four shown prior to his Presidency.

The ore car was used to haul granite out of the Hall of Records as it was blasted loose.

In the crevice behind the Faces, workers ascend to begin another day of work. These men worked in all kinds of weather to complete this work of art.

Drilled and blasted chunks of rock were eas removed leaving a solid carving surface of quali rock. Photo by National Park Servi

Not in use now, the old log studio at the foot of Doane Mountain afforded an inspirational view of the presidents as it made Mount Rushmore seem taller in comparison.

An automatic drill sharpener was in almos constant use in the blacksmith shop as the har granite rapidly dulled the drills.

Photo by National Park Service by Bert Be

One of the Mount Rushmore workers, Jack Zazadil, and the sculptor's assistant, Hugo Villa; both had the unique hobby of making violins.
Photo by State Travel Division

ompletely restored Borglum Studio and contain models and originals of the work of Borglums, as well as historic memorabilia uthentic furnishings.

Only a genius could have seen that this bare rocky pinnacle on the Harney Range would be suitable for a great memorial.

The Hall of Records

Some day the following scene could take place. Perhaps in the year 159,186 a big government has ordered an aerial survey of a mountainous area which had been covered with snow for a long time. Men and women archeologists on Uniwings accompany the Earth Energy Corps and the Arctic Recovery Team. The glaciers have slid from the peaks and the snow has melted. There are mighty crevices, tall pinnacles, weirdly erratic boulders of silvery gray rock. Suddenly an archeologist cries out and the team zeroes in on the most amazing sight in the history of their civilization. Here are four mammoth faces of men carved in rock. Incredible. The scientists rub their eyes with disbelief, aware that the tale of this find will shake their world.

The explorers crowd onto a ledge below. Their porta-computers tell them that the faces are 60 feet tall, that the rock is granite, and that the carvings were done by people who had not even learned to harness the earth's magma.

"Must be a tomb," says one, "we must organize a dig."

"Preposterous," replies another. "It is obvious these were their Gods, and they came to this mountain for special religious occasions."

"The one with the beard and the one with the mustache are obviously male, so perhaps the other two are female."

"Built by slaves, no doubt."

"Could there have been giants as tall as this scale?"

"How can we ever beam this to Tela-International without being laughed at!"

"What in the world is the arch over that figure's nose and the frame around his eyes?"

The questions go on and on. All without answers. Then and forever. For there are no answers. No word of explanation, title, or signature . . .

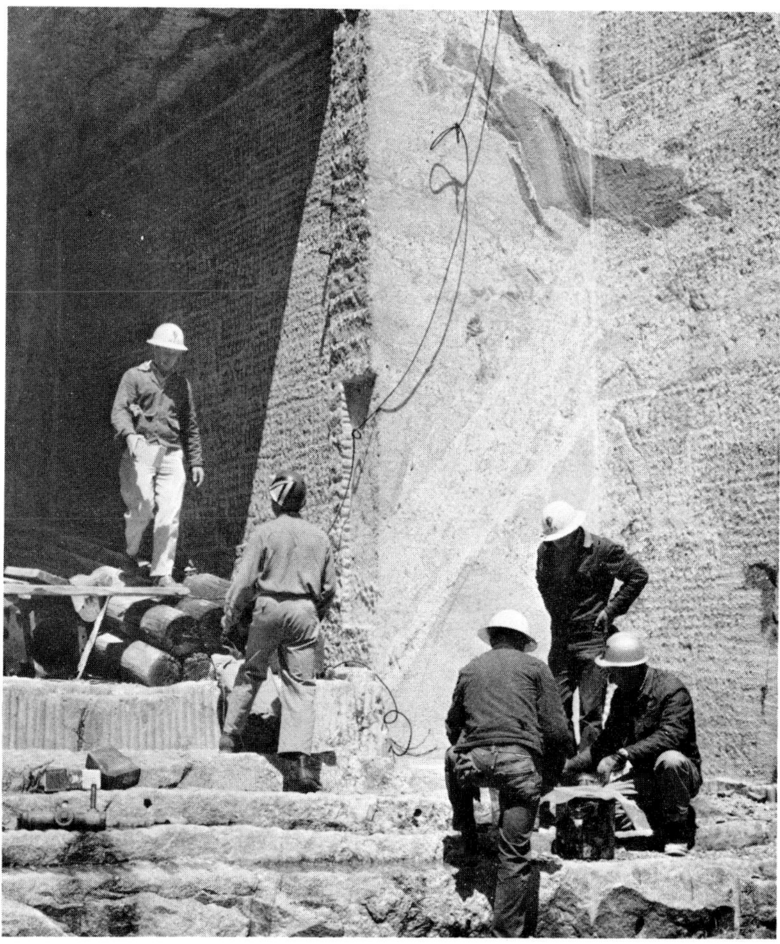

A start was made on the Hall Of Records, before an order from Washington, D.C., halted any farther work. Mountain goats took over the Hall for many years.

nothing which will endure for hundreds of thousands of years, except the faces in the rock. When the Sphinx has ceased to be, when the Easter Island faces have fallen apart, the Memorial will still be there, doomed to be another unfathomable mystery which future scientists may regard as the remnant of an artistic but illiterate people.

We know our libraries, our cities, and our roads will *not* endure 200,000 years. We know Rushmore *will.* Shall Rushmore fail to provide a clue to our times? Gutzon planned the answer . . . A *Hall of Records.*

Gutzon wanted the Hall of Records for several reasons, and he left behind plans for the completion of his magnificent dream. This permanent Hall of Records was planned for the rock across the narrow canyon from the faces. Gutzon realized that at some distant time, Rushmore might be the sole remnant of our civilization. He foresaw the interpretations of future archeologists who might mistake the figures as our gods. He knew that complete records of who we are and what we tried to accomplish, could be easily housed in the solid and enduring granite walls.

Since both Gutzon and Lincoln saw the necessity for interpreting the Memorial and our Democracy which it honors, the Hall of Records has been a major part of the overall plan since almost the beginning. Secure within the walls of defiant granite, reached by graceful stairs of solid stone, the Hall of Records could become almost as important as the Monument itself.

Every civilization asks searching questions about the past. Should they ask such questions about a nation which has the wealth, intelligence, and ability to leave the answers for the meaning of the Memorial, the accomplishments of America, the ideals and aspirations of the people of the nation?

Since contemporary leaders realize this culture will not survive for 200,000 years, but that Mount Rushmore will, the nation owes it to itself to leave a Hall of Records here. This built-in, future mystery about the Memorial and its purpose is not a part of the plan, for both Borglums knew the importance of documenting the Memorial.

A basic tenet of our sciences is to label everything. A basic policy of our government is to have full reports on everything in triplicate, yet the nation could become as guilty as the most primitive people of ignoring the importance of history, by not completing the Shrine of Democracy.

It seems now that plans are being revised and renewed and that the actual work on the Hall of Records may start soon. The Park Service is interested, and Lincoln Borglum has been contacted about finishing the job. This is good news, as it is most important that this work should be done soon. There has been a lot of correspondence and talk previously, but most of it was either double-talk or wishful thinking.

In one letter Lincoln Borglum had a couple of years ago from the Park Service, the explanation was made that the Hall could not be built because it would be hazardous to the environment and to the Monument itself, and the same letter went on to tell about considerable blasting which should be done in the immediate area to clear more scenic areas for additional parking space.

Russell Arundel is working with Lincoln in activating the completion

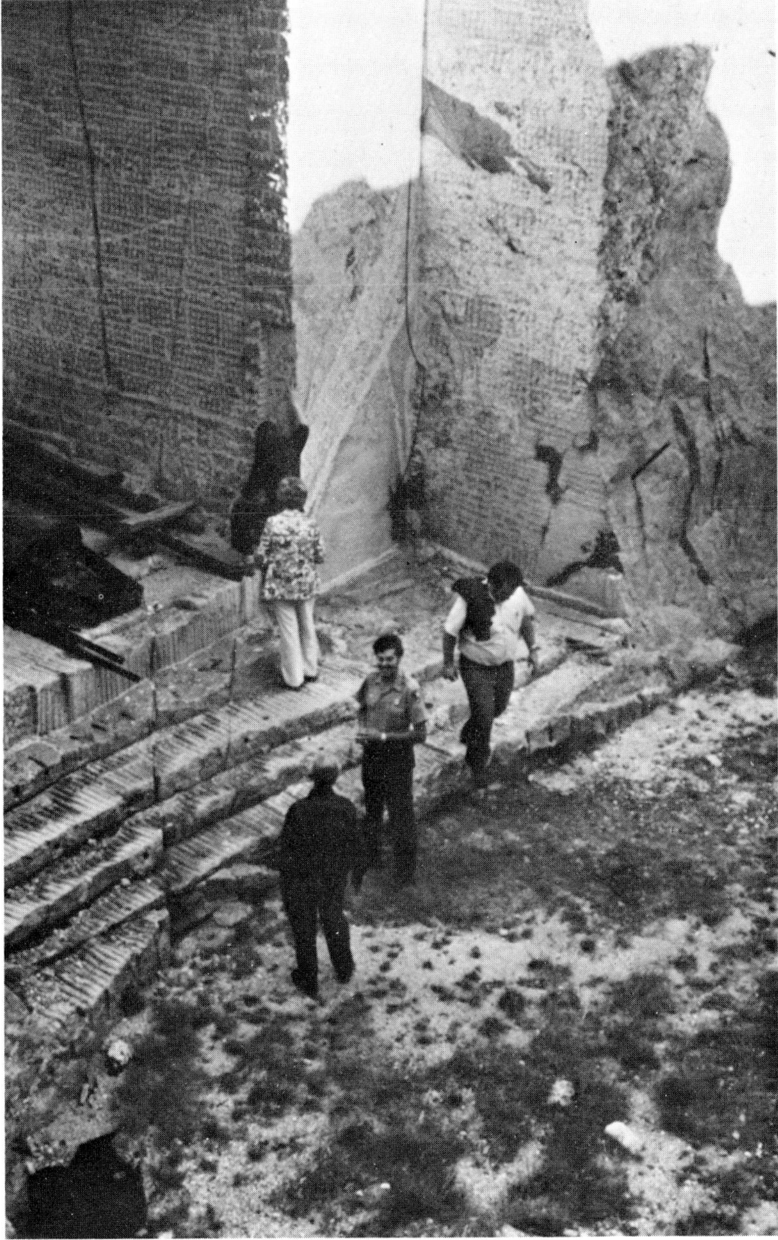

The Hall of Records, intended as the history book of our Democracy and the signature of the memorial, had actually been started when orders came to abandon it.

Photo by Jack Michelsen

of the Hall. There should not be too many problems, except financing, since Gutzon already left complete plans, and the bill allowing the Hall already passed Congress many years ago.

Modern technology should make it possible to complete the Hall speedily with no danger to the surrounding rock. If finances were carefully estimated and funding forthcoming at once, the Borglum dream could soon be fully realized. Mount Rushmore, itself, could have been completed in a fraction of the time it took, had the financial situation not been so serious.

The amount of money the Hall takes, should not really be questioned. If the truth were known, Mount Rushmore is probably one of the government's best investments. The Memorial has paid for itself many times over in gas taxes alone. A conservative estimate of the revenue brought in over the years on federal gas taxes, based on the number of cars coming to Mount Rushmore, is 30 million dollars. In addition, the government has collected excise taxes from the concessions, and also gets a percentage from the concessionaire. In the long run the Hall would pay for itself with the additional people it would bring to the area.

Considering that the U.S. government represents the capitalistic system, it is odd that a better way of funding government enterprises has not been devised before now. For example the Park Service brought out a beautiful full color book about the *Badlands National Monument* which it has sold for $2.00 per copy. With the high cost of color, private business would have sold the book for at least $5.00 and would sell as many copies and make a reasonable profit on its investment. Although the original Rushmore bill specified that there should never be any charge to see Mount Rushmore, if some way were found to raise only 50 cents per person, the completion of the Hall according to plans could be assured. There could be special programs, seminars, publications, but the most certain way to raise a large sum and at the same time beautify the area, would be to sell pieces of the granite from the rubble pile below the faces. This is high quality, attractive and polishable granite. It could be easily converted to book ends, paper weights, desk sets, carvings, or other rough or polished stone objects which would sell readily to collectors. Even pendants and key chains could be made from the granite. Or brass legends about Rushmore could be attached to rough or partially dressed pieces of granite. Commercial enterprises would be glad to bid on doing such work.

It is possible that private funds will be solicited for the Hall. This may be more feasible now than it was in Gutzon's day, partly because South Dakota has now become a household word, by courtesy of Mount Rushmore. There are various sources of such funds, such as foundations, endowments for arts and history, historical societies, civic groups, art organizations, and the businesses in the Black Hills which have benefited so greatly from Mount Rushmore.

Tourism is the biggest industry of the Black Hills and the second largest industry of the state. Most tourist oriented businesses in South Dakota owe their success to Mount Rushmore. With a few exceptions South Dakota businesses invested nothing in the Memorial nor did most of the cities, and as a state South Dakota gave nothing.

The state has been highly criticized for not giving Rushmore financial support when it was so badly needed. But South Dakota had a severe drouth during the Rushmore years, which were also deep depression years. Combining the natural conservatism of the people who homesteaded South Dakota with drouth and depression, resulted in the state government being very cautious about spending money.

Even Doane Robinson, who first started the push for the mountain sculpture in the Black Hills, was ashamed of South Dakota for making such a poor showing when it came to helping with the project.

Lincoln Borglum was once giving a talk in the Mount Rushmore Studio to a group of people who were holding a convention in Rapid City. He diplomatically glossed over South Dakota's lack of support when he noticed Doane Robinson in the back of the room. Lincoln paused momentarily to introduce the distinguished historian.

Robinson answered, "It is very kind of Lincoln to overlook South Dakota's part in Mount Rushmore, but I want you all to know the truth . . . that South Dakota as a state never gave a nickel toward the Memorial."

Since the completion of the carvings, South Dakota has spent large sums on roads and the promotion of Mount Rushmore and the Black Hills, but this should not prohibit the state from taking the lead in helping with the Hall of Records, should it be necessary.

Almost everyone agrees with the concept of the Hall. The few dissuaders say the Hall would be redundant because of the Time Capsule of the New York World's Fair, or microfilm libraries in Washington. In 200,000 years the eastern seaboard will probably be under the sea, but Mount Rushmore will almost certainly look much as it does today. Other complaints are from radical environmentalists who wish the Monument had never been built.

All of the reasons Gutzon had for the Hall of Records are just as valid now as they were when he made the plans, perhaps even more so. He felt that these figures and our society should be interpreted and the history recorded as a sort of indestructible immortality. He felt that people should learn more about our civilization from their visit to the

Shrine. He knew that no work of art is complete without a signature, and that the mighty Hall would be a signature.

Because of these reasons, when Lincoln was asked what should be done at Mount Rushmore to honor the American Bicentennial, without hesitation Lincoln replied that the Hall of Records should be resumed.

Frank Lloyd Wright, the great architect, had agreed to work with Gutzon on the Hall of Records. It is interesting to contemplate about how well the two geniuses might have got along in such a partnership, and to imagine the magnificent cultural heritage they would have created.

Other difficulties, in addition to finance, which are bound to arise are decisions about who and what to include in the Hall. Also, others will worry about how to handle the mobs of people who will want to visit the area, which is much nearer the faces than the public has been before. There will have to be increased security, and increased maintenance people. There will have to be a commission to decide how best to use the space both inside and outside. However, the problems are minor in comparison to the satisfaction that millions of people will gain from having the Hall finished.

Many people trained in the arts could help with the Hall, and would not necessarily even have to be there. The inside work could proceed all the year around. Lack of sufficient power and water would not be barriers to progress, as they were before. People are more aware of our culture and history. The time for the Hall could never be better.

Borglum planned on including leaders of all aspects of American life in the Hall. There would be carved busts of great Americans such as Alexander Graham Bell, George Washington Carver, Susan B. Anthony, and Thomas Alva Edison. There would be great bas relief carvings on the walls. Sealed glass and bronze cabinets would hold the precious records of our days and those of our founders. The accomplishments of the Western World would be permanently inscribed on aluminum scrolls in protective tubes. There would be at least 360 feet of paneled and recessed wall space. Subjects covered would be art, science, transportation, inventions, literature, medicine, industry, government . . . the plans were comprehensive, elaborate and detailed.

Perhaps some of Gutzon's more extravagant concepts will have to be modified. Where he called for lapis and gold mosaics at the entrance, cheaper substitutes could be used. Lapis lazuli is a rich blue gem which then sold by the pound or kilo, and now sells by the *carat*. Gold has skyrocketed and the end is not in sight. There are other blue gems with vibrant color which are not so expensive, and new art metals which substitute for gold give similar results as far as appearance goes.

Borglum planned a dramatic series of stone steps leading up to a finely chiseled doorway to his Hall of Records. The Hall was to be across a canyon from the faces, not underneath them.

The Hall is about two-thirds of the way up the mountain, with the entrance in a small gorge cut by the elements eons ago, to the right of the carvings as seen from below. It is located on the opposite side of the ravine from the heads and is not directly under them.

Gutzon wrote in his memoirs that the planning of the impressive "Great Stairway" was influenced by the popular movie of his day, Rider Haggard's fantasy, "She". Gutzon and Senator Norbeck repeatedly attended the movie to watch the scene showing a glorious open stone stairway, leading to the stars.

The stone steps are to be 15 to 20 feet in width, 18 inches or more in depth, with an easy, gradual rise and graceful lines. At chosen intervals there are to be seats, in harmony with the scene. The distance from the

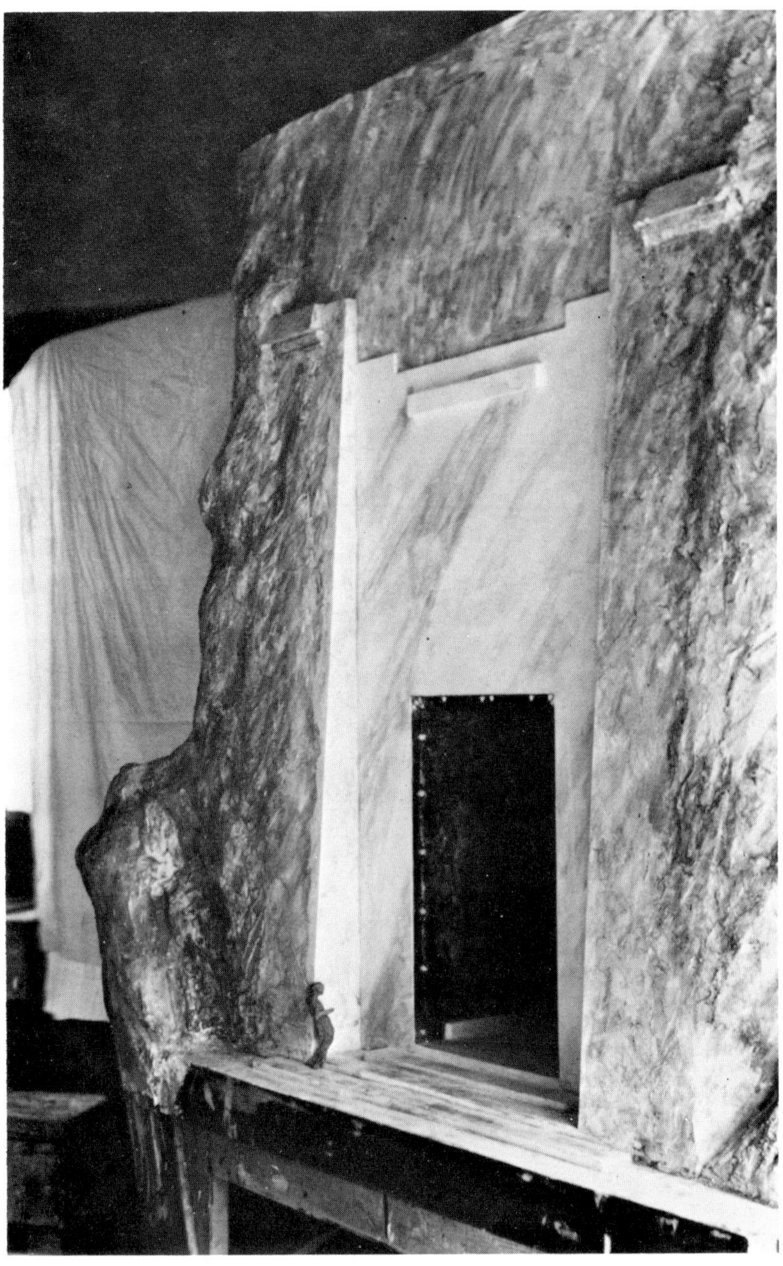

The model for the Hall of Records, an indispensable part of Borglum's dream, stands full of promise in the studio at the Borglum Ranch.

beginning of the stairs to the entrance of the Hall is 400 feet, so with 5-inch risers for each step there would be 80 or more steps.

Gutzon planned a stage and amphitheater at the foot of the stairs, and an enormous entranceway landing with a spectacular view. His plans even included such details as proper drainage from the canyon.

The facade to the Hall's entrance is to be 140 feet high, with supporting pylons of granite cut into the mountain flanking the entrance. The plans for the interior are inspiring, and will truly represent the most unique museum of American culture in existence. Many of the first ideas for a hall of historic records were planned by Gutzon when he was working on Stone Mountain.

Russell Arundel, who was helpful during the construction of the Memorial, is still in Washington and is very influential. The Mount Rushmore Society is also interested in the completion of the Hall of Records. Memorial Superintendent Harvey Wickware and the Rangers also favor the Hall, as it would be a positive interpretation of the meaning of the Shrine of Democracy, and would forever establish the who, what, when, and why, of the gigantic carvings.

At this writing, procedures are still to be worked out, but it is probable that visitors may be able to watch some of the work; to hear again the blasts of dynamite as workmen transform granite crags to graceful stairs; to observe artists sculpting statues of great Americans, perhaps in the Studio of the Borglum Ranch; to see trucks unloading great quantities of plate glass and bronze, of marble and redwood and steel; to feel the vibrations of the revitalized dream; to feel the intensity of the dream.

To write finis to the mighty project so many years after its inception is not as unusual as it may seem. No one knows how many years it took to build the pyramids, or to carve the strange figures of Easter Island. But in this case even a record of the time involved in the project can be preserved. Certainly nothing could be a more fitting enterprise for the Bicentennial, than the preservation of our history in everlasting stone.

In the meantime the true hall of records is the Borglum Ranch and Studio, where important historical facts about the mountain and about the life and times of Gutzon Borglum are carefully preserved. This is wonderful for the people of today, but after all, the old Studio is a wooden structure, and not even Lincoln Borglum expects that it will last tens of thousands of years. Moreover, if some of the items from the Studio were recovered several thousand years from now, it might take centuries for the discoverers to connect them with the 4 stone faces.

It is possible that the Bicentennial will renew enthusiasm for finishing the Memorial. Also South Dakota is becoming increasingly proud of its major attraction, and the political climate of the state has changed considerably since the Coolidge days, when the work was started. If enough people really care, it is probable the Memorial could be finished in the foreseeable future.

The Borglum Ranch and Studio

There are few drives in the world which surpass the one going to the newly opened Borglum Ranch and Studio from Mount Rushmore. Winding through aspens and pines, the trail is only a little more than 20 miles, but it may seem much farther because of the large number of irresistible scenic stops. Some stops offer a view of Mount Rushmore dramatically framed by tunnels blasted from the same type of granite. Another stop is on a broad mountaintop featuring the sight of the four presidents gleaming in the distance in spacious solitude, with the vast parking lots looking like the maze of a childhood game, and the pine forest looking like a great shag carpet. Or visitors may be tempted to stop to examine a dike of translucent rose quartz, or iridescent limonite. Or they will be thrilled by the appearance of wild game, antelope, deer, burros, bison, and mountain sheep. But when they reach the studio itself, that is the climax of this trip, for like Mount Rushmore, it is the culmination of a dream.

Over the years the Borglum story has captivated the public. After being enthralled by the Memorial, most people asked where they could see more of the work of the Borglums, the father and son. They wanted to learn more about this great family in the art of America. To see the first model for the monument, to see the house where Gutzon and Lincoln lived, the studio Gutzon had built, to temporarily house his visions, was the hope of many. Neither the Park Service nor the Rushmore Memorial Society had any provision for keeping the mementos and the history together where the public could recapture a little of the fascinating past.

Lincoln Borglum was an exceptionally devoted son, and as the last

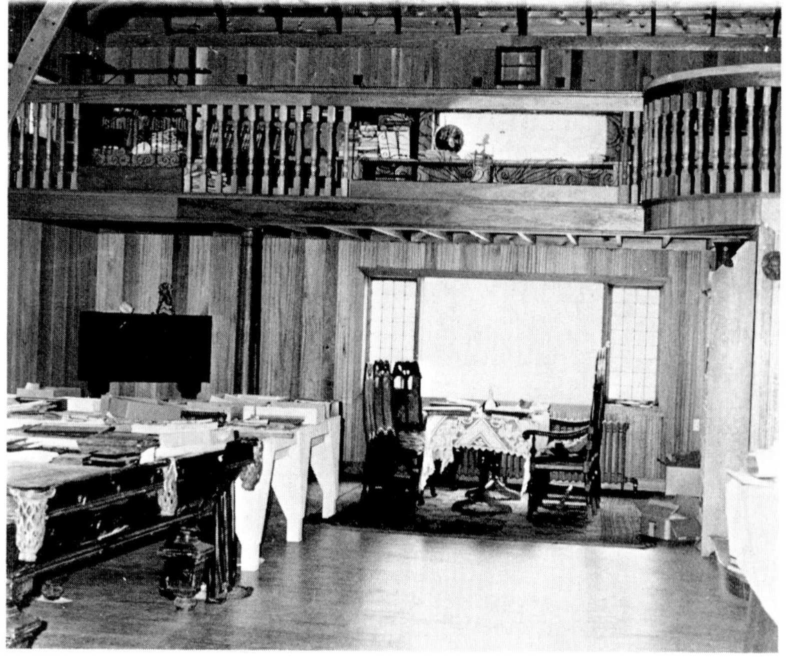

The interior of the Borglum home as it looked before the restoration undertaken by the Borglums and the Ellsworths in recent years. Floors and panelling are hardwood. The balcony, reached by graceful stairs, was designed by Gutzon.

living person who knew the entire history of Mount Rushmore, he knew it was up to him to see that the records were maintained and made available for future artists, historians, patriots, and visitors to the Shrine. It was such an overwhelming job that he tried for some years to push it from his mind. He was already busy with a full schedule of work in his Texas studio. He knew the establishment of a museum would be time consuming and expensive.

Lincoln had retained 25 acres of the original Borglum *Cloverleaf* Ranch near Hermosa, South Dakota. He had all of the Borglum letters and telegrams, the clippings and memos. The paintings, gifts, books and sculptures which Lincoln had retained, were mostly stored. Still standing were the original home, the newer home, and the tall sunswept studio. Some of the authentic furniture graced his Texas home. Neither Lincoln nor Mary Anne wanted to spend prolonged periods in South Dakota. They had found happiness in their peaceful, tropical home. Lincoln kept getting more commissions. With considerable property to maintain, and numerous civic and social activities, the job waiting in

This is the studio before the restoration. Now transformed to a showplace for the sculptures of the Borglums, the big building had been a storehouse for books, tools, boxes of artifacts, travel souvenirs, and family treasures.

South Dakota was no temptation. But Lincoln came to feel he could no longer postpone this task which his conscience and his love told him he must do. So in the cold winter of 1973, they prepared to open the Ranch and Studio to the public.

The historic site was run down, although a caretaker had always lived there. Weeds and grasshoppers had taken over much of the lawn. A mist of dust lay over the carefully packed boxes. Roofs needed repair, and the roads reflected the alternate floods and drouths. Lincoln and Mary Anne had never started a museum before, but working long hours in often bitter weather, they went over the bewildering assortment of materials with their assistants, and restored the historic home and studio as a living museum. Mary Anne's determination and devotion were equal to Lincoln's, and her artistic taste and instinctive flair provided just the right touch.

When the museum opened to the public in the summer of 1973, Borglums knew that their work was really only begun, but they sighed with relief at how much had been accomplished. They had been on the

The Borglum ranch is on Squaw Creek not far from Custer State Park. The first building is the studio and the farthest one is the old slaughter house of Keystone, which was the first of Gutzon's South Dakota Studios.

verge of giving up and moving the priceless collection to Texas, when a fortuitous event made the preservation possible. In 1972 the Stan Adelsteins, a Rapid City business family, expressed the wish to see a Borglum Museum in South Dakota. They offered financial backing to help renovate for the public, the old Borglum ranch site and buildings. Adelsteins and Borglums formed a partnership, and Mary Anne and Lincoln were able to keep the mementos and works in their natural locale.

Helping set up the displays for the opening season were Robert Ellsworth, Jimmy Borglum, Dr. and Mrs. David Garske, and Mrs. Willard Roberts. The Garskes and Mrs. Roberts had experience in a mineral museum (South Dakota School of Mines) but no one knew exactly how to go about transforming thousands of sometimes unrelated items into an important museum of art and history.

On a bright spring day the Ranch opened to the praise of area friends and residents. The gracious home and enormous Studio were ready for guests. Gay flowers edged the clipped, green lawn which slopes to the shaded creek. The roads were smooth, and well marked by

Paul and Pat Ellsworth, curators of the Ranch and Studio, stand by the new bronze Historical marker at the entrance just off state 36. Paul is Mary Anne Borglum's son. The inscription on the bronze marker was created by author June Culp Zeitner.

tasteful signs. The first season saw guests register from every state and many foreign countries. Some were so intrigued they came back several times. Often charter buses would bring large groups. It was with pride and gratitude that Lincoln noted the deep feeling of wonder, of respect, almost of awe, which the visitors had for the restoration.

A successful idea was the gift of a Borglum reproduction with every paid admission. Miniature authentic Rushmore models, carefully sculpted by Lincoln were placed on sale. Trained guides showed the visitors around, and all the while work on new displays progressed. Lincoln wanted more dioramas, a gallery a theater, and perhaps eventually picnic areas, or even resort facilities. He wanted a working studio for young people to study and practice their crafts.

He dreamed of having the former vitality and importance of the Ranch created anew. Borglums knew that all of their long range plans for the Ranch and Studio could not be realized by anyone but themselves, so in late 1973, Borglums agreed to buy out Adelsteins interest, and Lincoln and Mary Anne sought new funding to continue the work.

It almost seemed like Gutzon's story over again. The conservative South Dakota bankers and financiers, frightened by the widely publicized energy crisis threats to the tourist industry, refused to loan money for what they considered a risky business. So a family corporation was founded, including Lincoln and Mary Anne and all of their children. The gifted and dynamic young Paul Ellsworth of Dallas, Texas, was chosen as curator.

Paul, and his wife Pat, moved from Texas to the Dakota Ranch in the winter of 1973-1974. There, in a short time, Paul and Pat brought about a magnificent change. Paul, who had been a Chamber of Commerce official, grasped the public expectation of the enterprise, and as a family member, he knew what could and should be done. With masterful showmanship, he organized and revised the viewing areas, so that visitors could appreciate the Borglum Studio more fully, so they could understand more readily, the life and times of Gutzon Borglum.

Paul still provided guides for Studio-Ranch tours, but so well had he arranged the exhibits, that the casual visitors might browse through the exhibits unaccompanied and come out with a firm interpretation of the Borglum story from the beginning to the present.

On reaching the Studio from the new parking area, and getting tickets at the new admission office-gift shop, visitors are first struck by the sheer height of the building.

The exterior of the Studio is cream colored stucco, with the sheer expanse of sunny color being broken with natural wood trim, now weathered to a silvery gray. The steep roof of wooden shingles is stained a contrasting red. Windows of original design create a contemporary look, even though the Studio was built in the '30's.

When walking into the main entrance, one has the subtle feeling of stepping back into the period when the Studio was new. The huge room takes its character from the high ceiling of narrow, hardwood wainscoting, boards fitted together with tongue and groove. Walls are paneled in natural pine, and the sturdy beams and supports have been transformed to architectural accents with coats of vivid red.

The scrupulously clean cement floor is covered with plaster marks, hallmarks of a working sculptor's studio. Ancient kerosene lanterns hang on either side of the wonderful fireplace of native stone surrounded by a dark hearth of inlaid flagstone. The door is framed by panes of colored glass, a geometric pattern of ruby, sapphire, and aquamarine, transmitting moving beams of brightness.

To the right, open stairs lead to a wide balcony. Warm daylight floods every corner from mammoth well placed sky-lights. The largest windows, interesting arrangements of clear and frosted glass, face north. Replicas of Gutzons Gargoyles for Princeton University make dramatic decorations.

Cleverly divided into meaningful, uncluttered compartments by

Lincoln Borglum recently worked at preparing the Borglum art for exhibit at the Borglum Ranch and studio, now open to the public near Hermosa, South Dakota.

ropes and screens, the old Studio is revitalized. Each of the four major areas contributes a part of the story of the past, making it all seem like *now*.

Preceding the four major areas, is an exhibit under the balcony of the smaller tools of the sculptor's art and illustrations from the work of both Borglums, showing some of the techniques of the art of sculpture. The "trade secret" of making a wire armature to support the weight of the clay, is shown with Gutzon's graceful "Torso of a Dancer." On the wall is a portrait of Gutzon working on this dancer. How molds are made from the clay is a process revealed by Lincoln's reverse mold of his father, and by his bust of President Lyndon Johnson shown with the mold from which it was cast. Tools for working clay, plaster and stone are there, and in its original case, is a heavy, white block of unused marble, hiding a dream. Nearby is a studio ladder made by Gutzon.

The first of the major viewing areas is *Religious*. Near the entrance are the large hands and head of Christ, all that is left of the colossal statue which once dominated the Studio, the same statue Gutzon had created for Corpus Christi, and Lincoln was to have modified for the

Organizing and arranging the museum was a tremendous task for the Borglums, Ellsworths, and their helpers. In this picture are Lincoln's Francis Case and Lyndon Johnson, and Gutzon's Christ and standing Abraham Lincoln.

Spearfish "Christ on the Mountain." In this religious section there are the faces of the angels for the Cathedral of St. John the Divine in New York, together with articles about the controversy they precipitated. There is a marble statue of "Salome" by Gutzon. Arresting and unforgettable is Lincoln's calm and patient head of Christ. The focal point of the area is the full size statue of the transfixed figure of Mary Magdalene, as she softly calls "Rabboni". Backed with a plaster reproduction of a stone arch, the emotional statue is the original model for the bronze which stands in Rock Creek cemetery.

The next section is *Statesmen and Personalities.* Here again the work of both Borglums can be seen. Here are bronzes, marbles and plasters, small figures and large, bas reliefs and full, of young people and old, of those who were powerful and wealthy, and those who were family neighbors and friends. On specially designed pedestals, in keeping with the original period, a variety of individuals, stern, solemn, wise, tolerant, gracious or amused, show these qualities forever.

There is Dr. G. C. Watts from San Antonio, and Dr. William Frick, a surgeon from Kansas City. There is Frank Gannett, a newspaper publisher, William Maloney, once editor of the New York Tribune, and Herbert Myrick, who published *The Dakota Farmer.* Harvey Scott and Isadore Singer, are two more of Gutzon's journalists. John Reed, who was once mayor of Kansas City, W. W. Fuller, an attorney from North Carolina, and John Rainey, an Illinois Congressman, are some of the political figures.

The model for a famous patriotic statue with an interesting history is here. Borglum's statue of the American Revolution patriot and writer Thomas Paine was commissioned by a group called the Free Thinkers. Born in England, Paine was also a hero to the French, and it was in Paris that the statue was to be cast and installed for display. Borglum went to Paris to see about the casting some six months before the war (World War I) broke out. After the war, while again visiting France, Borglum inquired about the statue of Paine. He was shown the statue. It had been cast and was buried in a back yard during the war, and quietly resurrected once the war was over.

Another statue of Borglum's did not fare so well. The statue of Woodrow Wilson which Paderewski had commissioned for Poland met the fate of other fine statues during World War II. It was melted down for ammunitions by Hitler's armies.

For viewers of the extensive patriotic section of the studio a major interest is a half sized replica of the splendid marble head of President Lincoln which is in the Rotunda of the Capitol in Washington, which Robert Lincoln called the most true to life of all Lincoln likenesses. There is a standing figure of Robert Ingersoll. One of the most profound and appealing of all Borglum busts is of Sidney Lanier, the beloved poet of the south. Just as carefully executed as these well known figures, are Gutzon's interpretations of John Bovard, a Kansas City friend, and young Sidney Smith, Junior, the son of a geologist.

Interspersed with Gutzon's works are many fine sculptures by Lincoln, and if they were not labeled, it would be difficult for most people to tell the work of the father from that of the son. Indeed Gutzon had predicted that Lincoln could become a greater sculptor than he was, since Lincoln had been immersed in the art since childhood, and had perfected these techniques alone, rather than spending years at painting or another art form. However Gutzon did not anticipate a time when large sculptures, memorials, and monuments, would be in so little demand as they are now. Perhaps looking at all of Lincoln's work at once, one might feel that the extreme emotional qualities seen in Gutzon's work were more subdued. Gutzon's artistic exaggerations are replaced with Lincoln's candid ac-

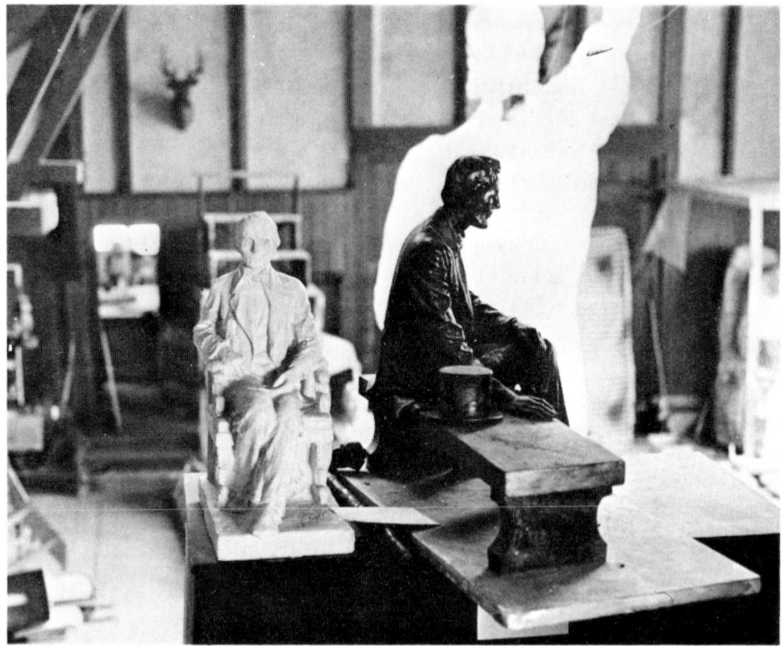

Two seated figures by Gutzon are shown before the studio restoration. They are Alexander Stevens and the seated Lincoln, which was made for Newark. Behind Lincoln is part of the massive Christ, Gutzon was doing for Corpus Christi.

ceptance of humanity. Anger, frustration, pride, and elation are replaced with patience, kindliness, and peace. The portrayal of true to life human beings is there in Lincoln's work, as it is in his father's, and his Uncle Solon's. As a craftsman, he is a perfectionist and the quality of his pieces compares favorably with Gutzon's. Perhaps the major difference is that Gutzon had greater egotism, ambition, and drive. He put all of his life's energy into sculpture and produced an overwhelming number of major works. Lincoln is a man with a more traditional life style, more humility, more satisfaction in participating in activities which have nothing to do with promoting his art.

Lincoln's loving bust of his son Jimmy as a child is similar to Gutzon's little Smith boy. Most imposing of Lincoln's works in this section is the life-sized bust of Thomas Brackett Reed, a former Speaker of the House. The original is in the Captitol in Washington. John F. Kennedy and Lyndon Baines Johnson are two of Lincoln's true to life busts. Ray Lemley and Russell Haley are two more Lincoln Borglum subjects, portrayed with understanding accuracy.

There has long been a need for a gallery to house Lincoln Borglum's art, as his contributions are many. So although the Studio restoration was started as a memorial to Gutzon and his art, it has also become the proper showcase for the work of Lincoln Borglum. This is a welcome bonus for the art world.

Lincoln has portrayed his father several times, some of these may be seen in the studio, the home, at Mount Rushmore and on the Memorial Highway. These are among his best works. The one in the Studio shows Gutzon as he was, a man of burning vision and ambition, ahead of his time. Senator Francis Case, a South Dakotan who worked long and hard for Rushmore, is interpreted by Lincoln with all the honesty and integrity South Dakotans knew Case to possess.

Reproductions of other works by Lincoln will be added as time goes by. In Abilene, Texas, is a much admired plaque in the courthouse, of three brothers who died in the Alamo. Beeville, Texas, is proud of its Christ statue by Lincoln. Rockport, Texas, boasts a benevolent St. Francis, a Lincoln Borglum creation. The Gladys Porter Zoo of Brownsville has a seated bronze figure of its benefactress holding a baby gorilla, executed by Lincoln with frankness and admiration. Lincoln has also made gold miniatures of family members and friends, and self portraits. He has designed jewelry, pendants, plaques, and awards. His western plaques and models of prize winning purebred cattle have won him an assured place in western art.

The next consecutive section of the Studio is dedicated to Gutzon's *Ladies.* It contains some of his most unusual and controversial works. There is his daring "Atlas", a graceful and determined young woman, lovingly bearing the entire weight of the world in her arms. "Earth" is a fulfilled statue, and "Conception" is the name of the exalted statue of young womanhood. A resigned "Martyr" rebukes civilization for discriminating against women. A bust of Edith Mathison, famous as an actress, immortalizes the comely lady who posed as Mary Magdalene. Mrs. William Van Horn, cool and serene, by Gutzon, is joined by her two small daughters, as sculpted by Hugo Villa, the Borglum protégé. Another Gutzon lady is named "Inspiration", and there are three sections of his famous group "I have Piped unto You and Ye have Not Danced."

The largest section, as it should be , is the *Rushmore* section. Here is another of Borglum's studies of his friend, Teddy Roosevelt, this one an unfamiliar work without glasses. William Williamson, the Dakota Congressman who helped the Rushmore project past some big hurdles, is in this section. Others who were burdened by the politics of Rushmore are here, but the main attractions are the models. Here is the stirring original model for Rushmore, featuring three patriotic figures instead of four, finished in the San Antonio studio, before the naked, granite peak in South Dakota was completely surveyed. There is an inspiring model of the finished Rushmore by Lincoln, and a precise diorama showing the work in progress, which also reveals the beginning of the Hall of Records across the ravine. At present this is the visitor's only chance of visualizing the location of the proposed Hall in relation to the Memorial itself.

Here is the drill which started it all. It is one of the four drills used by Gutzon at the first dedication when Calvin Coolidge was present. One of the actual harnesses from which the workmen first hung over the precipice hangs between the windows. This is on loan from Cliff Stygles, who took care of it all these years. There is an enlargement of a *Saturday Evening Post* cover showing one of Lincoln Borglum's inspirational photos of Rushmore. A gray chunk of granite with the smooth, round marks of the drill is against the wall. Such pieces of granite fell by the hundreds to the rubble pile below the faces, as the drilling and blasting progressed. Now collector's items, the igneous rock reveals the genesis of the Hills, as well as man's manner of transforming rough rock into art.

Bold headlines from yellowed papers, magazine articles, cartoons, photos in sepia, black and white, and color, clippings from leading papers, brochures, all neatly framed and organized, further interpret the Rushmore section, and also the others. The Rushmore years are presented chronologically, with the pictures and printed work augmenting the instant impact of the models, the tools and the granite.

Here are the first reports of the exciting Borglum dedications, the trials and triumphs over money and policy, the intriguing maneuvers of politicians, news of the heralded Rushmore contest sponsored by the Hearst papers, and the sad story of the sudden death of Gutzon. Here are the announcements of Lincoln's succession as head artist, designer, and later Superintendent. Pictures show everything from the isolated, granite mountain standing alone, to its use later, as the United States symbol, the Shrine of Democracy, as seen on the first Telstar broadcast, with the Mormon Tabernacle Choir in the foreground.

There is a big elk head over the door, given to Gutzon by his loyal workers. In the central corridor between the dividing screens is the pool table, once used by Rushmore workmen at the mountain. At the door is a Gutzon Borglum bas relief of innocent, carefree childhood, entitled "Babes in the Woods."

The walkways to the old home, and other parts of the Ranch, are of crushed native stone, outlined with water-rounded native rocks.

Lincoln Borglum often greets Ranch visitors such as the group shown here at the little theater where Borglum films are shown.

Towering beside the Studio entrance is a regal Black Hills spruce. It is only a short walk past the circular driveway, the spreading cottonwood, and terraced lawn to the door of the "homestead" house, which was once a buggy shed. In landscaped areas near the entrance are driftwood, day lilies, rocks, and a marble sculpture of a Centaur. The old log section of the house, with crisp white trim, is shaded by an ash tree and a tall, spreading willow. Joined to the new home, which was never finished, by a weathered wood hallway, the old part of the building seems small, but oddly, not incongruous. The high, new section is walled with ivory colored stucco, emphasizing the big fireplace, carefully built of random, narrow stone. The shingled roof has been stained red.

Beyond the slatted wood fence, is the modern house where the Ellsworths live. There is also the rustic log studio building which was once the slaughter house at Keystone. This was the original Borglum studio in South Dakota, where the first scale models of Rushmore were done. Lincoln had every log of the building numbered and the position recorded, then it was all moved to a site on the Ranch near the creek.

The old house has wainscoting on the ceiling. The fir boards of the floor have been painted long ago, and the paint is almost worn away. A staircase leads to the sleeping loft, and a door directly opposite the outside entrance went into the kitchen. The main room, once a living room in the old section, is now a restored bedroom. On one side is a much used trunk which had held the lovely clothes of Mary, as she traveled long miles fulfilling her obligations. The unusual canopied wood bed, designed by Gutzon, is the one in which his son was born. There are several handmade bookcases in the room. From the north window, sheer, white curtains are hanging. On the table is a statue of Nero, and a finely woven Pima Indian basket.

A gold carpet covers the floor of the white plastered hall, which matches the bedroom. On log "sawhorses" are two well cared-for leather saddles, one a favorite of the sculptor's, and the other, the sidesaddle his Mary used when riding with him. To carry out this theme, there are pictures of horses, the animals Borglum loved, and which helped carry him to fame. Narrow vertical windows line the north wall. Next is the huge "new" living room. It is typically Gutzon. With cathedral ceilings, gracefully curved open stairs, immense fireplace, and Philippine mahogany panelling, the spacious room looks elegant enough to entertain royalty, and warm enough for the family to gather on a winter's evening to make popcorn over the fire.

The furniture represents no particular style or period. Many of the pieces were gifts, or were selected on momentous trips abroad, or were acquired during the Connecticut years. Some were moved from the east to Georgia, to Texas, then to South Dakota. Two chairs, rare antiques, were among the pieces which made an additional trip to Texas and back to South Dakota, as they were in the Borglum home in Harlingen. One of these chairs is hardwood and Egyptian in style. The other, a large brass studded wood and leather chair, is both Spanish and Western in design.

Hard to describe is the ornate, gilded Spanish traveling desk, a lavish piece made by an artisan in the Court of Philip II of Spain. The gesso drawers are elaborately carved, painted and gilded.

A Borglum dining set on display here is of walnut with Spanish styled, tall backed chairs, set off by caning and red velvet upholstery. A matching settee is on one side of the table. On the hardwood floor is an ornately patterned area rug in harmonious and luminous colors.

Over the door and flanking the fireplace are spears, probably dating back to the Crusades. A distinguished looking firescreen is a Medieval chain coat-of-mail. Under plate glass which covers the large fireplace table, is an intricately embroidered Turkish tapestry. On this table is standing a statue of Abraham Lincoln. Above the fireplace is the Borglum coat-of-arms.

"Rabboni" is an impressive Borglum statue standing in Rock Creek Cemetery near the nation's capital. Photo by Jack Michelsen

At the east end of the room an airy balcony is supported by graceful pillars, bordered by a rail with baroque inserts of wrought iron. Leading to the balcony, which was designed as a library, are unique open stairs, designed by Gutzon. The Borglum library is valuable not only for its wide range of subjects, but for its many autographed volumes, such as one lovingly inscribed by Helen Keller.

Beneath the balcony is a pleasant alcove where some of the Borglum airplane designs hang from the ceiling. On a glass case stands the bust of James McConnell, first American pilot to be killed in World War I. In the case are models of propellers, flaps and other Borglum inventions for early airplanes.

In the alcove is an arresting oil painting of Gutzon's lovely Mary, a little lady in a big hat, looking very much like the true hostess of the magnificent room and the Clover Leaf Ranch.

"Womanhood of the South" is a Borglum work, which should have become one of his best known, except that funds for its completion for Fort Worth were never raised. The model of five figures stands near the home's south door. General Lee is shown on horseback, and beside him stands an indomitable woman, while at her feet two soldiers are helping a seriously wounded man.

In front of the south facing windows, with their ivory and rust hand screened drapes, stand more statues of significance. One of the most meaningful is Lincoln's portrayal of brave and gentle Sacajawea, the Sioux Indian maiden who befriended Lewis and Clark. Lincoln's sturdy likeness of Potato Creek Johnny, the South Dakota gold panner who came up with the state's largest gold nugget, and his carving of the courageous Jim Bowie with his rifle, serve to emphasize Lincoln's preoccupation with the West. Gutzon's love of the West is vibrant in his "Apache Pursued", his "Texas Ranger", and "Trail Drivers".

A replica of Borglum's seated Abraham Lincoln in Newark, often called the Children's Lincoln, is a scale model. There is also a stately bronze of General Sheridan and another of General Primm, who led a Spanish expedition into Mexico.

Over the door is a detailed and arresting relief carving which represents Gutzon's controversial plans for another mountain, far away Stone Mountain, Georgia. Though never finished, the sculpture is one of the most magnificent interpretations of the South.

A Gutzon Borglum masterpiece is General Sam Houston. Portrayed with vigor and strength of character, the original stands in Houston, Texas.

Although most things in this room are on a large scale for easy viewing and dramatic effect, there are some small items of note, too.

Huge native stone fireplaces are a feature of Borglum Buildings. This is the exterior of the big ranch house which Borglum had not quite finished when he died.
Photo by S.D. Travel Division

One of these is the gold medal Gutzon won for his "Mares of Diomedes" at the St. Louis World Fair in 1904. A pen used by Franklin Delano Roosevelt to sign a major Rushmore bill is on exhibit. In this case too, is the Masonic apron of Gutzon.

No attempt was made to modernize the room, or change its interior design in any way. Everything in the restoration is authentic. Visitors will see in this room, as in the others, that the arrangements have been made so that it is easy to study one item, or survey a group. The flow of lines and space, the thought of the groupings are done for the minimum distraction and maximum enjoyment.

Unlike many American artists, the works of the Borglums do not fall into any definite labeled period of influence by widely variant schools of art. For example some artists try realism, followed by impressionism, cubism, and abstracts, and soon become known and accepted chiefly for one period of work. Gutzon, when he first determined to become a sculptor, decided that his art would be American, that it would be true to life as he saw it, and that he would honestly and accurately portray only that which he considered to be worthwhile, good, true, and beautiful. He followed these ideals all of his life, and Lincoln, who learned well from his father, did likewise. Lincoln's work on his miniature gold charms is as precise and detailed and faithful as the work he finished on the president on the granite mountain, for whom he was named.

Going out the south door towards the new theater, where Borglum documentaries are shown, visitors view the wooded slopes of Squaw Creek. Old-fashioned flowers and lichen-covered stones, are in the shade of the oaks and native elms. Several species of fish live in the stream, and the trees vibrate with the movement of robins and bluebirds. This is a spot where the Prairies meet the Hills. To the west, the pines become numerous and after the red rock valley which encircles the Hills, is the sprawling, game-filled Custer State Park. To the east, are miles and miles of rich grasslands.

Eventually the log "slaughter-house" studio may be restored and added to the exhibits. It is now sometimes used as a studio by Lincoln, when he is in South Dakota. Another possibility is that the large working model of Mount Rushmore, now housed in the abandoned studio at the foot of Doane Mountain, could be brought to the Ranch Studio for display.

Lincoln dreams that the historic ranch will become again a center of arts for this part of the West, the area which held such great appeal for the Borglums. Since Lincoln recorded the Rushmore years with superb photographs, large sections could be devoted to this art.

The Studio and Ranch have been designated as National Historical Landmarks. Numerous artists and museum people as well as the press and media have been watching the progress of the new enterprise with intense interest. Now that there is a good chance that the Hall of Records will be revived, the roll of the Studio will grow even more important, as Gutzon's own plans for the Hall of Records are here, and it is here that Lincoln will do much of the planning and designing.

As of now, the real repository of the records of Rushmore and its artists is here at the Borglum Ranch and Studio, in the shadow of the Black Hills. The popularity of the Studio will certainly keep pace with the nation's deep feeling for its Shrine of Democracy. The Studio could become the first place where visitors could get a look at what the finished Hall of Records will be.

There are many projects which Borglums would like to see develop, when the Studio becomes self-sustaining. Mary Anne would like to see the gardens enlarged, including perhaps an array of native flowers of the Hills and Prairies. Lincoln would like to see facilities for seminars and symposiums. There are still more clippings and letters to be reread, catalogued and prepared for display or preserved so scholars could study them. A larger amphitheater suitable for outdoor pageants would be an attraction. Bicentennial events could be programmed. Since quiet spots for meditation add to any gallery, it is almost inevitable that more space will be needed in the buildings as more Borglum displays are added.

The ideas of sound tapes or closed circuit TV instead of guides could also be explored, and special areas be set aside for those who want to study or work at the arts.

Borglums feel very strongly that there should be no gross feeling of commercialization, no feeling of being crowded or rushed, for any visitor. They want an atmosphere of peace and dignity, of learning and appreciation, of rest and inspiration, and this is what they have produced. They are both happy that they have gone ahead with the Borglum Studio restoration and the museum or gallery, but they look forward to the time that their efforts will pay off financially, so that they can keep improving and building. It is almost too much for the artistic and historic communities to expect one family to keep this enormous project going.

Some years ago the South Dakota legislature passed a bill to purchase the old Borglum buildings and the part of the ranch which Lincoln owned. The idea was for the state to restore it to a Historic Park. However, funding was never appropriated and negotations fell through, with the state losing interest in the task of preservation of this cultural heritage. There is no doubt, though, that the devotion of the Borglums has produced a far better restoration than any other group could have done.

Departing guests have a choice of routes. The area is sparsely populated, but the roads are good. A new campground is near the Studio. Most of the neighbors are working ranchers. The chief crops are foods for livestock, and the natural competitors are the elk, the antelope, and the deer.

Those who have come over the dramatic Iron Mountain Road, may wish to return to Custer State Park, and take in the Needles, Sylvan Lake, or the State Game Lodge. Highway 16A goes to Custer. Some may wish to follow State 36 to its junction with State 79 which goes north to Rapid City or south to Hot Springs. There are accommodations, rest facilities, and interesting places to eat in all of the cities which are located in the southern Hills, and are all less than an hour's drive from the Borglum Studio.

As visitors depart, thoughts are with the man who conquered a mountain, and with his son who really finished the job, including the marvelous restoration of the historic ranch and family home. The Ranch and Studio interpret the true meaning of the National Memorial, the only National Memorial in the world to be planned and built by contemporary man. Perhaps, after seeing the Ranch, some will turn around and go right back again to take another look at the mountain the Borglums carved, a mountain which has become a part of our national life.

The Men Who Worked on Rushmore

Gutzon Borglum
Lincoln Borglum
Norman Anderson
Otto Anderson
Cecil Andrews
Carl Baird
H. E. Baird
Aldolph Bames
Alfred Berg
Luigi del Bianco
Ramond L. Berg
Pat Bintliff
Alvin Bradford
Glen Bradford
Floyd Brainard
Roy Brandt
Joe Bruner
Lee Burrow
Chester Calve
Albert Canfield
Kenneth Carson
Arthur Cerasini
James Champion
Charles Claney
Robert Christian
Charles Clifford
Donald Clifford
M. I. Cindel
Ralph Crane
Raleigh Crane
Lewis Davis
J. C. Dennison
Clyde Denton
W. F. Ducolon
W. L. Dunmire
Ray Daley
B. Eilbeck
Donald Ely
Charles Flathers
Miles Garner
Clyde H. Gates
Albert Gensler
Eldon Gordon
Chauncey Green
Jeff Grier
Ray Grover
Charles Halsted
Edward Halsted
Herbert B. Ham
Martin Hartman
John Hayes
Joseph Henry
Edward C. Hopner
George Hesnard
Robert Himebaugh
Arthur Hough
Ivan Houser
E. A. Hudson
H. V. Huntimer
Jens Ikast
Pete Jensen
Alfred Johnson
J. A. Johnson
Frank Jones
Glen T. Jones
Gustav Jurisch
Walter Katsch
Charles V. Kerston
Charles P. King
Bert Kinzey
Orland Kieffer
R. G. Kingsbury
James La Rue
Nils Ledon
Floyd A. Leach
Lawrence L. Lewis
John Lintz
E. A. Long
Waldo Madill
Frank C. Marsh
Frank Maxwell
Floyd McDonald
Robert McNally
R. F. Meiners
John C. Merrick
Giles Montgomery
Donald P. Morrison
Tom Miner
H. P. Munch
John Nickels, Jr.
Earl Oaks
Forest Payne
Frank Payne
Jack Payne
James T. Payne
Stephen Peabody
Howard L. Peterson
Merle E. Pertson
Bob Philip
H. Pierce
Ervin Pietz
Ernest Raga
John Raga
Matthew P. Reilley
Ernest Reynolds
Fred Richardson
Edward Roush
F. G. Robertson
George Rumple
R. H. Schuler
Gustav Schram
Charles S. Sheeley
Ray Shepard
J. C. Spotts
A. L. Spriggs
Boyd Swensen
William Tallman
J. G. Tucker
Leo Valdez
Hugo Villa
Lloyd Virtue
Ralph Virtue
Chris Vranick
Marian Watson
Ivan Wellman
Walter D. Wilkinson
Gale Wilcox
George Wilcox
Orville Worman
Edward E. Young
Jack Zazadil
K. Ziolkowski
John Boland
D. S. Blacksmith
Louis Beck
Rufous Evans
Jim Holmes

The Superintendents of Mount Rushmore National Memorial

*Lincoln Borglum	1941-1943
*Albert R. Taylor	1944-1944
*Estes Suter, Custodian	1944-1948
*Albert Elliott	1948-1951
*Charles E. Humberger	1951-1954
Charles E. Humberger	1954-1958
Leon Evans	1958-1966
Wallace O. McCaw	1966-1973
Harvey D. Wickware	1973-Present

*Coordinating Superintendent Harvey J. Liek

Presidents of the Mount Rushmore National Memorial Society Since Its Inception

Joseph Cullinan
Gutzon Borglum
John A. Boland
William Williamson
John A. Boland, Jr.
Hoadley Dean

About the Author

June Culp Zeitner (Mrs. C.A.) is a well-known writer and lecturer in the fields of earth sciences, lapidary arts, and travel. Author of four other books, she is Contributing Editor and columnist of the Lapidary Journal, Associate Editor of the American Federation of Mineralogical Societies Newsletter, and was previously an editor of Earth Science. She is a past-president and first honorary member of the Midwest Federation of Mineralogical Societies.

After graduating from Northern State College in Aberdeen, South Dakota, Mrs. Zeitner taught school for several years and was principal and superintendent of Todd County High School in Mission. She quit teaching while still in her 30's and with her husband traveled in every state, Mexico and Canada, visiting historic mines, scenic rocks, and areas of geological phenomena. For many years the Zeitners had their Geological Museum open to the public in Mission. Since starting her many years of travel, Mrs. Zeitner has been a free-lance writer, co-sponsored an annual gem safari to Mexico, and been guest lecturer in 68 major American Cities. She also taught several courses in gems and jewelry at Pan American Univeristy in Texas. Mrs. Zeitner was selected as the South Dakota Woman of Achievement for 1976. She is listed in Who's Who of American Women and the World Who's Who of Women and is a member of the National Press Women.

A South Dakota booster, Mrs. Zeitner was instrumental in bringing the Midwest Federation convention to South Dakota for the largest field trip ever held. As State Director for the Federation she helped start 12 clubs and started the annual South Dakota-Midwest Federation picnic. She has featured South Dakota in many of her articles and lectures. Her article for the Lapidary Journal about Mount Rushmore, brought her a letter of praise from Lincoln Borglum. Borglum sent the letter from his home in Texas, but instead of reaching

Mrs. Zeitner at her South Dakota address it was forwarded to her in Texas, only 30 miles from the Borglums. Soon after they became acquainted, the Zeitners and the Borglums started talking about setting parts of the Rushmore story straight, and recording aspects of the Rushmore-Borglum story which have never been told. This book is the culmination of that effort.

Mrs. Zeitner says the hardest thing she ever wrote was the legend for the bronze historical marker at the Borglum Ranch near Hermosa. "It is easy to write lots of words about this great American story," she asserts, "but to try and condense the essence of it all in 300 words or less was a real challenge."

The life and accomplishments of co-author Lincoln Borglum are described in detail in the text.

Bibliography

Books about the Borglums and Mount Rushmore:

Fite, Gilbert C. **Mount Rushmore.** University of Oklahoma Press

Dean, Robert J. **Living Granite.** Viking Press

Price, Willadene. **Gutzon Borglum.**

Borglum, Lincoln. **My Father's Mountain.** Fennwyn

Casey, Robert and Borglum, Mary. **Give The Man Room.**

Magazine Articles:

Lubell, S., and W. Everett. "Man who Carves Mountains" **Reader's Digest** (May 1940) Adelstein, Stanford M. "The Man who Made Mount Rushmore" **Why?** (Spring 1973) Cannon, M. Samuel, and Palkuti, Gabriel. "Who Was Gutzon Borglum?" **American History Illustrated** (Dec. 1974)

Index